Southwest Conference Football 1969

Published by
FOOTBALL HISTORY, INC.
Houston, Texas

Edited and Designed by
Ralph Wall and Ray Herndon

CONTENTS

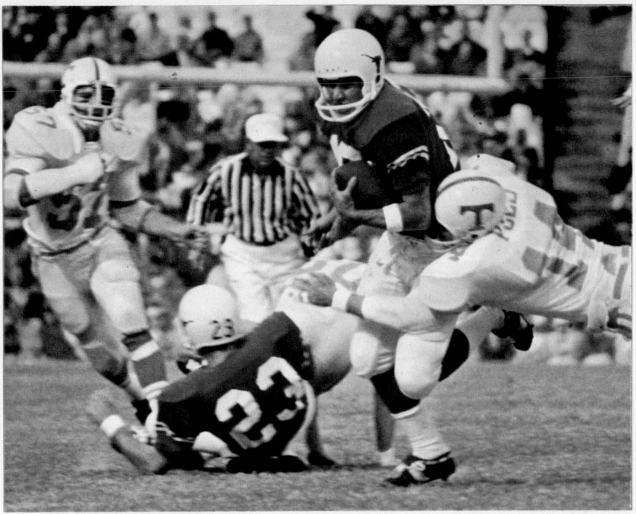

Danny Lester (23), takes out one man, but Bill Young (14) gets through to tackle James Street. Steve Kiner approaches from the right.

TEXAS 36 - TENNESSEE 13

Before the dust had settled, the Longhorns were long gone.

Texas matched the Cotton Bowl full house with a full house of their own. The dealer stands pat with James Street, Chris Gilbert, Ted Koy, Steve Worster and Cotton Speyrer. On each play the Volunteers had to guess which one of these five would end up with the ball. They guessed wrong all afternoon.

It was a chilly 33 degrees as the teams opened play in this 33rd Cotton Bowl game. Texas warmed up to the occasion early as they scored on their second possession. Starting from their 20, quarterback Street guided the Steers 80 yards in 13 plays. A crunching drive, on the ground all

the way. The Tennessee end zone was reached when Worster blasted up the middle behind Danny Abbott's blocking, veered to his left, and lunged across 14 yards later. Happy Feller kicked the point after and Texas led 7-0.

Holding the Volunteers, Texas put the ball in play again at their 22, following the Tennessee punt. Street faked a handoff to Worster, drawing in the Tennessee defense, then stepped back and passed to Speyrer at the Vol 42-yard line. Speyrer pulled up, caught the ball, outstepped safety Bill Young and outraced Young and Jim Weatherford to the end zone. Only one minute, forty-eight sec-

Cotton Speyrer (88), is off and running for his first touchdown. In futile pursuit are Steve Kiner (57), Dick Williams (74) and Bill Young (14). Texas tackle Bob McKay (62) is following the play from the rear.

ands and 78 yards had elapsed since Texas had scored its first touchdown. Feller missed the extra point and Texas now led 13-0.

In the early moments of the second period, the Longhorns cranked up another scoring sortie. Combining both running and passing, this one covered 71 yards in seven plays. Big gainers in the drive were two Gilbert runs of 16 and 12 yards, and a Street to Speyrer pass of 11 yards. Koy got the call this time and Bobby Wuensch led him through the Vol defense. Nine yards and a Tennessee gasp later, Koy reached paydirt. Feller's successful kick upped the Longhorn's lead to three touchdowns and two extra points.

With Bobby Scott having replaced Bubba Wyche at quarterback the Vols still remained mired down offensively. After Texas' second touchdown, Wyche took the Volunteers to the Horn 19, before losing the ball on downs. A score at that time might have changed the complexion of the game, but like Linus' Great Pumpkin, it wasn't meant to be.

Halftime was approaching and Texas beat the clock to score once more before giving Tennessee a rest to collect whatever remained of their game plan. In the 54-yard, eight play drive, Gilbert had a 13-yard run and Danny Lester caught a Street pass for 14 yards. Gilbert went wide for the final five yards as Koy threw the clearing block. Street passed to Speyrer for two points. The half ended with the score, Texas 28—Tennessee 0.

One half of the game was gone. Worster, Speyrer, Koy and Gilbert had all scored one touchdown apiece and Tennessee seemed powerless to stop the onslaught. Texas had met the Vols in the 1951 Cotton Bowl and lost, 20-14. Two years later the two teams met again, same place. This time the Longhorns prevailed, 16-0. Now 16 years later, with identical 8-1-1 records, the two powerful orange and white T's are meeting again. The Texas defense stopped Tennessee in the first half and the offensive line opened monumental holes for the ball carriers. Down four touchdowns, the Volunteers were looking toward better times

With Loyd Wainscott around his ankles, Leo Brooks around his waist and Glen Halsell and Scott Henderson divebombing from the front, Vol fullback Richard Pickens never had a chance.

as the second half got under way.

On the Longhorn's first possession they lost tight end Deryl Comer. He suffered a knee injury as he collided with teammate Bob McKay on a block. Both teams jockeyed back and forth until Young intercepted a Speyrer-bound aerial from Street at the Texas 38. Four plays later, from the 17, Scott passed complete to split end Gary Kreis for the Tennessee ice-breaker. Karl Kremser kicked the extra point to cut the Longhorn lead to three touchdowns. With almost ten minutes still to play in the third quarter, Volunteer rooters were hoping the worm had turned.

Linebacker Tom Campbell was instrumental in stopping the next two Vol drives. Twice he intercepted a Scott pass intended for Kreis. Then with 5:57 left before the final quarter, on first down, Street uncorked the bomb again to a flying Speyrer who outran Weatherford to the Tennessee end zone. Fumbling the snap back, Bill Bradley picked up the ball and ran across for a two point conversion. This put Texas back into a four touchdown

lead, 36-7, and dampened hopes of any Tennessee uprising.

Using their reserves in the fourth quarter, Texas got to the Vol three before losing the ball on downs. The big play in the drive, was a pass from quarterback Joe Norwood to Bradley, who was switched from defense to offense, good for 34 yards.

From their three, Scott took the Volunteers 97 yards in five plays. Two plays ate up most of the yardage, a pass to Kreis for 41 yards and a pass to Lester McClain for 40 yards. Scott's pass to Mike Price was good for three yards and the game's final touchdown. A pass failed for the extra point and 56 seconds later it was all over.

Street won the best offensive player award and teammate Tom Campbell picked up the best defensive player award.

Texas piled up a total offense of 513 yards, which missed the Cotton Bowl record by one yard, while holding Tennessee to a total of 275 yards, 97 of it coming on their last series.

5

Chris Gilbert (25), takes James Street's (16) handoff and slips by Steve Kiner (57). Jim McDonald (81), is just coming out of the starting blocks.

What do players on a team beaten 36-13 have to say after the battle is over? All-American guard Charles Rosenfelder observed that Texas had four good backs. He was also impressed by All-American Loyd Wainscott. Weatherford said Speyrer was the best he had played against this season. Dick Williams said that Tennessee didn't underestimate Texas, that their execution killed the Vols, their defense couldn't tell what was happening. All-American Steve Kiner thought Gilbert was the best he'd seen. Being a junior, Kiner has another year, and wants to play on a winning bowl team. He said that it was a long summer when you lose a bowl game. Summing up Tennessee's view of the game, Coach Doug Dickey said, "They block well, run well, play fundamental football and ran over us."

In the jubilant Texas dressing room All-American Chris Gilbert was reflecting back four years ago as he said, "When I first came here, one of my ambitions was to play for one of the finest teams in the nation. That's exactly the way it has

been, especially today. A football player couldn't ask for much more." Neither could Chris, neither could Texas.

Longhorns wearing the burnt orange for the last time were: Danny Abbott, Denny Aldridge, Marvin Bendele, Bill Bradley, Ronnie Ehrig, Ken Gidney, Chris Gilbert, Guy Harrison, Benny Pace, Mike Perrin, Corby Robertson, Mike Robuck, Tommy Souders, Loyd Wainscott and Dick Watt.

	Tenn.	Tex.
First downs	16	22
Rushing yardage	83	279
Passing yardage	192	234
Return yardage	—1	24
Passes	16-41-3	8-14-1
Punts	8-24	7-40
Fumbles lost	0	2
Yards penalized	17	60

Tennessee	0	0	7	6—13
Texas	13	15	8	0—36

Tex—Worster 14 run (Feller kick)
Tex—Speyrer 78 pass from Street (kick failed)
Tex—Koy 9 run (Feller kick)
Tex—Gilbert 5 run (Speyrer pass from Street)
Tenn — Kreis 17 pass from Scott (Kremser kick)
Tex—Speyrer 79 pass from Street (Bradley run)
Tenn — Price 3 pass from Scott (pass failed)
Attendance—72,000

6

Chuck Dicus, beating All-American Jake Scott by two steps, makes a fingertip catch of a Montgomery pass at the two, then crosses the goal line to score the game's only touchdown. Dicus won the game's most outstanding player award.

ARKANSAS 16 - GEORGIA 2

The Arkansas defense is alive and in the Sugar Bowl

In the 1969 version of the "Battle of New Orleans," it was the Razorback defensive troops, not the British, that kept a-comin'. Unlike the British, in that famous battle of 154 years ago, the Hogs won. The Arkansas defense allowed Georgia zero points. The Bulldogs scored two points while the defense was sitting on the bench.

The temperature was a crisp 44 degrees as Arkansas kicked off to start the 1969 Sugar Bowl. On the third play from scrimmage, Georgia quarterback Mike Cavan fumbled on a keeper and Cliff Powell recovered for Arkansas on the Hog 45. Unable to move, Stockdell punted. From their 22 the Bulldogs picked up a first down on the 39. Three plays later, facing fourth and eleven, Spike Jones punted to the Hog 26.

Arkansas still couldn't get untracked and

punted to the Georgia 40. Cavan overthrew intended receiver Kent Lawrence, but not Jerry Moore, who intercepted for Arkansas. Georgia spoiled this bit of good fortune as quarterback Bill Montgomery, hit as he faded to pass, fumbled. Terry Osbolt recovered for Georgia on the Arkansas 35. Cavan returned the favor, as on third down he fumbled the snapback and Guy Parker claimed the ball for the Razorbacks. Montgomery passed twice from his 31. The first was incomplete and the second was intercepted by Mark Stewart at the Georgia 34. Cavan kept the game of give away going as on second down, he again fumbled the snap and Bruce James recovered for the Hogs. Bill Burnett made three the hard way and Montgomery kept over left tackle for six more. Montgomery sneaked for a first down at the 26.

7

Bob White boots one of his three field goals, over the outstretched Georgia defense. Holding for the successful kick is Razorback safety, Terry Stewart (24).

Stopped on the next series, Bob White tried a 41-yard field goal which fell short.

Holding Georgia, the Hogs had the ball on their 35 following the Bulldog punt. The Razorbacks then started moving toward the game's only touchdown. Burnett ran for four yards. Bruce Maxwell picked up three more and Montgomery got the first down on a four-yard keeper. Maxwell ran for three up the middle. Montgomery passed incomplete, then hit Chuck Dicus for 12 yards and a first and ten at the Georgia 39. Staying in the air, Montgomery passed to Max Peacock for three and to Dicus for nine and another first down at the Bulldog 27 as the first quarter ended. On the first play of the second quarter, Montgomery passed to Dicus, who after beating Scott on a post pattern, made a fingertip catch at the two and crossed the goal for a Razorback touchdown. White added the extra point and Arkansas led 7-0.

Georgia took the kickoff, made one first down, then Bruce James threw Cavan for a 14-yard loss. Georgia punted, held Arkansas and the Hogs punted. Georgia was held again and punted to the Arkansas 14-yard line. Penalized for clipping, Arkansas started from their six. Although Arkansas had the ball, Georgia scored on the next play. Montgomery handed off to Burnett on a sweep. The pulling guards were wiped out and Burnett was forced deep. David McKnigh slammed him down in the Arkansas end zone for a Georgia safety. Arkansas 7 — Georgia 2.

Stockdell free-kicked out of bounds at the Hog 44. The Bulldogs still couldn't penetrate the Arkansas defense and punted dead on the Razorback 16. Following a Montgomery fumble, recovered by teammate Bob Stankovich for a seven-yard loss, Arkansas punted to their own 47. Picking up one first down, Georgia faced a fourth and two at the Arkansas 29 and went for it. Lawrence fumbled the pitch-out and covered the ball for an eight-yard loss.

Taking possession on their 37, the Razorbacks didn't waste this opportunity. Smarting from a seven-yard loss, Montgomery backed up on the

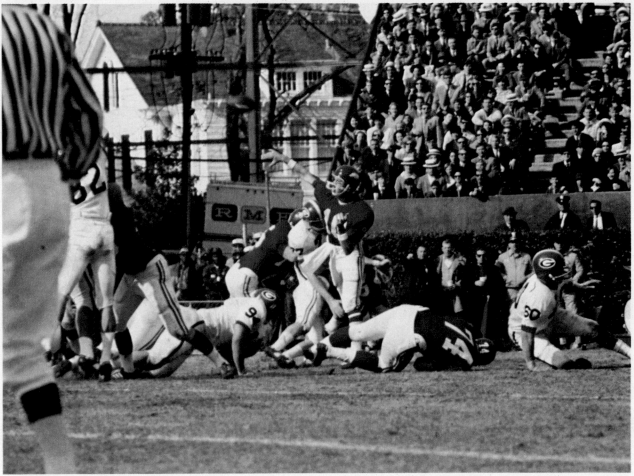

Surrounded by fallen bodies, Hog quarterback Bill Montgomery gets his pass away. Jerry Dossey (74), hits the turf after blocking Bulldog Steve Greer (60).

next play and threw deep to Dicus. Chuck caught the ball at the Georgia 35 for a 35-yard gain. Montgomery passed again to Dicus for 12 yards, then nine, then made five yards himself on a keeper. First down and goal to go at the Bulldog nine. Scott blitzed on a sweep to spill Burnett back on the 17. After two incomplete passes, Terry Stewart held for White's successful field goal from the 24. With just under two minutes left in the first half Arkansas led 10-2. Georgia got close enough, they thought, to try a field goal from the Hog 43. The kick was short and the half ended.

Georgia kicked off and John Rees fumbled after returning 12 yards. Trav Paine recovered for Georgia at the Razorback 20. Cavan passed to Charles Whittemore for a first down at the nine. Brad Johnson carried twice for five yards to the four. Johnson chose the middle on his next carry. Rick Kersey and Dick Bumpas hit him low and as he catapulted forward, Cliff Powell and Guy Parker hit him high. Out of the tangle of bodies

the ball came booming like a cannon shot, took one bounce and went out of the end zone. The Hogs took over the ball at their 20.

Arkansas was unable to move and Stockdell punted to the Bulldog 39. Cavan hit Lawrence on a pass, good for 21 yards, to the Arkansas 40. Cavan was then dumped for a 15-yard loss by Kersey. Georgia punted to the Arkansas 15. Three plays later Stockdell got off a punt of only 16 yards and Georgia took over at the Hog 32. Georgia picked up 10 yards on a carry by Craig Elrod. Bruce Kemp then made four yards, but on the next play, a blitzing Garner dropped Cavan for a minus 11 yards. Jim McCullough tried a 45-yard three pointer, which was short.

Three punts later Georgia had possession as the third quarter ended. Unable to move they punted to the Arkansas 34. The Razorbacks just missed a first down and punted to the Georgia 34. Gangbusters again as McNulty threw Donnie Hampton for a nine-yard loss, then an eight-yard loss. Jones punted to Adams on the Hog 45.

9

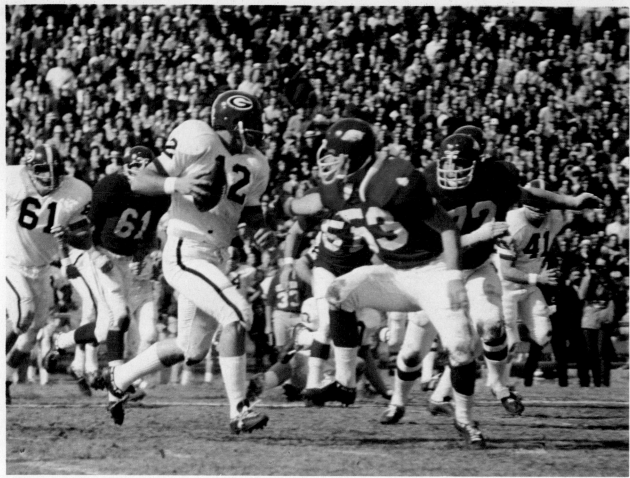

Georgia quarterback Mike Cavin saw red all day. On this play it was Dick Bumpas (61), Guy Parker (51), Lynn Garner (53) and Rick Kersey (72). Bulldog David Saye is the white clad 61.

Montgomery passed to Peacock for six yards. An incompletion, then a pass to Dicus, for 21 yards and a first down at the Georgia 28. Twice more Montgomery hit Dicus for 13 and six yards. Unable to get beyond the seven yard line, White kicked a 24-yard field goal to up the Razorback lead to 13-2. Georgia fumbled the kickoff to Mike Boschetti and White tried another field goal from the 46 which went to the right.

Georgia took over on their 20 and a Hampton pass was intercepted by Powell and returned to the Georgia 15. Arkansas was assessed a five-yard penalty for illegal procedure and settled for White's third field goal of the game. This one from 31 yards out, upped the Arkansas margin to 16-2. On Georgia's next attempt at moving the ball, Kemp was thrown for a one-yard loss by Powell and Hampton was thrown for a six-yard loss by Kersey.

After an exchange of punts, Georgia had their final chance at crossing the Hog goal. This ended when Moore intercepted a Hampton pass on the

Arkansas one and returned to the five. Montgomery took the snap, fell on the ball, and time ran out for the frustrated Georgia Bulldogs.

The Hog's offensive troops moved the ball well enough to put 16 points, one touchdown and three field goals, on their side of the Sugar Bowl scoreboard. Their defense was equivalent to a baseball no-hitter. Georgia had the football for 21 series. They forced the Bulldogs to punt ten times, recovered five fumbles, intercepted three passes, held on downs once and made Georgia try two abortive field goals. That adds up to nothing, but the offense gave up two points. The only thing that Georgia wasn't beat at was the coin toss before the game. Oh well, you can't win them all.

	Ark.	Ga.
First downs	13	13
Rushing yardage	40	75
Passing yardage	185	117
Return yardage	20	62
Passes	17-39-1	11-31-3
Punts	10-34	10-39
Fumbles lost	2	5
Yards penalized	31	25

Arkansas   0 10   0   6—16
Georgia   0   2   0   0— 2
Ark — Dicus 27 pass from Montgomery (White kick)
Ga — Safety Burnett tackled in end zone
Ark—FG White 34
Ark—FG White 24
Ark—FG White 31
Attendance—82,113

MVP Rufus Cormier (56), holds quarterback Bob Warmack to a one-yard gain in the first quarter. Joe Stutts, Jim Johnston and Tommy Fraser (94) follow up over OU's Jack Porter.

SMU 28 - OKLAHOMA 27
Bluebonnet Bowl breaks 24 records in wild upset

Endless chains of headlights marked the paths of 53,543 eager fans coming to Houston's Astrodome to watch the final answer to those who had given Oklahoma a twelve-point edge.

Both teams stepped into the Bluebonnet Bowl with a 7-3-0 record. Each had lost to the University of Texas and each had beaten North Carolina State. SMU had scored 283 points for the season, their opponents 246. Oklahoma topped their opponents 316 to 197.

SMU won the toss and elected to receive. Bruce Derr's kick was taken by Jerry Levias at the nine and returned to the Pony 17. The Sooner defense held and Daryl Doggett punted. Eddie Hinton took it on the Pony 43.

So it was that Oklahoma drew first blood. Steve Owens cut for three. Mike Harper banged guard to the 36, then Bob Warmack nearly made it all the way around left end on an option. Larry

Tunnell forced him out on the SMU three. Owens slammed over left guard into the end zone, but a penalty put the ball back on the five. Then Warmack ran a wide slant to the right, outrunning the pursuing Ponies to the corner of the end zone. The clock showed 12:05 left in the first quarter. Derr's extra point made it 7-0.

The kickoff dropped into Levias' hands on the SMU three. Like a souped-up Keystone Cop, he tucked the ball away and made a wild, zigzagging sprint through the Sooners before Dick Paaso and Forb Phillips jailed him on the SMU 26. The Ponies stalled with some help from OU left end Steve Zabel, who caught Chuck Hixson for a 12-yard loss. Tunnell boomed a 55-yard punt to the Oklahoma 25 where it rolled dead.

The next twelve plays featured Steve Owens for seven of them, but the drive stopped at the SMU five when Owens was hit for a two-yard loss by

11

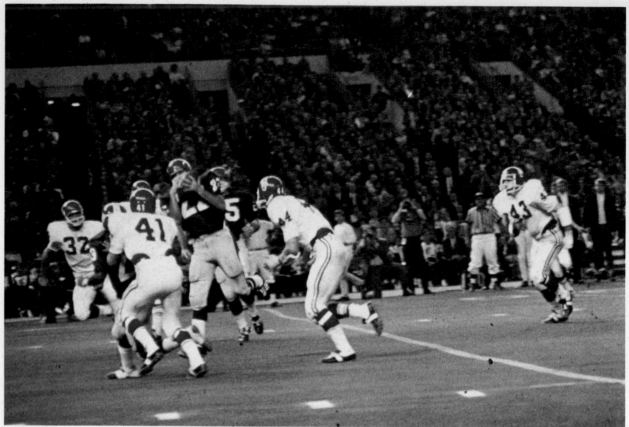

Clements (22) on a 17-yarder between Levias (23) and Fleming (85). Hetherington (32), Pearce (41), Casteel (44) and Pfrimmer (43) close in. Three plays later, Pearce intercepted in the end zone.

Jim Livingston and Tunnell. It was only Owens' second loss in two seasons.

On third-and-two, Zabel again cut down Hixson for a five-yard loss. Tunnell's punt was taken by Hinton on the SMU 46. But Oklahoma could get no farther than the 32, where Derr's field goal attempt fell short.

The Ponies ran three plays for no gain and Tunnell punted to Hinton who returned to the SMU 40. Owens was stopped by Rufus Cormier for a two-yard loss. Then a Warmack pass was intercepted by Livingston. Three plays made the SMU 28 for a first down at the end of the quarter. The Hixson aerial game began to click and the Pony offense moved into OU territory for the first time. On fourth-and-five at the OU 15, Buddy Echols' field goal attempt was wide to the right.

Oklahoma gained their 25, then Zabel punted 43 yards to Levias who returned eight yards to the SMU 40. The Mustangs moved to the Oklahoma 23 in six plays, but Bicky Lesser's 45-yard field goal attempt fell short.

In eleven plays, Oklahoma moved from their 20 to the SMU five, but a 15-yard holding penalty chilled things. They could not move past the Pony 20 and Derr's field goal attempt was wide to

the right. Warmack was forced to leave the game with a knee injury and the clouds were gathering for the Sooners.

The Ponies moved to their own 39 and punted out on the OU 27. Big Red was hit with a second bolt of bad luck when Zabel left the game with an injured knee. Now, it was Mickey Ripley at quarterback. On second down, Bruce Portillo intercepted a Ripley pass after Mike Nekuza tipped it. He was brought down on the OU 31.

Hixson threw to Sam Holden for 16. Holden cut into the left corner of the end zone and looked for the bomb. It came in the form of Sooner right half Joe Pearce who intercepted. But OU failed to get a first down as the half ended.

Lesser's kickoff to Oklahoma's Hinton started the second half. He returned 30 yards to the 32, but OU finally punted from the 36. Mike Richardson carried four times for 33 yards, then fumbled. Bruce Stensrud recovered for OU. On second-and-six, Owens fumbled and Cormier was in to recover for the Ponies.

Levias took an end around for four to the OU 37. Pinky Clements made ten. John Titsworth stopped Richardson for a loss of two, then Hixson connected with Levias who made a great catch

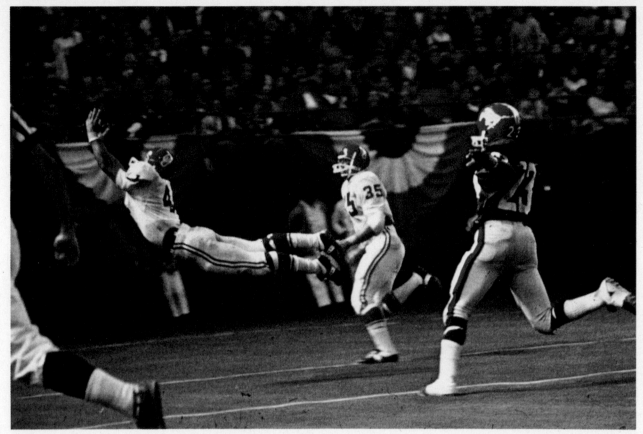

Oklahoma's MVP, Joe Pearce (41), narrowly misses a Hixson pass intended for Jerry Levias (23). Safety Steve Barrett is also covering.

and scrambled to the eight. Larry McDuff stopped Richardson up the middle for no gain. Levias and Pearce battled in the middle of the end zone for Hixson's next pass. Interference was called on Pearce, moving the ball to the one. Paaso stopped Richardson up the middle for no gain. But, it was still Richardson's night. He socked left tackle for the score. Lesser's extra point try was blocked by Pearce and the score stood at seven to six.

Oklahoma came storming back from their 20. Owens carried for one, then Ripley was hit by Cormier for a loss of ten. Owens carried three times into right guard for two yards each to the OU 47. A 14-yard interference call gave the Sooners the ball on the SMU 40. Owens carried twice more, once for 16 yards, bulling his way through six defenders. From the 21, Owens took a pitchout from Ripley, drew in the defense, then passed complete to split end Johnny Barr in the end zone. Derr's extra point put Oklahoma eight points ahead.

Two more possessions managed to get the Ponies to the OU 49 at the end of the third quarter. But things were beginning to click for the Mustangs.

Hixson hit Clements for 15 to the OU 35. After a couple of misses, he found Clements again for 17, then kept for six to the 12. His toss to Holden in the end zone was blocked by Pearce. It was Pearce again who intercepted a pass to Richardson in the end zone.

The Sooners failed to move from their 20. Levias took a fair catch on the SMU 43. This time, the Ponies would not be denied. Hixson passed to Richardson for 18, Ken Fleming for four, Richardson for 13 and Frank Stringer for 11. At the Oklahoma 1, Hixson rolled left and found Levias in the corner for the TD. Another pass to Clements, all alone over right tackle, tied the score at 14-all.

The Mustang defense squeezed the Sooner attack off at the OU eight. Doggett took Fred Malone's punt at the OU 37. Levias took a pass to the 35. Richardson rammed 17 yards down the OU throats, then slipped over right tackle, cut left and was gone for 18 yards and the TD. Lesser's kick made it 21-14, SMU. Pandemonium.

Ripley was learning fast. He hit Hinton for six to the 30. Johnny Barr took a well-executed look-in at the 42. Owens crunched for five to the 47. A sideline pass to Barr went to the SMU 42.

13

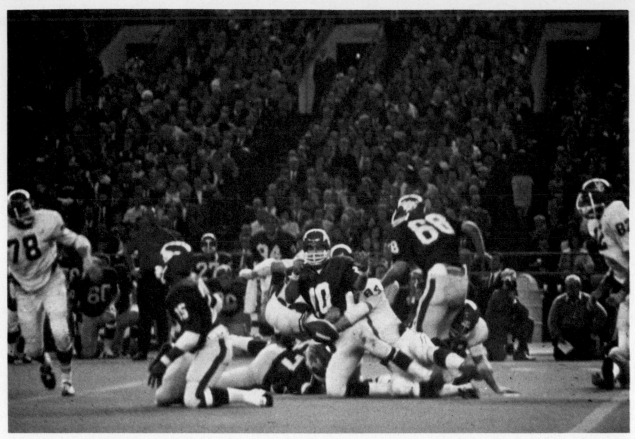

Third play on the SMU 19: Files (84) shakes Hixson loose from the ball. Hixson recovered. Haynes (25) watches Titsworth (78) as McMillan heads for his assignment and Zabel (82) moves in.

Owens again to the 22. The Mustangs broke up three passes, but on fourth-and-ten at the 22, Ripley bounced the ball off three Pony defenders and Bo Denton came down with the score. Derr's kick tied it up. *Boomer-Sooner* shook the place.

SMU couldn't make a first down. On second down, Ripley's pass was intercepted by the ever-ready Portillo, who made the Oklahoma 22. Richardson hit right guard for three. Hixson, rushed hard, shot a pass to Fleming in the end zone. He was a nose ahead of the defender, putting SMU ahead 27-21. Lesser's kick made it 28-21. The Pony band boomed *Peruna*.

But, this game was destined to be talked about for a long time. It was a fight to the finish, two minutes and 42 seconds away.

Hinton downed the kick in the end zone, then took a Ripley pass to the 42. Owens rammed to the 45. Ripley, forced to run, made the SMU 45. Two incompletes, then a screen to Owens at the 30. With 1:23 left, Barr made a great catch, barely outjumping the defense, to score. The noise level surpassed that of World War II. One point behind, the Sooners went for the win, but Ripley was knocked out-of-bounds by Mike Mitchell.

Peruna moved into the megaton class of sounds.

Derr tried an onside kick. Oklahoma's Ricky Heatherington covered it at the SMU 46. Doggett broke up Ripley's pass to Barr. Owens took the next pass to the SMU 32, then carried over left tackle to the 22. With 0:21 left, Ripley hit Denton for five and Derr lined up for a field goal with the ball on the 18. It was wide to the left.

Most Valuable Player awards were given to SMU noseguard, Rufus Cormier and OU cornerback, Joe Pearce. Twenty-four Bluebonnet Bowl records were broken along with thousands of ear drums.

	Okla.	SMU
First downs	23	22
Rushing yardage	176	72
Passing yardage	294	281
Return yardage	4	16
Passes	18-37-3	22-43-2
Punts	6-38	7-41
Fumbles lost	1	2
Yards penalized	55	34

SMU   0   0   6   22—28
Oklahoma   7   0   7   13—27
Okla—Warmack 8 run (Derr kick)
SMU—Richardson 1 run (kick failed)
Okla — Barr 21 pass from Owens (Derr kick)
SMU—Levias 11 pass from Hixson (Clements pass from Hixson)
SMU — Richardson 18 run (Lesser kick)
Okla—Denton 22 pass from Ripley (Derr kick)
SMU—Fleming 19 pass from Hixson (Lesser kick)
Okla—Barr 30 pass from Ripley (run failed)
Attendance—53,543

Preview
1969

By Dave Campbell,
President, Football Writers Association of America
Editor-Publisher, Texas Football Magazine

SEASON PREVIEW

September's two-a-day practice ordeal, where they let hot sun and hard knocks separate the players from the students, has finally ended. The journalists have come and gone, visiting each Southwest Conference football camp in its turn, quizzing coaches, interviewing players, sizing up mind and muscle, measuring attitudes, testing pulse-beats; and what really is not surprising at all is that it still looks like Texas and Arkansas.

Or, if you prefer, Arkansas and Texas.

"My feeling is that the race will be extremely close and well balanced," said SMU coach Hayden Fry, and he could have been speaking for all the coaches. Then he added: "I don't see how you could go with anyone but Texas and Arkansas. They're the co-champions, and there's no question that those two have got it going for them."

They sure do, and as the hours before the opening kickoffs come down to a precious few the big question before the house is whether there is another team or two or maybe three that also has plenty

going for it. Enough, that is, to seriously challenge Texas and Arkansas.

Take SMU, for instance, and that was something that was not easy to do in 1968. All the Mustangs did was make all the experts look silly by finishing a fast third instead of last, and then to compound the surprise they made highly-favored Oklahoma their eighth victim of the season in the Astro-Bluebonnet Bowl. Having been burned by a hot team once, a soothsayer is reluctant to challenge it again, especially when it continues to boast such combustibles as peerless passer Chuck Hixson, tight end Ken Fleming, a veteran defense and some live-wire sophomores. "We've got more size and experience and confidence. If you base it on what we did last year and what we have returning, we're going to have a good football team," predicts Fry, and he draws few arguments.

On the other hand, if you base it on the words of the opposition, Baylor is going to have a good team, too. The Bears just didn't loose much except their coach. Bill Beall, the man who replaced John Bridgers, inherited 18 returning regulars, and not

16

even Texas and Arkansas can make that statement. "I think Baylor is going to be a lot better than people think they are," Darrell Royal suggested in early September, and the players at Texas Tech were all in the amen corner. "If they had played everyone like they played us, they would have won the conference," said Raider quarterback Tom Sawyer. "That's why I think they'll do well this year."

If the Raider offense can keep pace with the defense, all of J. T. King's men may do well, too, because this is the best defense King has had at Tech, starting with those two fine ends, Richard Campbell and Bruce Dowdy. No team suffered greater manpower losses than the Aggies, yet no team is adding more good sophomores. "This team is not as good as last year's was potentially," analyzed Gene Stallings. "But I'll be disappointed if we don't have a better record." With a nucleus made up of such proven talent as Larry Stegent, Barney Harris, Ross Brupbacher and David Elmendorf, who can blame Stallings for such expectations as those?

Winless for the first time in their history in '68, the Rice Owls, too, are adding a flock of good sophomores. The Owls just have to be better. And the most improved team of all may be TCU, where rare running talent (Norman Bulaich, Marty Whelan) abounds, along with a large crop of seniors. But the boy who could make the big difference for TCU is a mere fledgling — sophomore Steve Judy, the best quarterback prospect the Frogs have welcomed to the varsity in ages.

"I think the conference is going to be as strong as it's ever been," said Frog grid boss Fred Taylor. "The way I look at it, one of those three teams (Texas, Arkansas, SMU) being picked at the top is going to come down, and one of the other five will come up. Which one? I don't know, but it could be us. I do think there are more people capable now of beating each other. It's going to be a real scramble."

Scramble it this way or that, it still comes out Texas and Arkansas.

In short, this is the season the Southwest Conference professes to be the land of football plenty and the Longhorns and Razorbacks are its peas-in-a-pod, one orange and the other red but both extravagantly armed, two old champions who last year reacquired both momentum and the winning habit. The shadow they now cast as the race prepares to start is like the tallest mountain: it is there, impossible to overlook.

Texas? By the end of the 1968 season, at the time of their landslide victory over Tennessee in the Cotton Bowl, not even the Longhorns knew their own strength. But after three consecutive 6-4 seasons

they did know they were back, all the way back, full to overflowing with fire and snap and dash and touchdowns, and if they are not starting this 1969 season with the same tools (not to mention many of the same faces), no one has been able to pinpoint any significant differences. Easier to land a man on the moon than to uncover a really serious flaw in the '69 'Horns.

Quarterback? James Street has never called a losing game. Runners? Steve Worster and Ted Koy somehow seem out of place this side of the pros, and maybe that prize newcomer, Jim Bertelsen, will, too. Receivers? Who has a more lethal one than Cotton Speyrer, the skinny kid with the long-distance clout? Size? Well, you can start with Large Leo (tackle Leo Brooks, 6-6, 244), the Big A (end Bill Atessis, 6-3, 257), and plain ol' Bob McKay 6-6, 245). If there isn't an All America or two in that crowd, Darrell Royal will miss his guess, and Royal is not a bad guesser.

But what Texas has Arkansas also has — quarterback Bill Montgomery, running backs Bill Burnett and Bruce Maxwell, receiver Chuck Dicus, a defense that Frank Broyles ranks second to none ("I'm just so proud of that defense") — and for good measure the Razorbacks also have a schedule made strictly in hog heaven.

When one boils it all down to the nitty-gritty — Street versus Montgomery, Speyrer versus Dicus, Texas power versus Arkansas deftness and versatility, the Longhorns' brute strength on defense versus the Hogs' big-play defense — it is that exceedingly favorable Arkansas schedule that may be the final difference. It seems sure to permit Frank Broyles to bring his team along just right.

There are other subtle differences between the league's two goliaths, of course. For instance, the Razorbacks are not having to replace a Chris Gilbert, a Loyd Wainscott, a Bill Bradley. The Longhorns are. For another instance, Texas has only one experienced quarterback but the Razorbacks have two, and if the course is as rugged as the coaches seem to think it will be, this is the season it may take two good quarterbacks to win.

"We lost more quality people than the people who are being picked up there with us," stressed Darrell Royal. "But yes, I think we're going to have a good football team."

In other words, from the AstroTurf at their feet to the quality in their ranks, the Longhorns and Razorbacks are strictly U. S. prime. They were all of that when they met last year in Austin, and Texas won. This year they meet in Fayetteville, and it's Arkansas's turn.

TEXAS TECH RED RAIDERS

Head Football Coach: J. T. King
Team Captains: Game Captains

Varsity

First Row: Left to Right
Marc Dove, R, Soph.
Tom Sawyer, QB, Sr.
Charles Napper, QB, Soph.
Lane Wade, FL, Jr.
Joe Matulich, QB, Sr.
Gary Doiron, DHB, Jr.
Andy Hoyle, R, Soph.
John Howard, R, Jr.
Bruce Bushong, S, Soph.
Jerry Watson, DHB, Jr.
Kevin Ormes, S, Sr.
Dale Rebold, S, Soph.
Ken Perkins, DHB, Soph.
Ken Kattner, FL, Jr.

Second Row: Left to Right
Reagan Young, FB, Soph.
Denton Fox, DHB, Sr.
Mark Fincannon, LB, Jr.
Jerry Don Sanders, KS, Sr.
Miles Langehennig, HB, Soph.

Doug McCutchen, FB, Soph.
Neil Mitchell, DHB, Jr.
Mike Brewer, HB, Jr.
Jimmy Bennett, FB, Sr.
Larry Hargrave, HB, Jr.
John Kleinert, FL, Soph.
Danny Hardaway, HB, Soph.
Don Crocker, FB, Soph.
Pat Rogers, R, Soph.
Charles Stewart, FL, Jr.

Third Row: Left to Right
Jesse Richardson, C, Jr.
Jon Hill, C, Soph.
Larry Molinaire, LB, Soph.
Jamie Hahn, C, Sr.
Mark Hazelwood, C, Jr.
Dicky Grigg, DT, Sr.
Carroll Sullivan, LB, Jr.
Scott Brady, LB, Soph.
Tom Newton, OG, Jr.
Tom Finley, OG, Soph.

Dennis Lane, LB, Sr.
Ted Lawson, DT, Jr.
Marty Criswell, OG, Soph.
Buddy Capps, OG, Soph.

Fourth Row: Left to Right
Pete Norwood, DG, Sr.
Walter Yarbrough, OG, Jr.
Bob Mooney, DG, Jr.
Joe Glenewinkel, DT, Soph.
Chuck Zeller, OT, Soph.
Jerry Ryan, OT, Soph.
Phillip Barney, OT, Soph.
Ronnie Mercer, OG, Jr.
Jim Dyer, DT, Jr.
Bob Browning, OT, Soph.
Wayne McDermand, DT, Jr.
Mike Holladay, OT, Sr.

Fifth Row: Left to Right
Johnny Odom, OE, Soph.
George Cox, DE, Sr.

Robbie Best, OE, Soph.
David May, OE, Jr.
Ernie Sheppard, OE, Soph.
Eddy Windom, DE, Sr.
Barney Oliver, DE, Sr.
Charles Evans, OE, Sr.
Richard Campbell, DE, Sr.
Ronnie Ross, OE, Soph.
Harold Hurst, DE, Soph.
Bruce Dowdy, DE, Jr.
Tom Tella, DE, Soph.

Sixth Row: Left to Right
J. T. King, Head Coach
Bradley Mills, AC
Gene Henderson, AC
Berl Huffman, AC
Tom Wilson, AC
Burl Bartlett, AC
Elwood Kettler, AC
Jim Acree, AC
John Conley, AC

TEXAS A&M AGGIES

Head Football Coach: Gene Stallings
Team Captains: Larry Stegent, Ross Brupbacher, Buster Adami

Varsity Team
First Row: Left to Right
Randy Maddox, OT, Soph.
Barney Harris, WB, Sr.
Larry Stegent, TB, Sr.
Bill Seely, WB, Sr.
Ross Brupbacher, TE, Sr.
Jim Piper, DE, Sr.
Jimmy Adams, SE, Sr.
Lynn Odom, DG, Sr.
Tom Sooy, SE, Sr.
Buster Adami, LB, Sr.
Mike Caswell, LB, Sr.
Jack Kovar, C, Sr.
Warren Moore, K, Sr.
Billy Bob Barnett, TE, Sr.
Mike DeNiro, DE, Jr.
Jack Whitmore, DB, Sr.
Edwin Ebrom, DB, Soph.

Second Row: Left to Right
Ronald Cole, DG, Jr.
Johnny Gardner, DB, Soph.
Mike Bellar, K, Soph.
Steve Burks, TB, Soph.
Mike Bunger, DB, Soph.
Billy Joe Polasek, WB, Soph.
Benny De Witt, C, Soph.
Joe Shaw, OT, Jr.
Barb Hinnant, OT, Soph.
Van Odom, DG, Soph.
Lee Hitt, DB, Soph.
Ted Davis, DE, Soph.
Mike Park, C, Soph.
James Duback, DE, Soph.
Andy Tewell, LB, Soph.
Dave Elmendorf, DB, Jr.
Rusty Stallings, OG, Jr.
Ted Smith, DE, Soph.
David Hoot, DB, Soph.
Bland Smith, DB, Soph.
Charles Crain, OG, Soph.

Third Row: Left to Right
Leonard Forey, OG, Soph.
Robin Davis, OG, Soph.
Hugh McElroy, WB, Soph.
Jim Tsitsiragos, TB, Soph.
Mike Stinson, C, Jr.
Lenard Millsap, OG, Soph.
Roy Kirkpatrick, TE, Soph.
Marc Black, FB, Soph.
Wayne Wheat, OT, Soph.
Clifford Thomas, TB, Soph.
Steve Luebbehusen, LB, Soph.
Joey Herr, WB, Soph.
Joe Mac King, QB, Soph.
Doug Neill, FB, Soph.
Mike Lord, LB, Soph.
Corky Sheffield, DB, Soph.
Tommy Deaton, DB, Soph.
Rae Albertini, OG, Soph.
James Pearce, OG, Soph.
Clifton Thomas, DE, Soph.

Fourth Row: Left to Right
Mitch Robertson, P, Soph.
Mike Tighe, DG, Soph.
Jimmy Sheffield, QB, Jr.
Gary Armbrister, FB, Soph.
Robert Stansberry, QB, Jr.
Chris Johnson, DB, Soph.
Mike Hedrick, DB, Soph.
David Odom, DB, Soph.
Greg Thompson, LB, Soph.
Tom Evans, DE, Soph.
Dale Watts, DB, Jr.
Andy Philley, OT, Soph.
Allan Hanson, OG, Jr.
Doug Robbins, FB, Soph.
John Cunningham, OT, Soph.
Mike Fields, OT, Jr.
Phil Adams, WB, Jr.
Jim Parker, OG, Sr.
Gary Kyle, QB, Soph.
Rocky Self, QB, Soph.

ARKANSAS RAZORBACKS

Head Football Coach: Frank Broyles
Team Captain: Game Captains

Varsity Team

Front Row: Left to Right	Second Row: Left to Right	Third Row: Left to Right	Fourth Row: Left to Right
John Eichler, QB, Sr.	Mike Hendren, TB, Jr.	Dewitt Smith, OG, Sr.	Gordon McNulty, DE, Sr.
David Cox, FL, Sr.	Tommy Hopper, LB, Sr.	Dick Fuller, FB, Jr.	Steve Birdwell, MM, Soph.
Walter Nelson, QB, Soph.	Roger Harnish, DE, Soph.	Steve Hockersmith, OG, Soph.	Cary Stockdell, P, Sr.
Louis Campbell, DB, Soph.	Pat Morrison, TE, Jr.	Bill Montgomery, QB, Jr.	Rodney Brand, C, Sr.
Bobby Field, MM, Jr.	Mike Boschetti, LB, Jr.	Chuck Dicus, SE, Jr.	Jerry Dossey, OG, Sr.
Tim Webster, K, Jr.	Tommy Dew, DE, Sr.	Bruce Maxwell, FB, Sr.	Ronnie Hammers, OG, Jr.
Russell Cody, TB, Sr.	Richard Coleman, LB, Jr.	Terry Don Phillips, DT, Sr.	Gary Parson, OT, Jr.
John Rees, FL, Jr.	Ronnie Jones, LB, Soph.	Bruce James, DE, Jr.	Jim Mullins, OG, Sr.
Rick Kersey, DT, Jr.	Gus Rusher, DB, Soph.	David Hogue, DB, Soph.	Don Wunderly, DT, Soph.
Robert Lewis, LB, Soph.	Russ Garber, FB, Soph.	Bill Burnett, TB, Jr.	Lendel Thomas, DT, Jr.
Dick Bumpas, DT, Jr.	Rick Vickers, DT, Soph.	Terry Hopkins, C, Jr.	Mike Kelson, OT, Soph.
Terry Stewart, DB, Sr.	Steve Vestal, LB, Soph.	Bill Carter, C, Soph.	Ronnie Bennett, OG, Soph.
Cliff Powell, LB, Sr.	Bobby Nichols, FB, Soph.	Bill McClard, K, Soph.	Bob Stankovich, OT, Sr.
Lynn Garner, LB, Sr.	Robert Dew, DB, Soph.	Dennis Berner, S, Sr.	John Turner, DT, Jr.
	Steve Benoit, DE, Soph.	Jerry Moore, DB, Jr.	
	Tom Mabry, OT, Soph.		

BAYLOR BEARS

Head Football Coach: Bill Beall
Team Captains: Game Captains

Varsity Team

First Row: Left to Right
Buddy Moore, OT, Sr.
Walt Groth, DT, Sr.
Richard Stevens, OT, Sr.
Calvin Hunt, C, Sr.
John Armstorn, C, Sr.
Mark Lewis, SE, Sr.
Jerral Landers, TB, Jr.
Gene Rogers, TB, Sr.
John Kelly, OT, Sr.
Roy McDearmon, DE, Sr.
Bob Stephenson, OG, Sr.
John Lerma, TB, Sr.
Mike Riley, DH, Soph.

Second Row: Left to Right
Preston Pitts, TB, Soph.
Lanus Treadwell, OG, Jr.
Robert Hucklebridge, DH, Soph.
Gordon Utgard, TB, Sr.
Joe Kopec, DT, Jr.
John Mosley, DT, Sr.
Tommy Reaux, DG, Sr.
Richard Dennard, OG, Sr.

Brian Blessing, LB, Sr.
Kent Starr, OG, Sr.
David Black, C, Jr.
Dennis Whitley, LB, Jr.
John Miller, S, Jr.
Ted Gillum, TE, Sr.
Phil Beall, QB, Soph.
Willie Stewart, DH, Soph.

Third Row: Left to Right
Joe Korenek, TE, Soph.
Gary Hughes, FK, Soph.
Mike Virdell, OG, Soph.
Martin Mathis, DE, Soph.
Griggs Dehay, TB, Soph.
Jim Sartain, OG, Jr.
Keith Wagner, OG, Jr.
Trent Phipps, OG, Jr.
Pete Lucas, OT, Soph.
Mike Hale, C, Soph.
Wayne Roberds, LB, Jr.
Terry Cozby, KS, Sr.
Orville Jansen, FK, Sr.
Gilbert Beall, OG, Jr.

Steve Parshall, DH, Soph.
Jerry Smith, FK, Sr.
Glen Chmelar, DE, Soph.
Clancy Dunigan, FB, Soph.
Mickey Ray, DH, Soph.
Pat Nunn, DE, Soph.
Derek Davis, TB, Jr.
Don Huggins, FK, Jr.
Terry Jackson, TB, Jr.
Barry Morgan, OG, Soph.

Fourth Row: Left to Right
Ron Steadman, TB, Soph.
David Walters, OT, Soph.
Ken Freitag, FK, Soph.
Si Southall, QB, Soph.
Mike Duckett, DG, Soph.
Joel Allison, DT, Jr.
Rollin Hunter, TE, Jr.
Laney Cook, QB, Jr.
Terry Newman, DE, Soph.
Greg Vardaman, LB, Soph.
Randy Cooper, FB, Jr.
Ed Marsh, DH, Jr.

Gary Sutton, DT, Soph.
Bob Garrett, DH, Soph.
Tom Fitzgerald, SE, Soph.
Dwayne Trammel, FB, Soph.
Jessie Young, OT, Jr.
Ron Evans, OT, Jr.
Joe Moore, FB, Jr.
Mike Conradt, FK, Soph.

Fifth Row: Left to Right
Don Stephenson, FB, Soph.
Dale Clark, C, Soph.
Steve Ables, DT, Soph.
Tom Bambrick, LB, Jr.
David Jones, LB, Jr.
Mike Beane, S, Sr.
Joe Allbright, OT, Soph.
Steve Stuart, QB, Jr.
Don Aylor, LB, Soph.
Dennis Watson, DE, Jr.
John Malone, DH, Soph.
Mike Morgan, SE, Soph.
Toby Toberny, TB, Soph.
Buddy Hartje, C, Soph.

TEXAS CHRISTIAN HORNED FROGS

Head Football Coach: Fred Taylor
Team Captains: James Ray, Norman Bulaich, Terry Shackelford, James Vanderslice

Varsity

First Row: Left to Right
Vernon Marlar, RB, Jr.
Bob Foster, DB, Soph.
Pat Walker, LB, Sr.
Linzy Cole, FL, Sr.
Jimmy Tidwell, DB, Jr.
David Holt, DG, Sr.
Billy Fondren, DB, Sr.
Larry Wright, DB, Sr.
Marty Whelan, RB, Sr.

Second Row: Left to Right
Greg Webb, DB, Jr.
Bobby Davis, RB, Soph.
Rusty Blair, C, Soph.
Ted Fay, DB, Sr.
John Nichols, LB, Jr.
Robert Lee, DB, Soph.

Paul Smith, OG, Sr.
Ronnie Woodman, C, Jr.
William Riley, OG, Sr.

Third Row: Left to Right
J. R. Eubanks, TE, Soph.
James Hodges, DB, Soph.
Steve Judy, QB, Soph.
Phil Birdwell, TE, Sr.
Busty Underwood, QB, Jr.
Steve Frost, OG, Soph.
Sammy Rabb, RB, Sr.
Norman Bulaich, RB, Sr.

Fourth Row: Left to Right
Charlie Pillow, DB, Soph.
Larry Speake, FL, Soph.
James Vanderslice, LB, Sr.

Craig Fife, DG, Soph.
Eddie Matthews, LB, Sr.
Mike Johnson, OT, Soph.
Bob Creech, DT, Jr.
Andy Durrett, LB, Sr.
Wayne Merritt, K, Sr.

Fifth Row: Left to Right
Joey Lawson, DG, Soph.
Chuck Forney, DG, Jr.
Larry Brogdon, DG, Soph.
Drake Farmer, OT, Soph.
John Meyers, DT, Sr.
Danny Lamb, OG, Jr.
Terry Shackelford, DT, Sr.
Jay Defee, DT, Soph.

Sixth Row: Left to Right

John Beilue, TE, Soph.
Bob Schobel, DT, Soph.
Jerry Miller, SE, Sr.
John Hetherly, SE, Soph.
Randy Hale, LB, Sr.
Doug McKinnon, LB, Soph.
Gary Stout, LB, Soph.
Gerald Kirby, OT, Jr.

Seventh Row: Left to Right
Gary Martinec, LB, Soph.
Jerry Cooper, OT, Jr.
Dan Carter, FL, Sr.
Clay Mitchell, DT, Sr.
John Ruthstrom, C, Jr.
Donnie Terveen, DG, Sr.
James Ray, OG, Sr.
Dean Wilkerson, OT, Jr.

TEXAS LONGHORNS

Head Football Coach: Darrell Royal   Team Captains: James Street, Ted Koy, Glen Halsell

Varsity Team

First Row: Left to Right
Roy Baldwin, Trainer
Jim Williamson, DE, Sr.
Leo Brooks, DT, Sr.
Bob McKay, OT, Sr.
Paul Kristynik, DHB, Sr.
Scooter Monzingo, DHB, Sr.
Ted Koy, HB, Sr.
Glen Halsell, LB, Sr.
Rob Layne, K. Sr.
Dick Johnston, DHB, Sr.
Forrest Wiegand, C, Sr.
Bobby Wuensch, OT, Jr.
Mack McKinney, LB, Sr.
Tom Campbell, DHB, Sr.
Randy Peschel, TE, Sr.
Bill Atessis, DE, Jr.
Steve Worster, FB, Jr.
Carl White, DT, Soph.
Jim Lemmon, Mgr.

Second Row: Left to Right
Jim Pippin, Trainer
Chris Young, DT, Sr.
Dean Campbell, SE, Jr.
Stan Mauldin, DE, Soph.
David Ballew, DHB, Soph.
Mike Campbell, LB, Sr.
James Street, QB, Sr.

Ken Ehrig, SE, Sr.
Charles Speyrer, SE, Jr.
Mike Dean, OG, Jr.
Fred Steinmark, S, Jr.
Scott Henderson, LB, Jr.
Happy Feller, K, Jr.
Danny Lester, DHB, Jr.
Jay Cormier, TE, Soph.
David Keeton, DHB, Soph.
George McIngvale, C. Soph.
Bill Hall, Mgr.
Jon Highbarger, Mgr.
David Fox. Mgr.

Third Row: Left to Right
Emory Bellard, AC
Fred Akers, AC
Mike Campbell, AC
Spanky Stephens, Trainer
Donnie Wigginton, QB, Soph.
Rick Troberman, LB, Soph.
Bob Huffman, DT, Soph.
Travis Roach, DT, Soph.
Tommy Asaff, HB, Sr.
Billy Dale, HB, Jr.
Raymond Fontenot, LB, Jr.
Bill Zapalac, DE, Jr.
David Richardson, LB, Jr.
George Cobb, DT, Sr.

Mike Hutchings, LB, Sr.
Mike Speer, OG, Soph.
Johnny Robinson, DHB, Jr.
Jeff Zapalac, C, Soph.
David Arledge, DE, Soph.
Tex Allshouse, QB, Soph.
Ronnie Tyler, OT, Soph.
Charles Rogers, OG, Soph.
Jimmy Kay, Mgr.
Paul Hobbs, Mgr.
Mike Cave, Mgr.
Leon Manley, AC
Buddy Simpson, Mgr.
R. M. Patterson, AC
Willie Zapalac, AC
Darrell Royal, Head Coach

Fourth Row: Left to Right
Jack Rushing, LB, Soph.
Ricky Martin, LB, Soph.
Robby Patman, SE, Sr.
Bobby Callison, HB, Jr.
Eddie Phillips, QB, Soph.
Robert Paine, HB, Soph.
Pat Macha, DT, Soph.
Johnny Otahal, LB, Soph.
Paul Robichau, HB, Soph.
Jim Achilles, C, Jr.
Bobby Mitchell, OG, Jr.

Greg Ploetz, LB, Jr.
Tommy Lee, OT, Soph.
Sammy McBrierty, OT, Soph.
Scott Palmer, OT, Jr.
Tommy Matula, DT, Soph.
Jimmy Gunn, LB, Soph.
Sid Keasler, OG, Soph.
Gary Rike, LB, Soph.
Bud Hudgins, LB, Sr.

Fifth Row: Left to Right
Jim Bertelsen, HB, Soph.
Tommy Woodard, LB, Soph.
Dan Terwelp, LB, Soph.
Randy Scott, QB, Soph.
Randy Braband, OG, Soph.
Rick Nabors, DHB, Jr.
Larry Webb, LB, Soph.
Jimmy Hull, OE, Soph.
Bill Catlett, DHB, Soph.
Rob Schultz, DT, Soph.
Kevin Hutson, DHB, Soph.
Jerrell Bolton, OG, Soph.
Sam Lawless, DHB, Soph.
Andy Banks, OT, Soph.
Will Wilson, LB, Jr.
Donnie Windham, HB, Soph.
Charles Crawford, OG, Soph.
Wayne Kirk, LB, Soph.

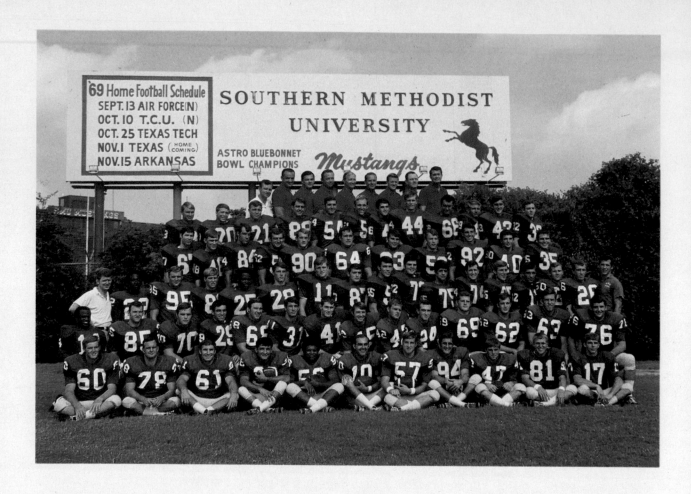

SOUTHERN METHODIST MUSTANGS

Head Football Coach: Hayden Fry
Captains: Off. Chuck Hixson, Daryl Doggett, Stan Poulos
Def. Bruce Portillo, Rufus Cormier, Tommy Fraser

Varsity Team

Front Row: Left to Right
Keith Cupples, OG, Sr.
Jim Higgins, OT, Sr.
Que Brittain, OG, Sr.
Bruce Portillo, LB, Sr.
Rufus Cormier, DG, Sr.
Chuck Hixson, QB, Jr.
Stan Poulos, C, Sr.
Tommy Fraser, R, Sr.
Daryl Doggett, FB, Sr.
Sam Holden, FL, Sr.
Garry Hammond, SE, Soph.

Second Row: Left to Right
Raymond Mapps, FL, Soph.
Ken Fleming, OE, Jr.
Jim Hodges, DG, Soph.
Bicky Lesser, HB, Sr.
Kemp McMillan, OG, Sr.
Joe Stutts, LB, Jr.
Larry Tunnell, DB, Jr.
Mike Nekuza, DB, Jr.

Danny Gordon, S, Sr.
Pat Curry, DB, Soph.
Bill Wright, DT, Jr.
Jim Johnston, DT, Jr.
Bill Line, DT, Jr.
Bill Jackson, OT, Jr.

Third Row: Left to Right
David Haines, ST, Jr.
Gordon Gilder, HB, Soph.
Buddy McGinnis, R, Sr.
Pelham Staples, FL, Jr.
Walter Haynes, FB, Jr.
Larry Guthrie, HB, Soph.
Gary Carter, QB, Jr.
David Thomas, OE, Jr.
Bill Hart, C, Jr.
Chuck Dannis, OT, Soph.
Gary Knee, OT, Jr.
Harry Hargrave, OT, Jr.
Vic Brittain, OG, Jr.
Wayne Delamater, QB, Jr.

Steve Parrott, OG, Jr.
Frank Stringer, FL, Sr.
Bill Glaros, ST, Jr.

Fourth Row: Left to Right
Dwight Houghton, DT, Sr.
Dave Smith, DB, Jr.
John Jordan, DT, Jr.
Mike Armstrong, DG, Sr.
Dan Jones, DB, Soph.
Pat O'Connell, DG, Sr.
Randy Dossett, SE, Soph.
Joe White, DG, Jr.
Mike Shelton, R, Soph.
Alan Everest, S, Soph.
Sherwood Blount, LB, Soph.

Fifth Row: Left to Right
Chipper Johnson, K, Soph.
Bill Dietz, HB, Sr.
Rob Floyd, FB, Jr.
Jim Shaw, DT, Sr.

Buddy Echols, OG, Jr.
Ken Kuesel, C, Soph.
Mike Jordan, DB, Jr.
T. D. Richardson, S, Jr.
Gerald Bowles, OG, Soph.
Cleve Whitener, S, Soph.
Robert Popelka, S, Soph.
Sam McLarty, S, Soph.

Sixth Row: Left to Right
Eddie Lane, Tr.
Bob McQueen, AC
Jerry Moore, AC
Dave Smith, AC
Herb Zimmerman, AC
Joe Boring, AC
Ray Utley, AC
Dudley Parker, AC
Hayden Fry, Head Coach

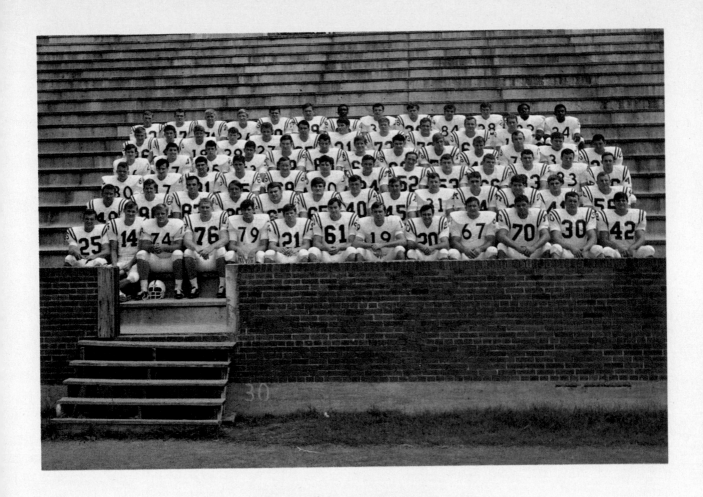

RICE OWLS

Head Football Coach: Harold R. (Bo) Hagan
Team Captain: Game Captains

Varsity Team
Front Row: Left to Right
Joe Henderson, FL, Sr.
Dennis Alexander, FS, Jr.
Joe Barron, DG, Sr.
Brownie Wheless, DG, Sr.
Jeff Schwartz, LB, Jr.
Dale Bernauer, FL, Sr.
Gary Carley, OG, Sr.
Tim Davis, K, Jr.
Ronnie Sollock, DHB, Sr.
Dwayne Phillips, OG, Sr.
Steve Bradshaw, DG, Sr.
Ron Marsh, LB, Sr.
Butch Robinson, TB, Jr.

Second Row: Left to Right
Randy Jinks, S, Sr.
Larry Davis, SE, Sr.
Sam Reed, TE, Sr.
Jack Neubauer, DE, Jr.
Roger Roitsch, DG, Jr.
David Stockwell, OG, Jr.

Bucky Allshouse, S, Jr.
Tommy Alexander, S, Jr.
Terry English, LB, Jr.
Larry Caldwell, TB, Soph.
Monte Hutchinson, LB, Jr.
Cliff Crabtree, TB, Soph.
Allen Arnold, C, Soph.

Third Row: Left to Right
Russ Russell, DE, Soph.
Ted Scruggs, FB, Soph.
James Garner, DE, Jr.
Roger Collins, DE, Jr.
Paul Strahan, OG, Jr.
Joe Buck, DE, Soph.
Dale Grounds, LB, Soph.
Wright Moody, C, Soph.
Dwayne Young, C, Soph.
Merideth Morton, OG, Soph.
Randy Lee, LB, Soph.
Mike Phillips, TE, Soph.
Mike Spruill, TB, Soph.

Fourth Row: Left to Right
Sammy Hudson, DHB, Soph.
Max Miller, FB, Soph.
Jerry Nacarrato, S, Soph.
Bill Holmes, LB, Soph.
Tommy Peel, OG, Jr.
Jack Faubion, FL, Jr.
Bill Galbraith, OG, Soph.
Cliff Hammond, DE, Jr.
Ron Waedemon, OT, Soph.
David Keys, DHB, Jr.
Tony Citti, LB, Soph.
Kim Malone, FB, Soph.
Jack Laurenzo, TB, Soph.

Fifth Row: Left to Right
Eddie Carnes, TE, Soph.
Phillip Wood, QB, Soph.
Mike Kramer, QB, Soph.
Bill Latourette, SE, Soph.
Gary Thomas, DHB, Jr.
Donnie Johnson, LB, Jr.

Tony Conley, FB, Jr.
Dan Carlton, OT, Soph.
Terry Mason, OT, Jr.
Tommy Countz, DG, Jr.
Jimmy Davis, QB, Soph.

Sixth Row: Left to Right
Charles Blackburn, FL, Soph.
John Cardwell, TB, Soph.
Walt Richardson, OT, Jr.
Gerald Simila, DHB, Soph.
Bill Batchelor, OT, Jr.
Ed Erwin, DG, Soph.
Stahle Vincent, QB, Soph.
John Swords, FB, Soph.
Ronnie Johnston, LB, Soph.
Bob Brown, SE, Soph.
Gilbert King, DHB, Soph.
Rodrigo Barnes, DE, Soph.
Mike Tyler, DHB, Soph.

PREDICTIONS AND SCHEDULES

POST BOWL TOP TEN — 1968
1. Ohio State
2. Penn State
3. Texas
4. Southern Cal
5. Notre Dame
6. Arkansas
7. Kansas
8. Georgia
9. Missouri
10. Purdue

1969 PRE-SEASON TOP TEN
1. Ohio State
2. Arkansas
3. Penn State
4. Texas
5. Southern Cal
6. Oklahoma
7. Houston
8. Georgia
9. Mississippi
10. Missouri

1969 SWC PRESS TOUR
1. Arkansas
2. Texas
3. (Tie) Baylor, SMU, Texas A & M
6. TCU
7. Texas Tech
8. Rice

1968 RECORDS

Team	SWC W	L	T	Season W	L	T
Arkansas	6	1	0	9	1	0
Texas	6	1	0	8	1	1
SMU	5	2	0	7	3	0
Texas Tech	4	3	0	5	3	2
Baylor	3	4	0	3	7	0
TCU	2	5	0	3	7	0
Texas A & M	2	5	0	3	7	0
Rice	0	7	0	0	9	1

ALL-TIME RECORDS

		W	L	T	Pct.
1.	Texas	489	187	28	.723
2.	Texas A & M	369	253	45	.593
3.	TCU	358	261	48	.578
4.	Arkansas	360	269	31	.572
5.	Texas Tech	241	189	25	.560
6.	Baylor	331	261	39	.559
7.	SMU	267	227	47	.540
8.	Rice	275	249	26	.524

1969 SCHEDULES

	BAYLOR	RICE	SMU	TEXAS A&M	TCU	TEXAS TECH	TEXAS	ARKANSAS
Sept. 13			Air Force					
Sept. 20	Kansas State	VMI	@ Georgia Tech	@ LSU	Purdue	Kansas	@ California	Oklahoma St.
Sept. 27	@ Georgia Tech	LSU	@ Michigan State	@ Nebraska	@ Ohio State	@ Texas	Texas Tech	Tulsa
Oct. 4	@ LSU	@ California		@ Army	@ Arkansas	@ Oklahoma State	Navy	TCU
Oct. 11	Arkansas		TCU (10th)	@ Texas Tech	@ SMU (10th)	Texas A & M	Oklahoma (Dallas)	@ Baylor
Oct. 18		SMU	@ Rice	@ TCU	Texas A & M	Mississippi State		
Oct. 25	@ Texas A & M	@ Texas	Texas Tech	Baylor	@ Miami (24th)	@ SMU	Rice	Wichita State
Nov. 1	TCU	@ Texas Tech	Texas	@ Arkansas	@ Baylor	Rice	@ SMU	Texas A & M
Nov. 8	@ Texas	Arkansas	@ Texas A & M	SMU	Texas Tech	@ TCU	Baylor	@ Rice
Nov. 15	@ Texas Tech	Texas A & M	Arkansas	@ Rice	@ Texas	Baylor	TCU	@ SMU
Nov. 22	SMU	@ TCU	@ Baylor		Rice			
Nov. 27				Texas		@ Arkansas	@ Texas A & M	Texas Tech
Nov. 29	@ Rice	Baylor						
Dec. 6							@ Arkansas	Texas

First Week
September 13, 20

NOTE: The SMU vs. Air Force game was moved from October 4 to September 13 to accommodate TV coverage. This game is included in the First Week.

This is a picture of half of the Mustang offense. The other half were the receivers as SMU rushed for —1 yard. Chuck Hixson throws under pressure from Harold Whaley (87). Bicky Lesser (29) blocks.

AIR FORCE 26-SMU 22

The beginning of college football's 100th season was celebrated in the Cotton Bowl by sacrificing a mustang. Chuck Hixson piloted the lopsided Pony offense for 356 yards in the air, but the total ground game amounted to one step backward, a —1 yard. In spite of their single threat offense and the fact that Air Force led at the half 23-0, the Mustangs owned the second half and kept the outcome in doubt until the final gun.

SMU took the kickoff, but failed to make a first down. An 11-yard punt by Larry Tunnell to their own 35 put the Mustangs in a hole. But the defense dug in and held the Falcons to a field goal try from the 44. Dennis Leuthauser's kick was good for three.

Again, SMU could not move and Hixson was dropped for a big loss from the 40 back to the 28. Lesser took a screen to the 35 and Tunnell's punt put Air Force on their 20.

In spite of some inspired defensive play led by Portillo and Stutts, Gary Baxter guided the Falcons to a score, depending often on Jim DeOrio, a work-horse of a fullback. On the 13th play, Baxter faked halfback Martin on a slant, then kept around right end for the score. Leuthauser's kick made it 10-0.

The Ponies managed to reach their own 31, then punted to the Falcons on their 35. Again, it was De-Orio, then Baxter up the middle for a first down. Longnecker took a 31-yard pass to the Pony 35. Martin ran to the 20, but the drive stalled on the 16. Leuthauser kicked another three points onto the scoreboard . . . 13-0. It was the first play of the second quarter.

Larry Guthrie took Leuthauser's kickoff to the SMU 38, then Hixson hit Larry Hammond down the left sideline with a beautiful pass to the Air Force 28. But, on fourth-and-three at the Falcons' ten, Hixson was dropped for a loss to the 22. Air Force, unable to move, kicked to the Ponies at their 32. A fumbled handoff on the next play was recovered by Ewig and Marietta of Air Force to set the Falcons up on the SMU 29. Two passes fell incomplete, then Baxter connected with Longnecker in heavy traffic. He made the 15 for a first down. Next, Baxter ran a convincing bootleg to the right corner of the end zone. Leuthauser's kick added up to 20-0.

SMU gained the Falcons' 18 before being stopped and Air Force, on the running of Baxter and DeOrio, took regular slices of the field before being stopped at the Pony 17. Leuthauser's 34-yard field goal brought the score to 23-0.

28

When Falcon fullback Jim DeOrio wasn't running, quarterback Gary Baxter was. Here Baxter's doing just that with Mike Keller (64) and Virgil Staponski (67) heading for safety Danny Gordon (42).

The second half began with the Mustangs trying an onsides kick. Air Force recovered. A good pass defense stopped the Falcons, then an equally good pass defense picked off a Mustang pass, but Air Force had to settle for a long field goal try from the 50. It was downed on the SMU 7. Finally, Hixson found his long lost arm. Frank Stringer made a good catch up the middle for 17, then Lesser took a short pass and added on a fine run to the 42. An interference penalty put the Mustangs on the Cadets' 39. Holden made a good snag up the middle to the 17. Haynes ran to the 15, then a well-covered Fleming took a needle-sharp pass on the two and bulled in to score. Fleming grabbed a pass over right tackle for a two-point conversion. Air Force led 23-8.

Another possession gained the Air Force nothing and the Ponies took over. In 11 plays, the Mustangs scored again. The march featured Fleming and Holden as receivers and Lesser going for first down yardage on the ground twice. Holden took the scoring pass as he twisted over the goal line. Fleming's reception in the right corner for two made it 23-16.

Again, Air Force had to try for a field goal from the 26. A hard Pony rush hurried the kick which missed. But, the Cadets were soon given another try when Charles Richardson intercepted a pass on his own 44. The defense, backed by Stutts and Portillo stopped Air Force on the two and the all-purpose

quarterback Baxter kicked for two more, making it 26-16.

The Ponies came close again, only to have a pass intercepted on the Cadet goal line by Leimbach. The ensuing punt was taken by Hammond on the 50 and returned to the 33. Holden took a pass to the 25, then Fleming took another to the four. Lesser pounded to the two, Hixson was dropped for no gain, then Haynes scored over the center. A run for two failed, leaving the Ponies behind 26-22.

Just to keep everybody standing, SMU recovered their onsides kick. Dan Jones pounced on it at the Air Force 49. Four plays later, the clock ran out on the 27.

	AF	SMU
First downs	21	21
Rushing yardage	178	—1
Passing yardage	206	356
Return yardage	1	31
Passes	15-34-0	34-55-3
Punts	6-40.8	6-37.3
Fumbles lost	1	1
Yards penalized	43	44

Air Force	10	13	0	3—26
SMU	0	0	16	6—22

AF — FG Leuthauser 44
AF — Baxter 2 run (Leuthauser kick)
AF — FG Leuthauser 33
AF — Baxter 15 run (Leuthauser kick)
AF — FG Leuthauser 34
SMU — Fleming 15 pass from Hixson (Fleming pass from Hixson)
SMU—Holden 6 pass from Hixson (Fleming pass from Hixson)
AF — FG Leuthauser 21
SMU — Lesser 2 run (run failed)
Attendance — 44,300

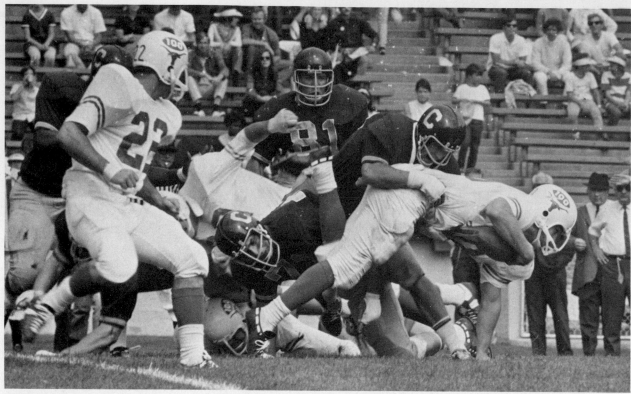

Fullback Steve Worster makes extra yardage as he stiff-arms the turf while driving upfield. Billy Dale (22) watches Steve's progress from the left.

TEXAS 17 - CALIFORNIA 0

Texas opened their 1969 gridiron season in Memorial Stadium before 31,000 people. 3,500 were Longhorn fans, the rest, well they didn't have much to cheer about. This Memorial Stadium belongs to the University of California and is planted firmly in Berkeley, California — home of the Golden Bears.

The Bears kicked off and Texas couldn't get the afterburners glowing until their second possession. The Longhorns then moved 70 yards in 11 plays. Halfback Ted Koy started things by thumping for five yards over right guard. Then repeated for two more. Quarterback James Street then pitched to halfback Jim Bertelsen on the triple option and Bertelsen gathered in nine yards on the right side. This play was also repeated and the yardage gained was again nine. Street then ran out of the pocket for seven yards. Bertelsen ran right tackle for five yards and pulled the old repeat act for another five. Koy then carried for three and a Bear penalty tacked on five more. Bertelsen, behind the blocking of tackle Bob McKay, gained seven yards. Repeated for two more, then followed McKay again wide right for 11 yards and the Longhorns first touchdown for 1969. Happy Feller, picking up where he left off last year, added the extra point. Texas led 7-0.

Fullback Steve Worster didn't carry the ball one time on the drive, but with Street faking to him before pitching out to Koy or Bertelsen, he decoyed the Bear offense into keying on him.

On the Horns next possession, Street was intercepted by the Bear's Jim Sheridan, who returned two to the Texas 38, where the Longhorn defense stopped the Bears. California, on their next possession, got close enough for Randy Wershing to try a field goal which fell short and was downed at the one-yard line. After a fumble-recovered snap and two incomplete passes, Scooter Monzingo punted for Texas.

Bertelsen burst through for a 20-yard gain on the Steer's next drive, but fumbled when gang tackled. California recovered on their own 19.

The splendid Longhorn defense again blunted the Bears offense and Texas next moved 65 yards in 11 plays. Worster carried twice for three and two yards. Then on third and five, Street hit tight end Randy Peschel for 11 yards and a first down. Bertelsen gained six and Koy five before Street recovered a fumble and gained six yards. At the Bear 32 now, Bertelsen got one and Koy four. Facing another third and five, Worster got the call and split the

This Golden Bear isn't going anywhere as an unidentified Longhorn bulldogs him for no gain. Stan Mauldin (85) joins in to secure the tackle.

middle for 20 yards to the California seven. Worster tried the middle again for three. Street then kept on the option and went over right end for four yards and a touchdown. Feller did his thing and Texas felt more comfortable at 14-0. The first half ended with no more scoring.

Texas kicked off to start the second half and created their own breaks right away. On the second play from scrimmage, defensive tackle Leo Brooks thumped Bear quarterback Randy Humphries causing a fumble. Mike Campbell recovered for Texas. From the California 36, Billy Dale ran for eight yards and Worster three more. Dale picked up two more and Worster gained six before the drive bogged down. Feller trotted on the field and got the Longhorns three more points with a 32-yard field goal. This made the score 17-0 in favor of Texas and with 10:27 left in the third quarter the scoreboard was through for the day.

Poor field position hurt Texas the rest of the game as they gained possession on their seven, one, six and five-yard lines. Feller tried a 40-yard field goal in the fourth quarter, which was blocked by Sheridan. From his own 32, the Bear's Bob Darby burst through right guard and was hauled down 47 yards later at the Texas 21. Paul Kristynik made the tackle. Coach Darrell Royal then returned his first stringers and closed the gate. Brooks dropped quar-

terback Dave Penhall, after two incomplete passes, for successive losses of two and 12 yards. The Texas defense never allowed California inside their 20.

Late in the fourth quarter the Longhorns cranked up another drive which ran out of steam as Royal freely used his sophomores.

Coach Ray Willsey of California, a former assistant coach to Royal at Texas, has nine Texans on his squad. Two standouts for the Bears, in a losing cause, were punter Gary Fowler and linebacker Phil Croyle. Fowler's booming punts kept the Longhorns backed up in the second half and Croyle was credited with 33 assists and 12 unassisted tackles.

So the Longhorns, after three straight years without an opening game win, played good solid football to snap that string and open the season with a victory. Cotton Speyrer didn't catch one pass and the end around, tried once, gained one yard. California lost, but not like Tennessee in the Cotton Bowl. They knew where Speyrer was on every play.

	Texas	Calif.
First downs	21	10
Rushing yardage	311	127
Passing yardage	18	79
Return yardage	31	86
Passes	2-7-2	12-23-1
Punts	7-30	6-41
Fumbles lost	1	1
Yards penalized	30	60

Texas	7 7 3	0—17
California	0 0 0	0— 0

Texas — Bertelsen 11 run (Feller kick)
Texas—Street 5 run (Feller kick)
Texas — FG Feller 32
Attendance — 31,000.

31

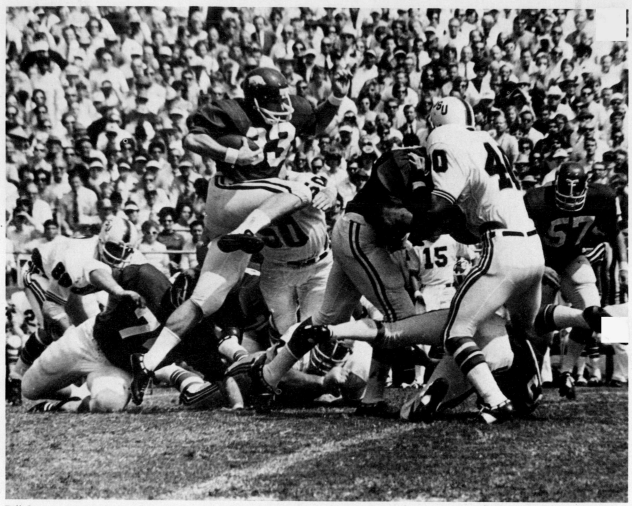

Bill Burnett goes up-up-and away for Arkansas as Cowpoke Steve Farris (40) is blocked out. Gary Darnell (50) misses as Burnett goes flying by. Hog center Rodney Brand (57) is to the right of Farris.

ARKANSAS 39-OKLA.STATE 0

The Razorbacks entertained the Cowboys from Oklahoma State in Little Rock's War Memorial Stadium before 51,000. They also entertained the Hog rooters as they matter-of-factly whipped the Cowboys with excellent defense and a routine offense. Because of the defense, the offense started from the State 40, 43, 32, 39, 33, 36 and 50 during the game. They recovered two fumbles and threw their runners for 19 yards more in losses than they could gain.

The Cowboys kicked off and after each team jockeyed back and forth, Terry Stewart returned an OSU punt 34 yards to their 40. Unable to move, the Hogs exchanged punts and started again from the Cowpoke 42. Quarterback Bill Montgomery kept for 17 yards and fullback Bruce Maxwell tacked on 19 more. Bill Burnett scored the touchdown from the two and Bill McClard kicked the extra point to put Arkansas ahead 7-0. All of this used four minutes.

OSU spurted after the kickoff, but after a 23-yard pass from quarterback Robert Cutburth to end Dick Graham, the offense stalled. The Hogs took over the ball, following a punt, at their 39. Arkansas scored in six plays. Montgomery passed to Chuck Dicus for eight yards. A personal foul penalty took the ball to the OSU 38. Pat Morrison, racing across the middle, gathered in a Montgomery pass and gained 16 yards. Burnett ran three straight times for 11, five and three yards to put the ball on the three. Montgomery kept inside left tackle for the three and the Razorback score mounted. With 7:41 remaining in the first period, the PAT was missed, Arkansas led 13-0.

Not all long drives end up in scores as the next one proved. From their 31, Maxwell went 10 yards up the middle. Burnett added nine more and Dicus caught a pass for eight which was enlarged to 20 as he fumbled forward and Mike Kelson recovered.

John Gates intercepted a Montgomery pass from the eight in the end zone and returned to the 10.

As the second quarter started, OSU moved to the Razorback 25 before failing on a fourth and two. Undaunted they came roaring back as Benny Goodwin returned a Hog punt to the Arkansas 35. On third down Cutburth passed to flanker Hermann Eben for 20 yards. The Razorback defense then held and the Hogs got the ball at the 13. A pass interception, again by Gates, set up the Cowboys on the Arkansas 28. In this case, the third time wasn't a charm. Following a five-yard gain, a 14-yard loss and an incomplete pass, Uwe Pruss unsuccessfully tried a field goal.

The Hogs got untracked and moved 80 yards in 13 plays. Burnett got 30 of those on a run around left end. Staying on the ground, Montgomery again got the final three. The extra point was missed and Arkansas led 19-0. Thirteen seconds later the first half ended.

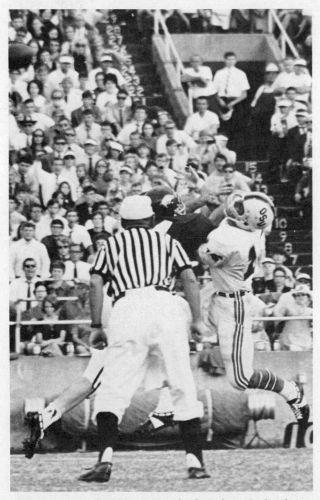

Cliff Powell reaches OSU quarterback Robert Cutburth just as he releases the ball. The Razorback defensive corps put the pressure on all the way as they looked in mid-season form for the season's opener.

Arkansas kicked off to start the second half. The Cowboys couldn't move and punted to the Hog 45. David Cox caught a pass for seven yards. Russell Cody took a screen pass 22 yards and Steve Hockersmith snagged one for 13. The runners took over then as Burnett used three carries to reach the three and Maxwell went the final three for the score. McClard found the range and added point number 26 with 8:14 left in the quarter.

With Oklahoma State unable to sustain a drive, the Razorbacks offense started from their 38. John Eichler took over the quarterbacking from Montgomery and didn't miss a beat as he guided the Hogs to scoreville in 13 plays. In the drive, Cox caught two passes for 15 and 13 yards. Eichler, unable to find anyone open, ran from the six for the touchdown. McClard missed the point and Arkansas led 32-0.

As the last quarter opened an Oklahoma State fumble was recovered by Gordon McNulty at the Cowboy 39. Aided by a 14-yard personal foul penalty the Razorbacks reached the State four. There the Cowboys held to stop the Hog effort.

After the punt return, Arkansas was back in business at the OSU 33. Eichler passed to Mike Hendren for eight and kept for six yards. At the seven Eichler was shaken up and replaced by Montgomery. Montgomery went to his left, kept the ball and scored on the next play. McClard put it through the uprights to close out the scoring. The Hogs led 39-0.

If the Cowpokes needed any proof that this wasn't their day, they got it on the ensuing kickoff. The line drive kick hit lineman Bob Bridges and bounced back toward Arkansas. Roger Harnish recovered at the 50 for the Razorbacks.

After an exchange of punts the Hogs reached the three. The biggest yardage being picked up on Eichler passes to William Powell, good for 12 and 11 yards. This time the Cowboys held at the three and shortly the game ended.

The Razorbacks' longest scoring play was seven yards as OSU contained the long gain. Although Montgomery's passing wasn't something to write home about, he ran for three touchdowns. If you can't beat them one way, you use another.

	OSU	Ark.
First downs	6	34
Rushing yardage	—19	349
Passing yardage	97	151
Passes	11-32-2	14-30-0
Punts	9-30.6	3-37.0
Return yardage	68	49
Fumbles lost	2	1
Yards penalized	34	60

OSU	0	0	0	0—	0
Arkansas	13	6	13	7—	39

Ark—Burnett 2 run (McClard kick)
Ark — Montgomery 3 run (kick failed)
Ark — Montgomery 3 pass (kick failed)
Ark — Maxwell 3 run (McClard kick)
Ark — Eichler 6 run (kick failed)
Ark — Montgomery 7 run (McClard kick)
Attendance — 51,386.

Norman Bulaich of TCU (23) finds a gaping hole and advances the ball 22 yards to the Purdue three in the third quarter. Purdue's Jim Renie (35) and Jim Kleidon couldn't quite reach the flying Bulaich. Frog guard William Riley (65) follows the action.

PURDUE 42 - TCU 36

TCU was meeting the Boilermakers from Purdue for the first time and after the pre-game, traditional handshake — it was Katy bar the door. Before a crowd of 25,000 at TCU-Amon Carter Stadium, eleven touchdowns and extra points were scored, which can't be divided equally. At games end Purdue was ahead six to five.

Purdue, the Irish tamers from Indiana, took the opening kickoff and a little over five minutes later Quarterback Mike Phipps, on a run-pass option, went five yards for the score. The big gainers in the drive were a Phipps to Stan Brown pass good for 32 yards, and a 20-yard run by Phipps. The Boilermakers didn't let 24 yards in penalties bother them either. Jeff Jones' extra point kick was good and Purdue led 7-0.

TCU, thanks to a 20-yard run by Norman Bulaich, got to within field goal range, but Busty Underwood missed and Purdue took over. A screen pass to John Bullock covered 80 yards, with Bullock bounced out of bounds on the Horned Frog five. With the help of a five-yard penalty TCU held and Jones missed a field goal from the 14.

This misfortune didn't stall Purdue for long as Tim Foley picked off TCU Quaterback Steve Judy's pass on the Frog nine. On second down Phipps passed to Ashley Bell for a touchdown. Jones' kick made it 14-0, Purdue.

Marty Whelan returned the kickoff 66 yards to the Purdue 33. This went for naught as Bulaich fumbled and Jim Kleidon recovered for Purdue on his 30. The Horned Frogs came back as Judy took to the air, completing passes to Linzy Cole for 16, to Jerry Miller for 25 and nine, then back to Cole again for five yards and a touchdown. The drive covered 71 yards in nine plays. Wayne Merritt added the extra point and TCU trailed 7-14.

Purdue was to add one more tally before half-time. A 74-yard sortie ended with a bit of the theatrical as Phipps' pass bounced off one receiver into the arms of Greg Fenner in the end zone. With Jones' conversion, the Boilermakers took a 21-7 lead into the dressing room at the half.

Purdue just about blew the Horned Frogs clear out of the stadium as the second half got underway. Phipps started the rout by lobbing a pass over the

Taking a Purdue punt on his own 30, Linzy Cole gives the Boilermaker bench a close-up of his 70-yard return for a TCU touchdown. This fourth quarter action narrowed the gap to a one touchdown advantage for Purdue. TCU's Jimmy Tidwell (27) gives escort.

Frog secondary to Bell, good for 23 yards and six points. Jones made it seven and Purdue upped its lead to 28-7.

Purdue, Phipps and Company did it again on their next possession. Stan Brown got behind Ted Fay and gathered in Phipps' pass, which when he reached paydirt, covered 67 yards. Jones footed a point and bang-bang, Purdue led 35-7.

The Horned Frogs could have folded after that, but sophomore Judy was just getting the feel of playing varsity football. He got the Frogs to moving on their next possession. Judy was throwing and Cole was catching as TCU moved downfield. Then as Judy dropped back to pass, he was hit from behind and the ball went end over end toward Sammy Rabb. Rabb was surprised, but Purdue was stunned, and Sammy went 35 yards down the sideline to score. Merritt converted and TCU trailed 14-35.

On their next possession the Frogs put it to them again. Judy passed to Cole for the final three and with Merritt's kick it was now 35-21, Purdue.

As the fourth quarter started Purdue had just recovered a Rabb fumble, this came after Andy Durrett had intercepted a Boilermaker pass to give TCU possession. Phipp pitched out to Randy Cooper and 54 yards later he was rolled out of bounds by Greg Webb on the Frog one. On third down Bullock scored and Purdue jumped out to a three-touchdown lead.

The Frogs weren't through though, far from it. After an exchange of interceptions, Billy Fondren recovered a Purdue fumble on the Boilermaker 19. Bulaich ran to the seven and Purdue was penalized for piling on, to the four. Judy passed to John Beilue for the score and with Merritt's PAT it was 42-28, Purdue.

The Frogs held after Purdue received and forced the punt. Cole was waiting. Taking the ball on his 30, he did a circleout, saw his way blocked, reversed his field and went 70 yards for the game's final score.

With four minutes left, Purdue made enough first downs to run out the clock. They were darn sure that they didn't want TCU in possession of the ball again. Final, Purdue 42 — TCU 35.

	Purdue	TCU
First downs	25	17
Rushing yardage	294	111
Passing yardage	286	213
Return yardage	83	213
Passes	11-26-2	19-36-2
Punts	4-39.2	5-35
Fumbles lost	1	2
Yards penalized	14-116	5-63

Purdue	7	14	14	7	—42
TCU	0	7	14	14	—35

Purdue — Phipps 5 run (Jones kick)
Purdue—Bell 8 pass from Phipps (Jones kick)

TCU — Cole 5 pass from Judy (Merritt kick)
Purdue — Fenner 8 pass from Phipps (Jones kick)
Purdue—Bell 23 pass from Phipps (Jones kick)
Purdue — Brown 67 pass from Phipps (Jones kick)
TCU — Rabb 35 pass from Judy (Merritt kick)
TCU — Cole 3 pass from Judy (Merritt kick)
Purdue — Bullock 1 run (Jones kick)
TCU — Beilue 3 pass from Judy (Merritt kick)
TCU — Cole 70 punt return (Merritt kick)
Attendance — 25,000.

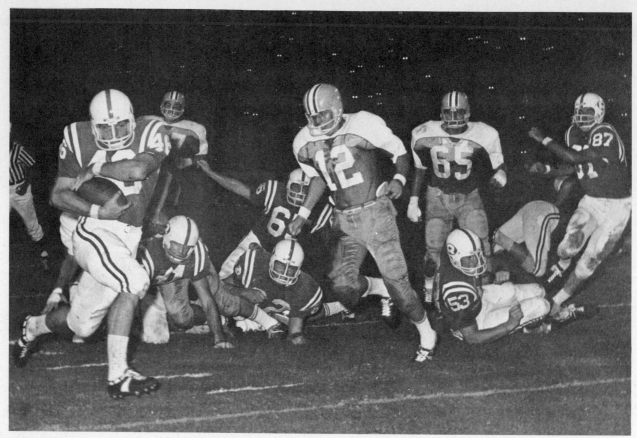

Tailback Mike Spruill (46) blasts through on the right as his Owl mates give him excellent blocking. Tony Conley (31), Tommy Peel (62), David Stockwell (65), Dwayne Young (53) and Sam Reed (87) are the Rice players. Eddie Blair (12) and Bob Copty (65) represent the Keydets.

RICE 55-VMI 0

Rice opened their season against the Keydets of Virginia Military Institute in Rice Stadium before 18,000 loyal fans, which probably were carry-overs from last year. Well, those faithful few were fully rewarded by the young Owls as they scored eight touchdowns to help erase some of the frustrations of last year.

The scoring started on a VMI bad center snap on fourth down. Punter Jim Bailey chased the ball down and miraculously avoided the onrushing Owls to get off a punt to the VMI 36.

Quarterback Stahle Vincent guided the Blue into the end zone in eight plays. Fullback Tony Conley, the only non-sophomore in the backfield turned in the big play on the drive with a run of 13 yards. Tailback Mike Spruill got seven and the TD behind excellent blocking by guard Tommy Peel and tackle Ron Waedemon. Tim Davis' extra point put Rice ahead 7-0.

No passing from Rice, so VMI started defending for runs only as Phillip Wood replaced Vincent at quarterback midway through the second quarter.

Wood put together a 53-yard scoring march, mixing in some passing along the way. Two to Bob Brown for 12 and 19 yards, and one of 14 yards to Larry Caldwell. The one to Caldwell was on fourth and four and was caught deep in the end zone. This added six points and Davis made it seven. Davis also tried a 44-yard field goal before halftime which missed. So at the break Rice led 14-0.

Rice had no victories last year. They played like a team possessed in the third period, making VMI's end zone very familiar in the process. They took the second half kickoff and zipped 66 yards in eight plays. Wood gained 20 on a keeper and Jack Laurenzo added 11 on a reverse. Dale Bernauer, a trackman playing his first football since high school, romped 24 yards on a wingback reverse to the Keydet nine. Wood kept and legged it around right end to score on fourth down. The extra point, by Davis, was good and the Owls led 21-0.

On Rice's next possession they moved 52 yards in six plays, with Vincent replacing a shaken up Wood in the process. Spruill got the touchdown by

Rice quarterback Phillip Wood (11) hurdles teammate Tony Conley (31) as he heads upfield. VMI right end Mike North (87) joins Tony on the turf as left end Steve Ballowe (84) takes up the chase.

diving over from the one. PAT by Davis and with 6:07 remaining in the third quarter, Rice had a 28-0 advantage.

With 2:26 left the Owls scored again as Vincent hit Brown for 35 yards and another score. Davis made it 35-0 for Rice.

Early in the fourth quarter the ball was lost on a bad pitchout at the VMI 17. This had no disheartening effects as the "whirlybirds" came back to score in five plays covering 62 yards. Spruill had the biggest gainer, a 33-yard run to the Keydet 17. Cliff Crabtree swept left end for all of it and with Davis contributing one, it was Rice, 42-0.

Third string tailback Crabtree found scoring to his liking, so the next time he went 70 yards. Vincent, after handing off, threw the block that sprung Crabtree. To break the monotony, Davis missed his first extra point in his varsity career after 26 in a row. His leg might have been getting tired. Rice led 48-0 with the game approaching its end.

A bad VMI punt set up the Owls final counter as they took control of the ball on the Keydet 25. On fourth down Vincent fired down the middle to Brown, good for 24 yards and another sixer. Davis started a new streak to make it 55-0, Rice.

VMI got into Rice territory, to the 48, once in the first half. They now penetrated Rice's end of the field as a result of a recovered fumble at the Rice 27 and reached the 24 before Don Cupit missed his field goal attempt. Thus the game ended, with no more scoring.

Stahle Vincent, the first black quarterback in Southwest Conference history, survived a rather conservative start to finish up strong. He completed three of six passes, two of which went for touchdowns. Equally as effective was Phillip Wood, who shared the signal calling chores with Vincent. Leading groundgainer for the Owls was a third-string tailback named Cliff Crabtree. On nine carries he chewed off 114 yards.

	VMI	Rice
First downs	5	25
Yards rushing	47	403
Yards passing	34	132
Return yardage	6	10
Passes	4-26-2	2-18-0
Punts	11-31	5-41
Fumbles lost	0	4
Yards penalized	38	60

VMI   0   0   0   0— 0
Rice   7   7 21 20—55

Rice — Spruill 7 run (Davis kick)
Rice — Caldwell 14 pass from Wood (Davis kick)
Rice — Wood 1 run (Davis kick)
Rice — Spruill 1 run (Davis kick)
Rice — Brown 35 pass from Vincent (Davis kick)
Rice — Crabtree 17 run (Davis kick)
Rice — Crabtree 70 run (kick failed)
Rice — Brown 24 pass from Vincent (Davis kick)
Attendance — 18,000 estimated.

37

Kansas State quarterback Lynn Dickey (11) throws to Mike Montgomery for the first score of the game. Bears are Trent Phipps (53), Walt Groth (71) and Tom Reaux (77).

KANSAS STATE 48-BAYLOR 15

Two teams in the rebuilding stage met at Waco Saturday night and one got torn down again. The Bears had not lost an opener in their home stadium in nine starts and it was the highest score an opponent had ever run up on the Bears on opening day. A tough opener for Baylor's new coach, Bill Beall.

The Bears kicked off to Kansas State, downing Mike Montgomery on the Wildcat 30. It took a couple of third down passes to keep things moving, one for 10 to Montgomery and one for 20 to wingback Mack Herron. And things kept going. A personal foul moved the Wildcats 15 yards closer. From the Baylor five, Dickey ran a swing pass play with Montgomery taking the TD toss. Max Arreguin's kick was good for 7-0.

On the Bears' first possession, they were stopped cold. Defensive tackle Ron Yankowski had a lot to do with that. He seemed to be everywhere.

Kansas State threw the bomb on their next possession, but Russell Serafin intercepted at the Baylor 13. A fumble cost the Bears the ball on their 25. Alan Steelman recovered for K-State. On third down, Dickey passed for an apparent TD, but it was ruled he had crossed the line of scrimmage before throwing. On fourth down, Max Arreguin kicked a field goal from the 37.

As soon as the Bears got possession, they couldn't wait to fumble it away. The Wildcats' alert Yankowski recovered for them on the 19. On the second play from scrimmage, Forrest Wells took a 17-yard Dickey pass for the score. The kick made it 17-0 and ended the scoring for the first tortuous quarter. But, there was still 4:30 remaining; enough time for the Bears to finally manage a first down. That was just about it . . . except for the following fourth-and-eleven situation at the Baylor 31, Bruin punter Ed Marsh was barely able to bring down a high snap. He knocked it down, picked it up and tried to pass. The Bears had an ineligible receiver downfield and the Wildcats took over on the Baylor 31. It took eight plays for KSU to get Herron over right tackle into the end zone, making it 24-0.

With four minutes gone in the second quarter, KSU's Mack Herron fumbled and Walter Groth recovered for the Bears on the Wildcat 25. It took only two plays to fumble the ball back again. On a fourth down punt two minutes later, Jim Crowl dropped the snap, picked it up and tried to kick, but Gary Sutton blocked it for the Bears. Tackle Earl Maxwell scooped up the bouncing ball and raced 22

Wildcat tailback Russell Harrison (32) picks up five yards and a bunch of Bears: Gilbert Beall (47), Trent Phipps (53), Russell Serafin (28), Tom Reaux (77) and Dennis Watson (86).

yards to score. Cozby's kick made it 24-7.

KSU jumped right back, moving 80 yards in 11 plays to score. A draw play sprang Lawson up the middle for 19 and Hawthorne made 31 more off tackle. Dickey bulled his way on a keeper like a fullback to the Bear 14. Another swing pass got Lawson into pay dirt from the eight. It was 31-7.

In spite of anything the Bears could do, the second half started. And so did the Cats. Again starting from their 30, Dickey passed to Yarnell for 21, Harrison rounded end for eight, another pass to Herron for nine, a 12-yard pass interference penalty against Serafin and, on the eighth play of the series, Harrison took right end for 12 yards and the TD. 38-7.

Again KSU got the ball and again they stuck it in the Bears' ear. A key block from Charles Collins sprung Herron loose from the Wildcat 32. The scoreboard sprung loose with another seven for a lopsided 45-7. Ed Marsh twisted an ankle on the play and the Bears lost their best punter as well as some more face.

The Bears got another pass intercepted by Clarence Scott, but Baylor forced a punt. This was not a good night for centers and punters for either side, however, and the snap sailed over Crowl's head and rolled into the end zone. Bruin end Roy McDearmon was the man who covered it for a Baylor score.

The offense was now allowed to make their only score of the evening. Steve Stuart passed to tailback Terry Jackson for a two-point conversion. The scoreboard was still tilted at 45-15.

As soon as the Wildcats got the ball, they started grinding Bear meat again. Arreguin took over at quarterback from Dickey. A fumble at the Baylor nine lost the ball to the Bears' John Miller.

An early fourth quarter drive by the Bruins moved the ball to the KSU 23, where Baylor tried a fake field goal to pick up the needed 16 yards for a first down. Their try fell six yards short.

Quaterback Arreguin was now running with an almost entirely new team, but they still made progress against the bruised Bears. They were finally stopped at the Baylor 21 where Arreguin's field goal ended the scoring at 48-15.

	KSU	Bay.
First downs	23	7
Rushing yardage	312	27
Passing yardage	173	110
Return yardage	5	183
Passes	18-29-1	12-35-2
Punts	2-38	8-42
Fumbles	4	4
Yards penalized	55	67

Kas. State	17	14	14	3—48	
Baylor	0	7	8	0—15	

KS — Montgomery 5 pass from Dickey (Arreguin kick)

KS — FG Arreguin 37

KS — Wells 17 pass from Dickey (Arreguin kick)

KS—Herron 1 run (Arreguin kick)

KS—Maxfield 22 run with blocked punt (Cozby kick)

KS — Lawson 8 pass from Dickey (Arreguin kick)

KS — Harrison 12 run (Arreguin kick)

KS — Herron 68 run (Arreguin kick)

Bay — McDearmon recover bad center in end zone (Stuart pass to Jackson)

KS — FG Arreguin 38

Attendance — 30,000

Quarterback Joe Matulich gets the pass away in spite of Jayhawk efforts. Gary Davenport (85), Jim Bailey (71) and a friend close in fast. Barney (73) delays Bailey.

TEXAS TECH 38-KANSAS 22

The pro odds favored Kansas by three points, but fate favored the Raiders to win their third straight contest with the Jayhawks. The bookies were undoubtedly happy through the first half as Kansas walked over the Raiders and then to the dressing room with a 16-3 lead.

Kansas' first possession wasn't planned that way. The Hawks' Jim Hatcher intercepted a Tom Sawyer pass at the Tech 31. On the fourth play from scrimmage, quarterback Jim Ettinger ran a sneak for the final yard to score. Bill Bell added the extra point for a 7-0 lead.

Tech was almost plowed under again on a miscue, but the defense managed to save the score. A fumble by Miles Langehennig was recovered by Kansas at the Tech 23. The Jayhawks made a first down at the 11. Another sneak by Ettinger made the two. Fullback John Riggins was blasted by left tackle Dicky Grigg and lost a yard. Same play, third down. Same Grigg, no gain. The old Ettinger sneak was pulled again on fourth down, but the Raiders were ready this time. No score.

J. D. Sanders was punting from the Raider five late in the first quarter when Kansas middle guard Al Jakobcic blew in to block the boot. The ball bounced into the end zone, then rolled out of bounds, scoring a safety on Tech and moving the score to 9-0.

Sanders' free kick, following the safety, only went to the Jayhawk 28. It took eleven plays for Kansas to again raid the Raider end zone. Ettinger threw from scrimmage at the 15 to wingback Willie Amison who had gotten loose behind the goal line. Bell's kick was good and the Jayhawks led 16-0 with 46 seconds gone in the second quarter.

Joe Matulich, battling for first chair quarterback, entered the game in the second quarter. His direction took Tech from its own 35 to the Jayhawks' 25. With a fourth down coming up, J. D. Sanders was called in for a 42-yard field goal. And Tech's side of the scoreboard lit up for the first time with a 16-3 deficit.

The tide was finally turned in Tech's direction midway through the third quarter. Eddy Windom tipped Jim Ettinger's pass and linebacker Dennis Lane picked it off on the Tech 45. Happily for Tech, Lane was standing in the midst of four teammates. The interception return went 55 yards to score. Sanders booted the tally to 16-10.

It was a different team that kicked off to the Jay-

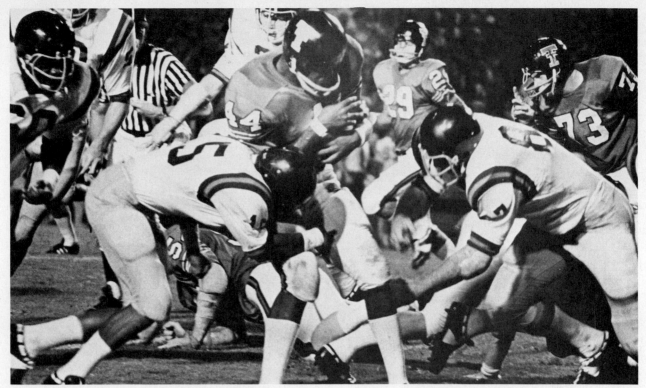

Danny Hardaway (44) is crunched between Jim Hatcher (15) and Steve Carmichael (87). Also pictured are Ken Kattner (29) and Philip Barney (73).

hawks. Kansas ran three plays for no gain and was forced to punt. Tech took the ball on their own 35. Matulich moved his troops into Kansas pay dirt on nine plays. Halfback Danny Hardaway ran for the final yard and Sanders' kick put the Raiders ahead 17-16. There were eighteen seconds left to play in the third quarter and the Tech New Look was something to get excited about.

A great Jayhawk punt by Bill Bell was killed on the Raider two, putting Tech in a hole that they were unable to scramble out of. Kicking under pressure in his end zone, Sanders' punt got only to the Tech 29. The elated Hawks poured it on the Raiders from there. With 8:45 remaining in the game, Jim Ettinger threw for seven yards and the score to wingback Steve Conley. Leading by only five points, the Jayhawks tried for two on the conversion, but a hard pass rush by Bruce Dowdy and Dicky Grigg broke up the play with the score still 22-17.

The remaining four minutes were a nightmare for the Jayhawks. Safety Kevin Ormes made a 24-yard return with one of Bill Bell's punts to the Tech 43. It only took one play from there. Matulich rolled out to his left. End David May had outrun the defense and Matulich's pass connected for the 57-yard score that put Tech ahead 23-22. Sanders made it 24-22.

Kansas was allowed possession of the ball for only

two plays after Tech kicked off. And they would have been better off not to have had the second. Defensive left halfback, Denton Fox got in the way of another of Ettinger's passes and ran it back 55 yards to rack another six points for Tech. Again, Sanders' toe added the point and it was 31-22.

Fox decided he liked intercepting passes. He set up Tech's last score with another steal of an Ettinger pass on the KU 47 and returned it to their 22. In spite of the efforts of the Kansas defense, a fifteen-yard penalty on third down kept the Raiders going. Reagan Young bulled over from the three. Sanders hit another kick for the final score of 38-22.

	Kas.	Tech
First downs	14	16
Yards rushing	220	123
Yards passing	78	145
Return yardage	11	159
Passes	8-19-3	12-19-1
Punts	6-37	6-36
Fumbles lost	0	1
Yards penalized	81	45

Kansas	9	7	6	0—22
Texas Tech	0	3	14	21—38

KU — Ettinger 1 run (Bell kick)
KU — Safety, Jakobcic blocked punt out of end zone
KU — Amison 15 pass from Ettinger (Bell kick)
Tech — FG Sanders 42
Tech — Lane 55 interception return (Sanders kick)
Tech — Hardaway 1 run (Sanders kick)
KU — Conley 7 pass from Ettinger (run failed)
Tech — May 57 pass from Matulich (Sanders kick)
Tech — Tech 55 interception return (Sanders kick)
Tech — Young 3 run (Sanders kick)
Attendance — 42,250

Jimmy Sheffield (11) hustles to avoid the clutches of LSU defensive left end Jerry Kober as fullback Marc Black readies a block.

LSU 35 - TEXAS A&M 6

It looks like, in ten years of repeat matches, the Tigers would have stumbled once, anyway. They almost did in 1966. That was a tie, 7-7. But, there was no sign of a false step at Baton Rouge Saturday night and it was the Aggies who fell into the Tiger trap.

Army was thoroughly defensed throughout the first half, but did manage one scoring threat when Jim Piper recovered an LSU fumble at the Tigers' 15. After three plays, the cadets found themselves only one yard closer to the goal, so they tried for a field goal. It was wide to the right.

Following an unproductive first quarter, the Bengals were first on the scoreboard early in the second period. In fact, they were first, second, third, fourth and fifth on the board. The first one started on the LSU 48-yard line with tailback Art Cantrelle ripping off nine yards. Two completions brought the Tigers to the A&M 23, then Cantrelle went down the left sideline with the scoring pass. Lumpkin's kick was good for a 7-0 lead.

The Aggies were almost stung again when they lost a fumble on their own 37 to LSU's Donnie

Bozeman. As the Tigers went for blood from the A&M ten, Dave Elmendorf intercepted in the end zone for the cadets.

It wasn't long before the Bengals were again in enemy territory, but the drive was stopped at the Aggie 13. Lumpkin's field goal try fell short from the 50.

With less than three minutes left in the half, LSU drew another six out of the Cadets' account. Again, Hillman's passing took the Tigers for a first down, after four completions, at the Aggie 25. Fullback Eddie Ray carried over tackle for five and a pass to Jimmy Gilbert netted six more. From the 14, Andy Hamilton carried a reverse around his right end, broke loose at the ten and crossed the Aggie threshold standing up. Lumpkin was again called to kick the score to 14-0. Two minutes were left in the half.

As the bands played, the respective coaches either asked for more of the same, or less of it, depending on his point of view . . . from which side of the field. Then came that awful third quarter which will be relived in a good many Aggie nightmares.

In spite of the fact that things started badly for the

Moving as well as possible on one leg, Aggie tailback Steve Burks (42) has his prop knocked from under him by Tiger left linebacker Mike Anderson (45).

Aggies, they got worse. On their first series, Sheffield was dropped for an 11-yard loss to his four. The ensuing punt was returned fourteen yards by Casanova on a razzle-dazzle handoff from Burns. From the 26, the Tigers stayed on the ground, picking up a first down, then another score after six jabs at the battered A&M defense. Del Walker carried over from the two. Another flex of the Lumpkin leg and the Bengals led by 21.

Again, the Aggie War Machine sputtered into action and coughed up the football on the Cadet 30. LSU's Jerry Kober recovered the bobbled handoff. It took five plays to dissect the Aggie defense. West took a big chunk with a 16-yard completion from Hillman. Two plays later, Hillman hit Ray on the left sideline. Caswell bounced him out of bounds on the Army two. Cantrelle vaulted the line twice, finding himself in the Aggie end zone for the second time of the night. Lumpkin's kick missed, but A&M was called on a roughing-the-kicker penalty. The second try was good enough for a 28-0 score.

The Tigers took the ball from their 20 to the Aggie 13, but lost possession when Wayne Wheat recovered a fumble for the Cadets. Army didn't breathe easy for long. They were forced to punt to the Shell Game Twins, Burns and Casanova. This time, it was Burns' turn to take the handoff. With opinion divided as to who had the ball, Burns reached the Aggie eight before Burks bumped him out. It took Hillman two carries to score. Leg Lumpkin added his fifth point, rounding it out to 35-0.

The Aggies had lost the game, but not their fight. Caswell recovered a fumbled pass on the LSU 41 to give the Cadets another chance to avoid a shutout. Rocky Self was now in at quarterback. Brupbacher took his pass for a first down at the 20, then Self ran for ten more. He threw incomplete twice, connected with Harris for three and faced a fourth down on the seven. He gambled it all and hit Brupbacher in the end zone for the TD. But, his try for two was no good.

	A&M	LSU
First downs	11	22
Rushing yardage	37	164
Passing yardage	135	191
Passes	17-39	17-31
Passes intercepted by	1	1
Fumbles lost	2	3
Punts	13-37.2	8-38.9

A&M	0	0	0	6— 6
LSU	0	14	21	0—35

LSU — Cantrelle 23 pass from Hillman (Lumpkin kick)
LSU — Walker 2 run (Lumpkin kick)
LSU — Cantrelle 1 run (Lumpkin kick)
LSU — Hillman 5 run (Lumpkin kick)
A&M — Brupbacher 7 pass from Self (pass failed)
Attendance — 67,510

Mustang split end Gary Hammond (17) does a fancy dance to avoid Georgia Tech pursuit by Dave Beavin (36) and Jack Paulk (24).

GEORGIA TECH 24 - SMU 21

It was a cool, cloudy and breezy afternoon in Atlanta. The Ramblin' Wrecks had the sophomore prodigy at quarterback, Charlie Dudish, while the Mustang hopes rested on the arm of last year's soph prodigy, Chuck Hixson.

It took only two Mustang plays to put Tech in the position of playing catch-up ball. The first play was a pass to tailback Bicky Lesser. Lesser took the pass at the right sideline from the 34 to the 48 of SMU. Then, Gary Hammond raced down the left side, got behind the Tech safety and grabbed Hixson's pass at the 22. He covered the rest of the ground with no defender in sight. Lesser's kick put the Mustangs ahead 7-0.

The first time Tech managed to cross into SMU territory was on a 21-yard run by Dudish, but Jordan caused him to fumble and Portillo recovered at the SMU 38. Only one other drive in the first half managed to get Tech across the 50. Again, the Pony defense, led by John Jordan, bowled over Dudish for three straight losses. And, after a five-yard penalty, the Wrecks found themselves punting from their own 24 in a fourth-and-41 situation. Often, the Mustang defense bulldogged the Tech offense to a halt with Jordan, Cormier, White, Fraser and Portillo turning a number of key plays.

After Hixson's touchdown pass, his 300th career completion, the Ponies were unable to get off the ground again. Tech was having its trouble with the Pony defense and a short punt against the wind gave the Mustangs the ball on the Tech 45. But the defense was still the name of the game and the Ponies had to settle for a try at a field goal from the Tech 47. Lesser's kick was no good.

Early in the second quarter, the Mustangs moved from their own 35 to the Tech 15 as Hixson was able to maintain his passing attack with receptions by Holden and Fleming. But outside linebacker Bubba Hoats got Hixson for a ten-yard loss. The next pass play to Sam Holden made up the yardage, but brought up a fourth down situation. Lesser came in for another field goal try, but the kick was wide.

Again, the Tech defense closed in on the harried Mustang attackers. Trying to move the Ponies out of their own end of the field, Hixson flung a pass to Hammond, but defensive back Jeff Ford snatched it at the 39 and, after a brief juggling act, raced untouched into the end zone. The extra point tied the score at 7-7.

Near the end of the half, Tech ran a pass pattern from their own 47, but Portillo dumped Dudish for a five-yard loss. That would have brought around the

Here comes the winning TD carried by quarterback Charlie Dudish (11) after picking up a fumbled snap. SMU defense is (L to R) Rufus Cormier, Joe Stutts and Bruce Portillo.

fourth down except for a personal foul penalty against a Tech receiver. With a first down on the SMU 38, Tech ground out a few more yards, but they reached a fourth down before they reached the Pony end zone. Pat Curry had just broken up a pass in the end zone, so Tech called in Johnny Duncan who put his 48-yard kick through the target and Tech led at halftime 10-7.

Halfway through the third quarter, Portillo recovered Dudish's errant pitchout on the SMU 43. It took seven plays and a 15-yard penalty to put the Mustangs back in the lead. The score came with a Fleming reception of a 12-yard pass from Hixson in the right corner of the end zone.

But the four-point Mustang lead evaporated quickly. Late in the third period, Tech recovered a Lesser fumble on the SMU 31. On first down, Tech lost 15 yards on a personal foul. Sophomore Jack O'Neill, Tech's third quarterback of the day, threw his first college pass. His target was split end Percy Helmer. Helmer ran a post pattern, got behind the Mustang defense and took O'Neill's inaugural pass for a 16-yard TD. The kick made it 17-14, Tech.

The alert Mustang defense was still very much alive. Early in the fourth quarter, Pat Curry intercepted O'Neill's pass at his own 37. It took only eight plays to cover the needed 63 yards. One of the flashiest was a double reverse pass by Hammond to Holden for 27 yards and a first down at the Tech

five. It took three more tries, but Hixson hit Lesser wide open in the end zone with 12:56 left in the game. Lesser's kick put the Ponies back ahead 21-17.

The Mustang kickoff was fumbled by Dudish and John Jordan recovered on the Tech 31, but a 15-yard offensive pass interference penalty put the Ponies out of reach and kept the Wrecks within reach of victory.

With 6:47 left, an errant Hixson pass was snatched away by Tech safety, Mike Wysong at the Mustang 49. Dudish returned to his quarterback post. Tight end Steve Foster took a pair of passes for 15 yards each, bulling his way for the extra yardage. On fourth-and-one for the TD, Dudish fumbled the snap, but he picked it up and just managed to dive far enough for the score. It didn't matter much, Moore kicked the extra point anyway.

The game did result in an individual victory for Chuck Hixson. It brought his career record of TD passes to 26, bettering Don Meredith's previous mark of 25.

	SMU	Tech
First downs	23	16
Rushing yardage	60	139
Passing yardage	270	101
Return yardage	58	46
Passes	26-48-2	8-17-1
Punts	5-31	7-40
Fumbles lost	1	4
Yards penalized	70	110

SMU	7	0	7	7—21
Ga. Tech	0	10	7	7—24

Attendance — 42,624

SMU — Hammond 52 pass from Hixson (Lesser kick)

Tech — Ford 39 pass interception (Moore kick)

Tech — FG Duncan 48

SMU — Fleming 12 pass from Hixson (Lesser kick)

Tech — Helmer 46 pass from O'Neil (Moore kick)

SMU — Lesser 3 pass from Hixson (Lesser kick)

Tech—Dudish 1 run (Moore kick)

SYNOPSIS

TOP TEN

1. Ohio State
2. Penn State
3. Arkansas
4. Texas
5. Southern Cal
6. Oklahoma
7. Georgia
8. Mississippi
9. Notre Dame
10. Indiana

SWC OFFENSIVE PLAYER OF WEEK

Steve Judy, Quarterback, TCU

SWC DEFENSIVE PLAYER OF WEEK

Leo Brooks, Defensive Tackle, Texas

TEAM LEADERS FOR SEASON

DEFENSE

Rushing ....Arkansas —19 yds.
Passing ....Rice 34 yds.
Total ....Arkansas 78 yds.

OFFENSE

Rushing ....Rice 403 yds.
Passing ....SMU 626 yds.
Total ....SMU 685 yds.

SEASON RECORDS

	W	L	T
Texas Tech	1	0	0
Rice	1	0	0
Arkansas	1	0	0
Texas	1	0	0
Baylor	0	1	0
Texas A & M	0	1	0
TCU	0	1	0
SMU	0	2	0

Second Week
September 27

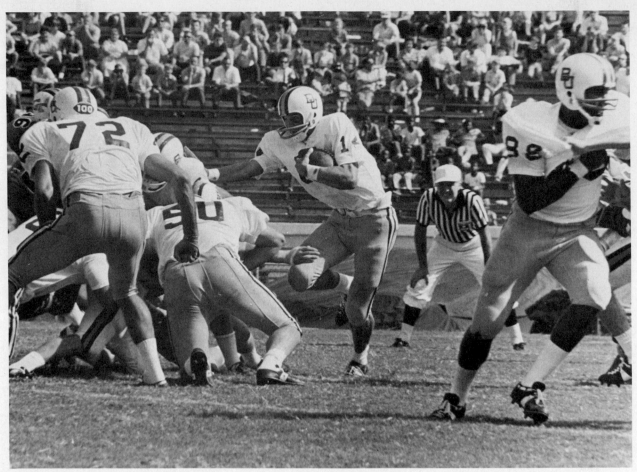

Laney Cook (14) sprints for good yardage in the third quarter behind blocking by Jessie Young (72) and Calvin Hunt (50) as Rollin Hunter (88) gets his jersey stretched.

GEORGIA TECH 17-BAYLOR 10

The underdog Bears met the Yellow Jackets in Atlanta mostly to test the aerial skill of three quarterbacks. Georgia Tech's sophomore quarterback, Charles Dudish, fresh from the previous week's win over SMU's fliers, was looking for a repeat with his quarterback spot firmly nailed down. Si Southall and Steve Stuart were each ready to turn in a performance that would secure the signal-calling job for himself.

Baylor won the toss and elected to receive. But the unhappy Bruins fumbled the ball away to Tech on their first play. Gene Rogers was hit hard by John Riggle on the Baylor 18 and Tash Van Dora recovered for Tech. That play set the tone for the rest of the game. It was to be a battle of the defenses. And now it was the Bears' turn in the pit.

Defensive Baylor end David Jones dropped Dudish for a one-yard loss on third-and-three at the eleven. The best the Wrecks could do was a field goal by Jack Moore from the 28. Only two minutes

and six seconds had elapsed and Tech led 3-0.

The Bears came fighting back, moving 70 yards to the Yellow Jacket four-yard line. Steve Stuart connected with passes to Jerry Smith for six, 18 and eleven yards, to Derek Davis for ten and Gene Rogers on a 21-yard screen pass. But the drive died on a eleven-yard pass which missed Randy Cooper at the goal line.

On Tech's next series, the Bear defense bristled and forced the Yellow Jackets to punt. Walt Groth, Brian Blessing and Gilbert Beall made the going rough enough to keep opponents' points off the board.

The Bears, under the direction of quarterback Si Southall managed to get to the Tech 18, but had to settle for a field goal try. Then, they had to settle for nothing. It was blocked by Tech.

The third quarter brought a little joy to the Baylor bench. It started when Bear safety, John Miller pounced on a Dudish fumble at the Baylor 36

48

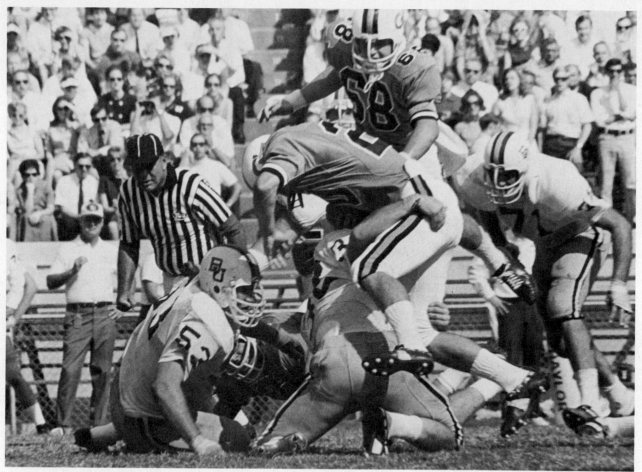

Pads pop as Baylor's Tom Bambrick (32) stops Eddie Hughes (20) for no gain. Trent Phipps (53) and Walt Groth (71) move in to help as Frank McCloskey (68) arrives too late to block.

after a 14-yard gain by the flashy "Dude". Quarterback Steve Stuart passed for 16 yards to Derek Davis, then hit Randy Cooper deep in the Tech secondary. Cooper was finally forced out of bounds on the Tech 17. Then Stuart was forced to run and picked up nine yards. Cooper bucked for a first down at the Tech six, then was dropped for a loss of three on the next play. Laney Cook carried to the three and Gene Rogers made the two, but it was fourth down coming up. Terry Cozby's kick tied the game at 3-3.

The fourth quarter began with the Bears in a hole and saw Tech cave it in on them. Stuart had a second-and-eight on his own nine. His pass was picked away by Jeff Ford, a 167 pound defensive halfback, who had scored in the same manner on SMU a week earlier. Ford acquired the ball at the Baylor 16 and ran untouched for the score. Jack Moore's kick made it 10-3.

But Baylor wasn't through, yet. Putting the ball in play on their own 29 after the Tech kickoff, Southall handed off to Jarrell Landers. He got a yard. Then Laney Cook took off down the field and

Southall opened the bomb doors. He took his time, letting Cook get behind the defense, then let go. Cook crawled into the air, just putting enough brakes on the ball to keep it dancing on his fingertips. His wild balancing act finally gave way to a footrace to the end zone with the ball tucked safely away. Again the score was tied.

But, Baylor was through for the afternoon and Georgia Tech wasn't. Dudish got a scoring pass to halfback Steve Harkey for the 21 yards needed to put Tech ahead for the day.

	Baylor	Tech
First downs	11	14
Rushing yardage	31	144
Passing yardage	217	111
Return yardage	15	20
Passes	12-26-3	11-22-2
Punts	7-36	7-41
Fumbles lost	1	1
Yards penalized	18	15
Baylor	0 0 3	7—10
Ga. Tech	3 0 0	14—17

Tech—FG Moore 28
Bay—FG Cozby 19
Tech—Ford 16 pass interception (Moore kick)
Bay—Cook 69 pass from Southall (Cozby kick)
Tech—Harkey 21 pass from Dudish (Moore kick)
Attendance—37,776

49

Nebraska quarterback Jerry Tagge (14) grits his teeth and looks for a receiver over Aggie defenders Jim Piper (40) and Billy Bob Barnett (85). John Hopkins and Gale Williams (77) block.

NEBRASKA 14-TEXAS A&M 0

The Huskers shucked the Aggies before 66,331, mostly Nebraska fans in Lincoln. A&M coach Gene Stallings wasn't sure whether it was the Nebraska defense or the Army offense, but the Aggies were unable to score on four different occasions inside the Nebraska ten.

Mike Bellar kicked off for A&M. Nebraska marched down to the Aggie 20, then lost the ball on a fumble. Jimmy Sheffield started at quarterback for A&M, but failed to move his team. On third-and-seven at his own 27, he was dropped by Mike Wynn for a nine-yard loss. He punted 36 yards to the Nebraska 46. Nebraska quarterback Van Brownson moved his team to the Aggie 26, but was thrown for a loss on the 40. The field goal attempt by Paul Rogers was short.

Then lightning hit the Aggie barn. Sheffield flung a pass from his 20, but Nebraska's right cornerback Jim Anderson snatched it and returned it to the three. It had been intended for Jimmy Adams, who tipped the high throw into the waiting hands of Anderson. It took only one play for halfback Jeff Kinney to bust over the middle for the score. With 6:50 left in the first quarter, Rogers' kick made

it 7-0.

The Aggies could not gain the Nebraska end of the field and kicked. Guy Ingles made a fair catch on the Nebraska 43. On second-and-eleven at the Cornhusker 44, a pass to Jeff Kinney was intercepted by Buster Adami and returned to the Nebraska 42. But A&M could not move and Sheffield kicked out-of-bounds on the Cornhusker three. Nebraska fumbled the ball away at the six on first down, but Larry Stegent lost six on the next carry. Then a pass to Barney Harris was intercepted by Randy Reeves at the goal line.

Nebraska made eight yards from their 20, then punted. The Aggies tried, then punted back. Again, punts were exchanged before the Cornhuskers finally found the gearshift.

Nebraska took Sheffield's punt at their own seven. Jerry Tagge was now running the Cornhusker offense and he conducted them through a steady drive with a good mixture of passing and running to the A&M 11. A five-yard offsides penalty against the Aggies move the ball to the six. Kinney made a tough run up the Aggie middle to the one, then Tagge took the sneak over for the score. Again,

50

A&M's Marc Black cuts behind the blocking of Barney Harris (15) and Larry Stegent (25). Stegent takes aim on Cornhusker monster man Al Larson (20).

Rogers made the extra point and the scoring was finished for the afternoon with 2:54 left in the first half.

But the excitement wasn't over. A&M again failed to make a first down and kicked to Guy Ingles at the Nebraska 34. Tagge dropped back to pass, was hit and fumbled. Lynn Odom recovered. A pass to Billy Joe Polasek was tipped away by Jim Anderson. Rocky Self was the new face at quarterback for the Aggies. He rolled right and was dropped for a one-yard loss, then passed complete to Polasek to the nine. Then a fumble was recovered by Marc Black for A&M back on the 16 followed by a holding penalty to the 31. So ended the threat and the half.

The Aggies took the second half kickoff, then had to punt. Nebraska took the punt on their 19 and returned to the 28, then moved steadily to the Aggie 36 to try for a field goal. It was short and Dave Elmendorf returned it to the A&M 30. Then the Aggies made a sustained march to the Nebraska eight, but a bobbled pitchout was picked up to Dana Stephenson and returned to the 16 of Nebraska. They pushed to their 23 and had to punt. The Aggies ran one play and lost the ball on an interception by Al Larson as the third quarter ended.

Tagge again marched his team to within striking distance of the Aggie end zone, but again had to be content with a field goal try from the 17-yard line. The angle was sharp from the right side of the field and the kick was no good.

A&M couldn't move from their 20. Sheffield's punt went to the Nebraska 35. Tagge threw the bomb and Jim McFarland made a fine diving catch on the A&M 24. But Mike Green fumbled and Edwin Ebrom recovered for the Aggies. A&M moved to their 44, then had to kick. Nebraska likewise made their 44 and punted to Dave Elmendorf on the A&M 20. He made a fantastic run before being stopped by the last Nebraska man, Mike Green at the Nebraska 23. But, with a third-and-goal on the Nebraska eight, Dana Stephenson intercepted the last Aggie threat and ran it back to the A&M 41 wih 3:29 left.

It was A&M's first shutout in 26 games. Arkansas did it 34-0 in 1966.

	A&M	Neb.
First downs	12	23
Rushing yardage	35	157
Passing yardage	136	209
Return yardage	131	100
Passes	16 34-3	17-24-1
Punts	9-39	5-37
Fumbles lost	1	4
Yards penalized	20	45

Texas A&M	0	0	0	0— 0
Nebraska	7	7	0	0—14

Neb—Kinney 3 run (Rogers kick)
Neb—Tagge 1 run (Rogers kick)
Attendance—66,331

51

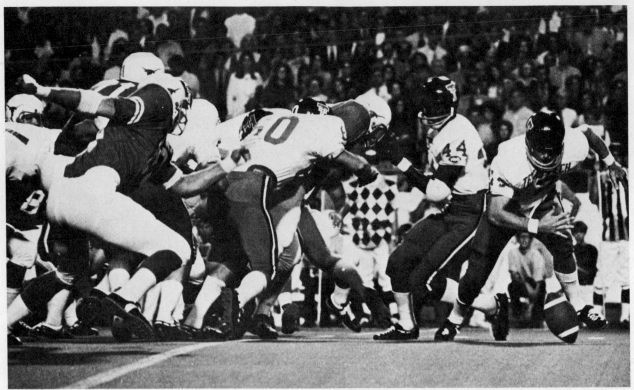

Tech quarterback Joe Matulich tries to run down his own fumble. Mike Campbell, on far left with outstretched arm, recovered for Texas. Danny Hardaway (44) suddenly realizes what has happened.

TEXAS 49-TEXAS TECH 7

Memorial Stadium was jammed with 65,200 football faithful as the Longhorns and Red Raiders opened the 55th Southwest Conference season. The two teams also christened the new artificial grass which now covers the playing field.

The big question preceding the game was, could Tech make it three in a row over Texas? The answer wasn't long in coming as the 'Horns came roaring out of the chute to score 28 points in the first half. While the offense was doing this, the defense allowed Tech to get past the mid-field stripe just once, before intermission.

On Tech's first possession quarterback Joe Matulich juggled the snapback and lost the ball for good as Bill Zapalac hit him. Mike Campbell recovered for Texas at the Tech 27. Steve Worster carried three times to move the ball to the 12. From there Billy Dale skirted right end, behind great blocking, and went leaping over bodies to score. Happy Feller tacked on the one-pointer and Texas led 7-0.

The second Texas touchdown came early in the second quarter on a 49-yard drive. The moment of truth came when quarterback James Street, facing a

fourth down and two, threw complete to Cotton Speyrer for 10 yards. This placed the pigskin on the five and Jim Bertelsen made that on the next play. Feller's boot made it 14-0.

This opened the floodgates for Texas. Two minutes and 40 seconds later they were again in the Red Raider end zone. Ted Koy exploded through the line and sped 42 yards to the Tech five-yard line. On third down, Worster crossed the goal and with Feller's PAT the Longhorns led 21-0.

Following the kickoff Texas held Tech and forced a punt. Speyrer gathered in the ball at the Longhorn 42 and returned almost all the way. Jesse Richardson hauled him down five yards shy of pay dirt. Bertelsen appeared to be heading for a TD on the next play, but fumbled into the end zone as he neared the goal line. Larry Molinaire recovered for the Red Raiders and the ball came out to the 20.

Unable to move, Tech punted and Street guided the Longhorns from midfield to the Red Raider 19. On fourth down Dicky Greg stopped Worster and Tech took possession.

On second down Matulich, with Bill Atessis ap-

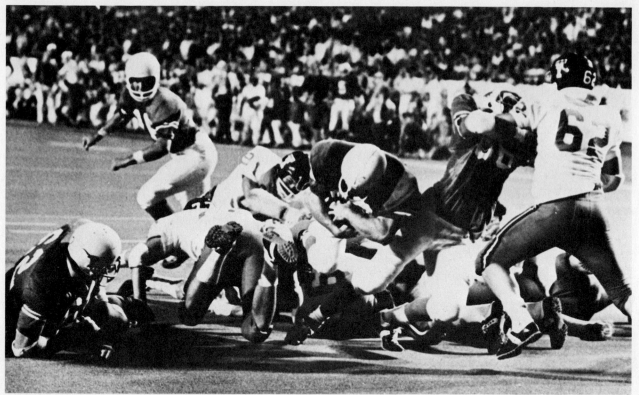

Steve Worster "guts" it up the middle for nine yards. Mike Dean (66) throws a block on Steven Bannat (62) as James Street watches play from the rear.

plying pressure, threw quickly and Mike Campbell intercepted for Texas. Campbell crossed the goal untouched, covering 26 yards in the process. Feller added the seventh point and it was now 28-0 with time running out in the first half.

Soon afterwards a Street aerial was intercepted by Jerry Watson at the Tech 18 and returned to the Texas 48. The Red Raiders had time for only two plays before the first half ended.

Charles Napper, who had replaced Matulich as Tech quarterback, had a rude welcome as the third quarter opened. Tom Campbell intercepted one of his passes at the Red Raider 34 and returned all but two yards. From the two, Worster scored his second touchdown. With an extra point by Feller the score mounted to 35-0.

The onslaught didn't slow down. Scott Henderson intercepted another Napper pass on the Tech 20. When one thing goes wrong, everything goes wrong. The Red Raiders drew a half-the-distance penalty to their 10 yard line. Facing a fourth and three, quarterback Eddie Phillips pitched back to Dale who crossed the final stripe for the score. That and Feller's kick made the tally read 42-0, Texas.

As the third quarter approached the end, Texas cranked out its last touchdown. Phillips took the

Longhorn reserves 54 yards in nine plays. He contributed 14 yards on a keeper and started the triple option to Paul Robichau, who turned the corner for the final 14 yards. Feller did it again and Texas led 49-0.

With just over 12 minutes left in the game, Tech broke the tape on the Longhorn goal line. They covered 79 yards in 10 plays. The big gainer was a Napper to Johnny Kleinert pass, good for 18 yards and setting up the ball on the Texas 12. From the nine Napper passed to Johnny Odom, who made a ground level catch as he went into the end zone.

With no more scoring the final read Texas 49 — Tech 7. The Longhorn defense played another outstanding game and gave the offense excellent field position all night.

For the Tech seniors — two out of three from Texas ain't bad. For their sophomores — welcome to Southwest Conference Football.

	Tech	Texas
First downs	9	14
Rushing yardage	42	257
Passing yardage	171	29
Return yardage	58	114
Passes	14-34-1	3-10-4
Punts	11-35	7-43
Fumbles lost	1	1
Yards penalized	80	59

Texas Tech 0 0 0 7— 7
Texas 7 21 21 0—49
UT — Dale 12 run (Feller kick)
UT — Bertelsen 5 run (Feller kick)
UT — Worster 2 run (Feller kick)
UT — M. Campbell 26 pass interception (Feller kick)
UT — Worster 2 run (Feller kick)
UT — Dale 2 run (Feller kick)
TT — Odom 9 pass from Napper (Sanders kick)
Attendance — 65,200.

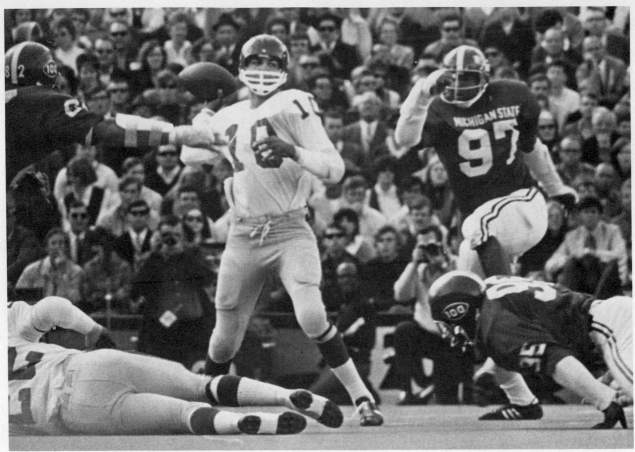

Mustang quarterback Chuck Hixson on a record-breaking, heart-breaking day. Closing in are defensive Spartans Gary Nowak (82), Wilt Martin (97) and Don Law (95). Gordon Gilder (22) on ground.

MICHIGAN STATE 23-SMU 15

SMU's great old grad, Doak Walker, drove down from his home in Detroit to East Lansing to watch his alma mater try to upset heavily-favored Michigan. And they almost did. Instead, they had to settle for their third straight loss of the season.

Michigan Sate quarterback Bill Triplett was his team's leading rusher with 122 yards. He got half of that total on his first carry of 95 yards to the Pony 15 on the third play of the game. Halfback Don Highsmith finished off the drive when be busted up the middle for the score. Gary Boyce's kick put the Spartans ahead 7-0 with 2:01 gone in the first period.

The Mustangs got their first scoring chance when Tommy Fraser recovered an MSU fumble on the Spartan 34, but Michigan State's defense held on and sent the Ponies scoreless back to the bench.

The Spartans almost scored again when left halfback Eric Allen raced 60 yards to the SMU one yard line, but the play was called back to the SMU 46 on a clipping penalty. Again, Michigan State failed to dent the SMU defense after Larry Tunnell's 17-yard

punt set the Spartans in business on the Mustang 34. It was Fraser again who recovered an MSU fumble on the 13.

Split end Gary Hammond took two of Chuck Hixson's passes for 42 yards. Daryl Doggett's reception added 19 more and, on the eleventh play from the one, Hixson kept for the score. Linebacker Ralph Wieleba blocked Bicky Lesser's extra point try and the score stood at 7-6.

It was in the third quarter that the Ponies finally moved ahead. They had moved from their own 20 to the Spartan 20 when Hixson was thrown for an 11-yard loss. The march had been highlighted by good runs by Daryl Doggett and Gordon Gilder and passes to Bicky Lesser and Ken Fleming. But the drive ended with Lesser trying a field goal from the 48. It was good and the Ponies led 9-7.

Eric Allen fumbled the Mustang kickoff and Chipper Johnson recovered for SMU on the Spartan 41. Capitalizing on the break, Hixson went for it all with a pass to Gilder, who had beaten the Spartan safety

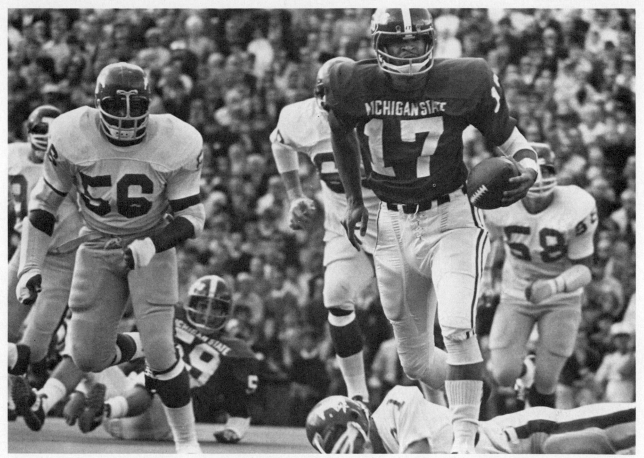

Rushing leader and quarterback for MSU, Bill Triplett hurdles Joe Stutts (31), pursued by Tommy Fraser (94), Rufus Cormier (56), Kemp McMillan (69) and Joe White (58).

and the Ponies had their third score just 15 seconds after their field goal. Again, Lesser's extra point try was blocked, this time by right tackle Ron Curl. The score was 15-7 for SMU.

The alert Mustang defense picked up another MSU fumble by Allen. It was right guard Rufus Cormier who recovered for SMU. But, the Ponies couldn't convert the break to a score as Lesser missed a 47-yard field goal try.

Spartan left half Harold Phillips intercepted a Hixson pass early in the fourth quarter. He picked it off on the Pony 32 and ran it back to the 19. The SMU defense answered the call again and held the Spartans to a field goal of 36 yards by Gary Boyce. The Spartans now trailed SMU 15-10.

Gary Hammond took the Michigan State kickoff for a 40-yard ride to the Spartan 45. Hixson's next play put the ball on the 35, but a fumbled snap was recovered by Ron Joseph for MSU.

On the first play from scrimmage, Joe Stutts belted the ball loose from Triplett and it was nearly recovered by Mike Shelton. But the Spartans regained their composure and, with Triplett gaining 41 yards on five carries, Don Highsmith punched it

over the middle for the last five yards to score. Joe Stutts stopped Steve Piro short of a two-point attempt. The Spartans again took the lead 16-15.

The Ponies took the kickoff and, on the second play, a pitchout to Doggett was fumbled. Joseph recovered for MSU on the Mustang 22. The scoring play came from the five on a pass to tight end Bruce Kuleska. Boyce's kick made the final score 23-15.

During the course of the game Doak Walker watched Mustang quarterback Chuck Hixson break Walker's old total offense record of 3592 yards. Hixson netted 206 yards, bringing his total to 3729 yards in just one season and three games.

	SMU	Mich.
First downs	17	21
Rushing yardage	49	302
Passing yardage	244	37
Return yardage	11	0
Passes	17-31-1	6-16-0
Punts	6-31	6-33
Fumbles lost	2	4
Yards penalized	40	20

SMU	0	6	9	0—15
Mich. St.	7	0	0	16—23

Mich—Highsmith 15 run (Boyce kick)
SMU—Hixson 1 run (kick failed)
SMU—FG Lesser 48
SMU—Gilder 41 pass from Hixson (kick failed)
Mich—FG Boyce 36
Mich—Highsmith 5 run (run failed)
Mich—Kulesza 5 pass from Triplett (Boyce kick)
Attendance—72,189

Rice fullback Kim Malone (32) gets excellent blocking from Mike Spruill (46), Paul Strahan (68) and Ron Waedemon (75) as he picks up short yardage over left guard.

LSU 42 - RICE 0

The Rice Owls went from riches to rags in Rice Stadium before a crowd of 55,000, of whom at least half were LSU Tiger rooters. The week before the Owls completely overwhelmed VMI. The shoe was on the other foot this time.

LSU kicked off and on Rice's second punt Tommy Casanova received, faked a handoff, then ran a parallel route before cutting upfield and going 68 yards to the Owl end zone. Mark Lumpkin kicked this extra point and five more before the match was over. LSU led 7-0.

The Tigers scored again on their next possession. It took them seven plays to cover 66 yards. Two plays gobbled up most of the yardage. Left-handed quarterback Mike Hillman ran on a roll-out for 21 yards and Bill Stober caught a throwback pass for 22 yards. Jim West made the last seven yards standing up. The Tigers moved up to a 14-0 lead.

On LSU's next drive, second-team quarterback Buddy Lee directed the Tigers all the way in six plays. On one of those plays, Lee faked then kept for 18 yards. Stober scored from the four on a pass

and LSU led by three touchdowns and extra points.

The Baton Rouge based Tigers didn't score anymore during the first quarter, but they tacked on another touchdown in the second quarter. It was half way through the stanza when the LSU first string drove 47 yards in six plays. A Hillman to West pass picked up 23 yards of the distance. For the touchdown, Hillman passed four yards to Lonny Myles. The Tigers lead increased to 28-0.

Shortly after this score, Rice made its initial first down. Mike Kramer, an intended red-shirt, was now at the quarterback helm. He passed complete to Bob Brown for 13 yards. The Bengals then stiffened and held. The LSU third offensive unit got close enough to try a field goal before the half closed. The 47-yard effort missed and the Louisianans led at the half by four touchdowns, 28-0.

LSU had a statistical edge in the first half of 12-1 in first downs, 137-13 yards rushing and 68-24 yards in the air. The Owls never got beyond their 35.

Rice kicked off to start the final half and LSU's Eddie Ray fumbled when hit. John Swords recov-

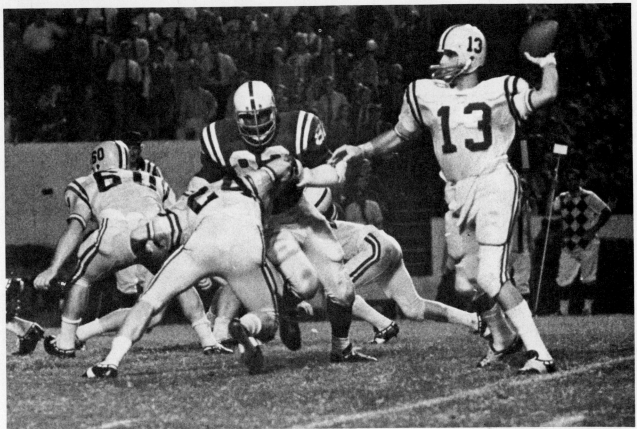

LSU quarterback Mike Hillman (13) passes four yards for the fourth Tiger touchdown. The onrushing Rodrigo Barnes (82) is slowed by LSU tailback Art Cantrelle (24), the game's leading rusher.

ered for Rice at the Tiger 19. Quarterback Phillip Wood tried two rollouts and netted one yard. Stahle Vincent replaced Wood and threw an incompletion. Then Wood re-entered and had his pass intercepted by linebacker Bill Thompson at the five.

Vincent got the Owls to moving late in the third quarter as he passed to Brown for nine yards, then swept left end for 23 yards. Unable to sustain the drive, Rice punted on a fourth and two situation at the LSU 35. Rice held and the Tiger punt was fumbled by Dale Bernauer. LSU recovered on the Owl 22, but Rice stiffened and took over at its 15. Vincent hit Brown with an 11-yard pass. Soon facing a second and eight, Wood tried to hit Brown in the flat. LSU linebacker Lloyd Frye intercepted the pass and ran 42 yards to score. He bowled over Wood, the last defender, at the 10 during his journey. Lumpkin's kick put LSU ahead 35-0.

In the fourth quarter Hillman led LSU to its final score. The Tigers moved 74 yards in 11 plays, Hillman scoring the touchdown on a fourth down run of two yards. The Bengals now led 42-0.

Kramer then, on the next Rice possession, gave the Owl fans their biggest moment to cheer about. He threw a 46-yard pass that Brown caught at the LSU 35. That was it though, as three straight passes were incompleted and Bernauer was dropped for an eight-yard loss.

The Tigers then moved to the Rice seven-yard line. Time ran out as Rodrigo Barnes tackled Lee for a two-yard loss. Final score 42-0 in LSU's favor.

LSU has now won six in a row over Southwest Conference teams. The Tigers all-time record against the SWC reads: 72 wins, 37 losses and nine ties. This all started with a 14-0 victory over Texas in 1896.

Rice coach Bo Hagan shuttled three quarterbacks all during the game, but they were unable to mount any consistent threat. The Owls lost starting guard Tommy Peel, on their first possession, with a leg injury. He will be out for the rest of the season.

	LSU	Rice
First downs	21	6
Rushing yardage	272	60
Passing yardage	132	101
Return yardage	141	—15
Passes	13-22-0	9-31-2
Punts	9-45	12-36
Fumbles lost	1	1
Yards penalized	38	30

LSU	21	7 7	7—42
Rice	0	0 0	0— 0

LSU — Burns 68 punt return (Lumpkin kick)

LSU — West 7 pass (Lumpkin kick)

LSU — Stober pass from Lee (Lumpkin kick)

LSU — Myles 4 pass from Hillman (Lumpkin kick)

LSU — Frye 42 pass interception (Lumpkin kick)

LSU — Hillman 2 run (Lumpkin kick)

Attendance — 55,000.

Ohio State safety Mike Sensibaugh (3) breaks up this pass intended for TCU's Linzy Cole, in first quarter action. Shortly afterwards Sensibaugh intercepted a Horned Frog pass.

OHIO STATE 62-TCU 0

TCU first played the Buckeyes from Ohio State in 1937 and lost 14-0. Twenty years later TCU won 18-14. In 1961 it was a 7-7 standoff. Five years after the tie, Ohio State won 14-7. With those close scores to reflect on, the Horned Frogs wouldn't have dreamed what was in store for them as they invaded Columbus to engage the Buckeyes for the fifth time.

The largest crowd in Ohio Stadium history —

86,412 — was on hand to watch the Christians fed to the Buckeyes. Quarterback Rex Kern started the scoring orgy after his first-play pass to Bruce Jankowski, good to the TCU 8, was rubbed out by a penalty. On the next play Kern threw again to Jankowski, this one good for 58 yards and a TD. Stan White added the placement and OS led 7-0.

TCU couldn't move the ball and the Buckeyes,

following a punt, took over at the Frog 41-yard line. On the eighth play, all on the ground, Jim Otis went outside left tackle for one yard and the 13th point. White missed the extra point.

The Horned Frogs made a first down on their next possession, but that was all as punt formation time rolled around again. After receiving the punt, the Buckeyes rolled goalward again. Kern passed to Larry Zelina for 30 yards. Zelina ran from scrimmage the next time and made 28 yards up the sideline. Otis then took the ball to the TCU two on two carries. John Brockington scored on a dive over the middle. Greg Webb blocked the extra point kick and Ohio State led 19-0.

Mike Sensibaugh intercepted a Steve Judy pass at the State 40 and returned to the TCU 38. The Frogs held at their 27 and a drizzling rain started as the quarter came to an end.

The second quarter started with another Buckeye interception at the TCU 41. Otis almost scored singlehandedly as he ran over, under and through the Horned Frogs. He ran for eight, for 17, then went over standing up from eight yards out. White's kick made it 26-0.

Marty Whelan gained ten yards, then fumbled after a vicious tackle by rover back Jack Tatum. Ohio State and Otis took over again at the TCU 47. Otis carried three straight times to push the pigskin

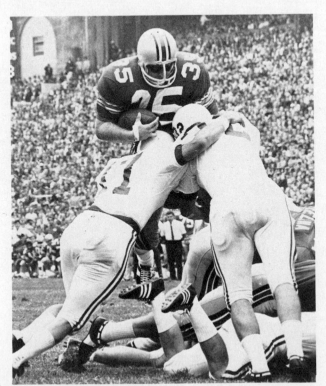

One of the few times that Ohio State fullback Jim Otis was held for no gain. Applying the binders to Otis are Ted Fay (17) and Andy Durrett (32).

to the Frog five. Brockington carried the final five and with White's successful point, the Buckeyes led 33-0. The first half ended with no more scoring.

TCU's deepest penetration in the first half was their own 45 yard line. They had three first downs and 71 yards gained. On the other side of the scrimmage line, the Buckeyes made 13 first downs and 326 yards. The Horned Frogs lost Norman Bulaich on his first carry and Linzy Cole soon afterwards. Both sat out the balance of the game.

The Buckeyes scored twice more in the third quarter. Both tallies were scored by quarterback Kern, the first one on a weaving 17-yard run through the Purple defense, making the score 40-0. The second came after Jimmy Tidwell set up the Buckeyes by fumbling the kickoff. Kern made the final five yards on a slanting quarterback sneak. The computer at the end of the field now read Ohio State 47 — TCU 0. This included White's extra points.

Ohio State coach Woody Hayes sent in his reserves to finish out the game. Naturally each boy is trying to make the starting eleven, so the difference really wasn't apparent. Brockington got the next touchdown in the fourth quarter. He ran over from two yards out and when TCU was penalized to the one and a half yard before the conversion try, he ran that over too. It was 55-0 and not over yet.

As the clock got down in the short rows, quarterback Kevin Rusknik dropped back and passed to Tom Campana. The ball was caught by Campana at the Horned Frog 40 and he crossed the goal line untouched by human hands. White added the last point to make it 62-0.

With time running out quarterback Busty Underwood threw the bomb to John Beileu who, after the catch and run, was downed at the Buckeye 14. This was TCU's deepest penetration, but the clock had run out and the game ended.

Ohio State played everyone, a total of 71 players. TCU coach Fred Taylor, after viewing Ohio State on the film prior to the game said, "The Buckeyes are the greatest football team I've ever seen." When the game was over he decided that he had underestimated them. It was a gray, rainy day for the weather and TCU.

	TCU	OS
First downs	9	26
Rushing yardage	44	373
Passing yardage	152	192
Return yardage	23	102
Passes	5-36-4	9-19-1
Punts	10-37	5-42
Fumbles lost	2	0
Yards penalized	5	47

TCU .... 0 0 0 0— 0
Ohio State .... 19 14 14 15—62
OSU — Jankowski 58 pass from Kern (White kick)
OSU — Otis 2 run (kick failed)
OSU — Brockington 2 run (kick failed)
OSU — Otis 9 run (White kick)
OSU — Brockington 5 run (White kick)
OSU — Kern 17 run (White kick)
OSU — Kern 5 run (White kick)
OSU — Brockington 2 run (Brockington run)
OSU — Campana 62 pass from Rusknik (White kick)
Attendance — 86,412.

Tulsa defensive tackle Tom Brady is about to lower the boom on Arkansas quarterback Bill Montgomery. The Hog signal caller had just made a blind pitchout to Bill Burnett, shown reaching for the ball. Burnett fumbled and recovered for a loss.

ARKANSAS 55-TULSA 0

The Razorbacks met Tulsa on their new artificial grass in Razorback Stadium. In the stands sat 43,000 fans, eager to see the new turf initiated. Arkansas won 55-0. Their defense recovered five of seven Hurricane fumbles and intercepted three passes.

Tulsa won the toss and elected to defend the south goal. Arkansas chose to receive. Bill Burnett took the kickoff at the eight and returned to the 33. After three short running plays, Bruce Maxwell took a pitchout and skirted right end for 26 yards to the Tulsa 29. Burnett then carried six straight times, the last for one yard and a touchdown. Bill McClard's kick made it Arkansas 7 — Tulsa 0.

On Tulsa's next possession Josh Ashton fumbled and Bruce James recovered for Arkansas. Following a penalty and an 11-yard loss, the Hogs punted. Facing a fourth and eight, Ken Duncan fumbled on a Tulsa punt attempt. He picked up the ball and passed incomplete. In three plays Arkansas lost 15 yards, then punted. On the next series Tulsa quarterback Dave Ellis' pass was intercepted by Bobby Field and returned to the Tulsa 37. Arkansas then reached the three early in the second period, but on second down Maxwell fumbled and Tim Jones captured the

elusive pigskin for Tulsa. The Razorback defense then scored, as on second down Steve Birdwell intercepted an Ellis pass on the 11 and returned it into the end zone. McClard kicked the conversion and Arkansas led 14-0.

Tulsa couldn't move and punted dead on the Hog 39. A Montgomery bomb was intercepted by safety Jon Long at the Hurricane 14. Arkansas held and on fourth down Duncan again fumbled on the snap, then ran to the 22. This was two yards shy of a first down. Burnett hit the middle for seven, Montgomery on a counter for five and Burnett again around right end for 11 and a touchdown. With McClard's kick it was 21-0, Hogs.

On second down following the kickoff, new Tulsa quarterback Rick Arrington fumbled the snap and Rick Kersey recovered for Arkansas at the Tulsa 43. Rick to Rick. The Razorbacks reached the Tulsa eight, but then Montgomery lost three and McClard kicked a 28-yard field goal.

The Hurricane came back, mainly on an Arrington to Bill Robey pass of 22 yards, to reach the Arkansas 37. But disaster struck again as Arrington fumbled the handoff and Bruce James hugged the

Dave Ellis, the Tulsa quarterback, is soon to see a disastrous happening. The pass he is to throw will be intercepted by Steve Birdwell who is seen to the left of Ellis' left elbow. Birdwell returned 11 yards for a touchdown. The pressure being applied by Dick Bumpas (61) and Rick Kersey (72) caused the hurried pass.

ball for Arkansas. Two punts later the first half ended with the Razorbacks leading 24-0.

Tulsa received the kickoff as second half action started. No first down, so Duncan punted to the Hurricane 46. The Hogs moved to the Tulsa five as Montgomery passed to Steve Hockersmith for 14 yards and Maxwell ran three times for seven, 18 and two yards respectively. The offense bogged down at this point and McClard kicked a 23-yard field goal to put Arkansas ahead 27-0.

After an exchange of punts, Tulsa faced a fourth and five at their six. Duncan punted 52 yards and Terry Stewart returned 25 to the Hurricane 33. An errant pitchout stopped the Hogs this time as Pedro Williams recovered for Tulsa. The Oklahomans failed to move and Duncan punted only 14 yards, out of bounds at the Arkansas 44. The Razorbacks scored, in seven plays, on a Montgomery to Pat Morrison pass for the final five yards. A Montgomery pass to Chuck Dicus, good for 36 yards, was the big play in this drive. McClard put it through the uprights to make the score 34-0, Arkansas.

On their next possession Tulsa fumbled to Arkansas's Gordon McNulty. Russ Garber then ran for six yards and fumbled to Tulsa's Williams. Robey ran for four yards and guess what? He fumbled and Cliff Powell reclaimed for the Hogs at the Tulsa 47.

Play moved into the fourth quarter before Arkansas could crank up another scoring drive. From the Hog 40, quarterback John Eichler took them home in nine plays. Eichler got 25 of the 60 yards on a keeper around left end. Mike Hendren scored from one yard out and McClard converted to put Arkansas ahead 41 to 0.

Shortly after the kickoff a John Dobbs pass was intercepted by David Hogue. He returned to the one and Eichler sneaked for the yard. McClard's good PAT brought the score to 48-0.

The Razorbacks were to make one more touchdown before game's end. The big gainer was an unsportsmanlike conduct penalty against Tulsa. On the next play Eichler passed 13 yards to David Cox for the score. With McClard's point adding one, the scoring ended, and so did the game a moment later. Final, Arkansas 55 — Tulsa 0.

	Tulsa	Ark.
First downs	15	24
Yards rushing	166	217
Yards passing	113	138
Passes	9-28-3	13-28-1
Punts	8-38.1	6-44.1
Fumbles lost	5	3
Return yardage	13	98
Yards penalized	84	53

Tulsa	0	0	0	0—	0
Arkansas	7	17	10	21—	55

Ark — Burnett 1 run (McClard kick)

Ark — Birdwell 13 interception return (McClard kick)
Ark — Burnett 10 run (McClard kick)
Ark — FG McClard 28
Ark — FG McClard 23
Ark — Morrison 5 pass from Montgomery (McClard kick)
Ark — Hendren 1 run (McClard kick)
Ark — Eichler 1 run (McClard kick)
Ark — Cox 13 pass from Eichler (McClard kick)
Attendance — 43,000.

SYNOPSIS

TOP TEN

1. Ohio State
2. Penn State
3. Arkansas
4. Texas
5. Southern Cal
6. Oklahoma
7. Georgia
8. Purdue
9. Missouri
10. Tennessee

TEAM LEADERS FOR SEASON

OFFENSE

Rushing ....Texas 568 yds.
Passing ....SMU 870 yds.
Total ....SMU 978 yds.

SWC OFFENSIVE PLAYER OF WEEK

Daryl Doggett, Fullback, SMU

DEFENSE

Rushing ....Arkansas 147 yds.
Passing.................Texas Tech 107 yds.
Total ....Arkansas 357 yds.

SWC DEFENSIVE PLAYER OF WEEK

Mike Campbell, Linebacker, Texas

CONFERENCE

	W	L	T
Texas	1	0	0
Arkansas	0	0	0
Rice	0	0	0
TCU	0	0	0
Texas A & M	0	0	0
SMU	0	0	0
Baylor	0	0	0
Texas Tech	0	1	0

SEASON RECORDS

	W	L	T
Texas	2	0	0
Arkansas	2	0	0
Rice	1	1	0
Texas Tech	1	1	0
Texas A & M	0	2	0
TCU	0	2	0
Baylor	0	2	0
SMU	0	3	0

Third Week
October 4

The Owls' speedy Dale Bernauer beats Bear Jim Sheridan to gather in this 38-yard Vincent pass. Rice scored their first touchdown on the next play.

CALIFORNIA 31 - RICE 21

Before a crowd of 37,000 in the Bears' Memorial Stadium, California snapped a SWC losing streak. Scoring twice in the last minute of play, the desperate Bears grabbed the money away from a stubborn underdog Owl team. This was Cal's first win, in six tries, against a SWC team.

A tribute to the Owls' tenaciousness, was the fact they stayed in contention despite three pass interceptions and four lost fumbles. On the other hand, the Rice defense recovered four Bear fumbles.

Rice kicked off and held California on their first series, but jumped offside on the punting down. This gave the Bears a first down and they moved close enough for soccer-style kicker Randy Wersching to kick a 34-yard field goal. California led 3-0.

This was all the scoring in the first quarter, but the second period proved more fruitful as each team scored a touchdown.

First California put together a 10-play 67-yard drive. The score coming on a 10-yard run through a boulevard opening at the Owls' right tackle. Gary Fowler was the ball carrier for the Bears. Wersching added the exta point and it was 10-0, Bears.

Shortly Randy Lee recovered a Fowler fumble, which gave Rice possession on the California 44. On the first play Rice quarterback Stahle Vincent passed complete to speedster Dave Bernauer for 38 yards. With first and goal at the six, quarterback Phillip Wood checked in at halfback. Vincent pitched out to Wood, who passed complete to Bob Brown in the left corner of the promised land. Tim Davis kicked good on the conversion and the Bears' led was cut to three points, 10-7.

The half ended with no more scoring, as each team was trying to unravel its offense.

On an exchange of punts early in the second half, Gilbert King fumbled the Bear punt on his own 21. Tackle Bob Richards recovered at that spot for the Bears. Three plays later California had added another touchdown. The score came on an 11-yard smash up the middle by tailback Bob Darby. Wersching's kick made the score 17-7, Bears.

The Owls retaliated quickly following the Bear kickoff. Vincent took them 74 yards in nine plays. back to the 27 for clipping. Vincent then hit Conley for five yards. Then Mike Phillips caught a blue-darter at the Cal six-yard marker. Larry Caldwell ran for two. Mike Spruill ran for two and Vincent

Rice quarterback Stahle Vincent pitches out just before being hit from both sides. O. Z. White (70) and Andy Westfall (58) met with Vincent in between.

ran for two. That used up all the yardage left as the Owls went ahead, including the good one-pointer by Davis, 21-17.

In the fourth quarter both teams developed a bad case of fumbleitis. Driving at the Rice 27, Curtis ran the option and fumbled when hit, to Rice's Lee. After one first down, Spruill lost a fumble at the Owl 13. On the second down, Cal's Curtis was hit as he lateraled and Rodrigo Barnes recovered the ball for Rice at their 20. Vincent, while sweeping left, had the ball knocked out of his hands and Cal's O. Z. White recovered at the Owl 19.

The Bears moved to a first and goal at the four, but the Owls held and after three time-consuming runs Bucky Allshouse punted to the Rice 44. Jim Calkins caught a Curtis pass for 17 yards. On second down, Fowler gained five. On third down Curtis rolled out to the right with Roger Roitsch in hot pursuit. As Roitsch hit Curtis he lofted a lazy flyer into Something of value was a 15-yard piling on penalty against California. The shocker in the drive was a run up the middle by Tony Conley, good for 25 yards. On fourth down at the four, Bernauer skirted right end for the touchdown. Davis' kick was good and Rice trailed 17-14.

On the following Rice kickoff, Stan Murphy fumbled when hit and David Keyes smothered the ball

for Rice at the California 17. Vincent ran a keeper-sweep for eight yards, but the Owls were penalized the end zone. Heavily covered, Calkins made his leap at the precise moment and came down with the ball and ball game. Wersching's kick made it 24-21 in favor of California.

With less than a minute to play the Owls had to throw caution to the wind and try to move the football. And as usual, the Bears could do no wrong. In a prevent defense, Paul Martyr intercepted a fourth-down pass by Vincent. He returned it 25 yards for the game's final score. The game ended with California winning 31-21.

Rice coach Bo Hagan said the only thing California did that surprised them, was win. Bear coach Ray Willsey added that Rice had a good football team which was perhaps the best on the field today.

	Rice	Calif.
First downs	10	18
Rushing yardage	129	273
Passing yardage	138	85
Return yardage	—2	85
Passes	12-21-3	7-18-0
Punts	8-41.9	7-38.3
Fumbles lost	4	4
Yards penalized	45	51

Rice	0	7	14	0—21
California	3	7	7	14—31

Cal — FG Wersching 34
Cal — Fowler 10 run (Wersching kick)
Rice — Brown 6 pass from Wood (Davis kick)
Cal — Darby 11 run (Wersching kick)
Rice — Bernauer 4 run (Davis kick)
Rice — Vincent 2 run (Davis kick)
Cal — Calkins 19 pass from Curtis (Wersching kick)
Cal — Martyr 24 pass interception (Wersching kick)
Attendance — 37,000.

Horned Frog Gerald Kirby throws the block to spring fullback Marty Whelan (40) loose into the Arkansas secondary.

ARKANSAS 24-TCU 6

Arkansas and TCU opened their SWC season at the Razorback's home away from home — War Memorial Stadium in Little Rock. The home folk, some 50,000, settled back to enjoy a game in which Arkansas was a 25-point favorite. The final score was close to the odds, the game was something else.

The Hogs kicked off and TCU was unable to move. TCU punted to the Arkansas 35. Terry Stewart returned five yards. Arkansas reached the Horned Frog 29, where Bruce Maxwell fumbled and Andy Durrett recovered for TCU at the 24.

Quarterback Steve Judy then showed the Arkansas fans what the edge of the seat feels like. After a penalty rubbed out his 13-yard pass on first down, he gave to Sammy Rabb on a draw for six yards. Marty Whelan hit left guard for eight. Judy passed to Rabb for 12 yards. After Whelan made two, Judy passed to J. R. Eubanks for nine yards. Then on a third and nine, Judy kept for 15 yards. Next a pass to Linzy Cole was good for 17 yards. Whelan ran for seven more and Judy kept for two. Arkansas drew a five yard penalty for offsides. Following an incomplete pass from the Razorback four, Whelan fumbled at left tackle. Bruce James reclaimed the ball for Arkansas at the 14.

The Hogs used three downs and made three yards.

Cary Stockdell punted to the TCU 41. Rabb made five yards at left tackle. Whelan exploded around right end for 19 yards, but then fumbled. Bobby Field recovered for Arkansas at their 35. This time after three downs the Hogs had lost eight yards. Stockdell then punted 70 yards, his best ever.

After all of the knocking, the Horned Frogs finally opened the door and got on the scoreboard early in the second quarter. Judy, starting from his three, passed 14 yards to Eubanks. Bobby Davis made six on two rushes. Judy then passed deep to Jerry Miller and the speedster grabbed the ball and burnt rubber. Safety Dennis Berner hauled Miller down 40 yards later at the Hog 37. After reaching the 25, Judy found Miller open again, good to the eight. The Arkansas defense held and Wayne Merritt kicked an 11-yard field goal. TCU led 3-0.

TCU kicked off and quarterback Bill Montgomery warmed up by throwing to Chuck Dicus for eight yards. He went to the well again and Dicus went all the way, 73 yards. Bill McClard's point after put the Razorbacks up 7-3.

After an exchange of punts, TCU was starting from the Arkansas 35. On second down, Whelan fumbled again and Stewart recovered for Arkansas at their 41. The Hogs then got to the TCU 22,

Tailback Bill Burnett (33), behind the blocking of Ronnie Hammers (70) and Jerry Dossey (74), picks up good yardage for the Razorbacks.

mainly on the running of Bill Burnett and Maxwell, and the Montgomery to Dicus passes. Unable to move further, McClard kicked a 38-yard field goal. Arkansas 10 — TCU 3.

Judy and the Horned Frogs came right back. He passed to Miller, Davis, Miller, Cole and Miller again to reach the Razorback 17. On a blitz he kept for nine, then kept again for a first down at the five. The Frogs had to settle for a field goal again and Merritt kicked it from the 12. The half ended with Arkansas leading 10-6.

Arkansas chose to kick off to open the second half. TCU moved to the Arkansas 46, before an 11-yard loss put the clamps on that drive. Whelan punted over the goal and Montgomery and Company started at their 20. Montgomery kept for 10, passed to Dicus for 12 and sent Burnett on a sweep for 22. On second down at the TCU 23, Dicus caught a pass at the seven, was hit, did a fake here and a fake there and scored. With a good kick from McClard, the Razorbacks led 17-6.

On the next TCU series, Stewart intercepted a Judy pass at the Arkansas 45. The Hogs got to the TCU 30, from where McClard tried a 46-yard field goal which was wide.

The Frogs had one more drive in their system as they passed and ran to the Arkansas 35. There the Hogs were penalized to their 20. Their defense held

and took over at the 21 right after the fourth quarter began.

From there Arkansas began its last scoring drive, which was dominated by penalties. The Horned Frogs held and forced a punt, but roughed the kicker and Arkansas had the ball back, courtesy of the penalty, on the 50. A clipping penalty set Arkansas back 15 yards, but then TCU retaliated by getting penalized 21 yards for holding. On the next play TCU was penalized again, for grabbing Montgomery's face mask. With the ball now on the 13, Burnett swept for six and also plunged for the final yard and score as McClard wrapped up the scoring. The Razorbacks led 24-6.

Arkansas used up most of the four minutes left to reach the TCU 17, where the Horned Frogs took over on downs. Judy passed to Whelan for 18 yards. Following a TCU time out Judy passed for 13 yards to Miller on the final play of the game.

	TCU	Ark
First downs	21	22
Rushing yardage	121	150
Passing yardage	245	208
Return yardage	25	21
Passes	20-38-1	13-26-0
Punts	4-45	3-49.3
Fumbles lost	3	1
Yards penalized	74	35

TCU	0 6 0	0— 6
Arkansas	0 10 7	7—24

TCU — FG 21 Merritt
Ark — Dicus 73 pass from Montgomery (McClard kick)
Ark — FG 38 McClard
TCU — FG 22 Merritt
Ark — Dicus 23 pass from Montgomery (McClard kick)
Ark — Burnett 1 run (McClard kick)
Attendance — 50,000.

Larry Stegent (25) rolls behind the blocking of Jim Parker (64) and Ross Brupbacher (80). Jack Kovar hits Joe Neuman (62) and Larry Horacek moves for the stop.

TEXAS A&M 20-ARMY 13

The Army marched in, but the Aggies took over at West Point. They played to the largest crowd in the history of Army's Michie Stadium.

Army took the kick at their own 18. Lynn Moore returned it to the 36, but they could not make a first down and punted. The Aggies began their drive on their 32, had to gamble on a fourth and two feet with a keeper by quarterback Rocky Self. He made the first down on the Knights' 43. Then Larry Stegent hit right guard for 19 and Self carried up the middle to the Army 14. The Aggies were halted at the six and Mike Bellar put three points on the board for the Aggies from 24 yards out.

Then, it was Army's turn. Quarterback Bernie Wall pitched out to fullback Lynn Moore who sprinted from his 24 to the A&M 11. Three plays put Moore into the end zone over right guard. Arden Jensen's kick put the Black Knights ahead 7-3.

The Aggies nearly came all the way back, but bogged down on a fourth-and-goal pass from Self to Stegent that got only to the three. But Army took over in the hole and couldn't get out. Their punt

only moved the Aggies back to the Cadet 32.

Fullback Marc Black carried over left tackle to the 25, then Steve Burks banged right guard for 17 to the eight. The Cadets drew a penalty to the four on that play, giving the Aggies first and goal from there. Tailback Steve Burks lost a yard, Self kept for four to the Army one. Center Jack Kovar led the charge that got Self into the end zone and put the Aggies back in the lead, 10-7.

The Cadets managed to reach the Aggie 15, but could go no farther. Jensen added three points from 27 yards out to tie the Aggies 10-10 at the half.

Larry Stegent took the second half kickoff at the Aggie eight and returned it to his own 31. Ross Brupbacher took a pass from Self to the 50 and Stegent ran to the Cadets' 35. There, things stalled for A&M, but a roughing-the-kicker penalty was called on Jimmy Sheffield's punt, giving the Aggies a first down on the Army 17. They made another first down at the Knights' seven, but couldn't gain the end zone. Once again, it was Mike Bellar who was called to add to the score. His 24-yard kick gave

Aggies' Barney Harris (15) runs for good yardage pursued by Army's Bob Coonan (54), John Brenner (20), Chuck Blakely (29) and Dave Smith (60). Jimmy Adams (88) and Ross Brupbacher (80) follow.

A&M a 13-10 edge.

Army was unable to move against the Aggie defense and had to punt. A&M was back in business at their own 33. The Aggies used up lots of time, but couldn't score as Bellar's third field goal attempt was wide to the right.

Army was forced to punt after a series of downs, ending the third quarter in which the Aggies had controlled the ball for nearly twelve minutes and had not allowed Army one first down.

A roughing-the-kicker penalty got the ball back for Army at their own 35 after they had failed in another series to gain ten yards. That was the beginning of the first sustained Army drive in the second half. It ended 44 yards later when Aggie defensive halfback Ed Ebrom intercepted at the A&M 21.

For the first time in the second half, the Aggies were forced to punt. Army took the ball on their 20, after a touchback, to begin the fourth quarter. Then the Aggies had to return the punt with Sheffield blasting a 46-yarder to the Army 26.

The Army decided to try an air attack. Wall's first pass bounced off his receiver's fingertips into the waiting hands of A&M's defensive halfback, David Hoot. Hoot had been knocked down and he caught the ball flat on his back at the Army 40.

Self was forced to run on first down when his receivers were covered. He scrambled to the 29 for an 11-yard pick up. Marc Black smacked left tackle for two and Self dropped back to pass again. He found Brupbacher wide open down the right sideline and dropped the ball in his hands at the 13. He dodged three defenders and hopped into another six points. Bellar's kick made it 20-10.

Lynn Moore, Army's wheel horse, took the kick-off for an 80-yard ride before finally being stopped by Dave Elmendorf at the Aggie ten. Army put quarterback Bob Mohn in, but he threw incomplete for three downs and the Cadets had to settle for a field goal by Jensen from the 26, stopping the scoring at 20-13.

	A&M	Army
First downs	21	11
Rushing yardage	230	193
Passing yardage	167	28
Return yardage	54	173
Passes	11-20-0	3-20-3
Punts	6-46	7-37
Fumbles lost	0	0
Yards penalized	70	43

A&M—FG Beller 24
Army—Moore 1 run (Bellar kick)
Army—FG Jensen 27
A&M — Brupbacher 27 pass from Self (Bellar kick)
A&M—FG Bellar 22
Army—FG Jensen 26
Attendance—41,000

Texas A&M	10	0	3	7—20
Army	7	3	0	3—13

Fred Steinmark(28) returns a Navy punt for 36 yards, but a clipping call nullified the run. Leading is Rick Nabors(41).

TEXAS 56 - NAVY 17

Another capacity crowd jammed its way into Memorial Stadium to watch the Longhorns confront the Middies from Annapolis. This was the second meeting of the two teams. The first was in the 1964 Cotton Bowl, where Texas prevailed 28-6. Led again by a stone wall defense, Texas pulled the plug and swamped the sailors. The offense also got in the sinking by running up the largest score ever against Navy in the 90 years of midshipmen football.

Texas kicked off and Navy, unable to move, punted. The punt was partially blocked by Mike Campbell and the Longhorns started their first series at the Navy 43. On the opening play halfback Jim Bertelsen went through right guard, veered to the sideline and went all the way. Happy Feller kicked the first of his six straight extra points and Texas led 7-0.

The Longhorn kickoff was followed by another Navy punt, after three plays failed to pick up a first down. Although unblocked, this kick traveled only 22 yards. Texas started their second series from the Middies 33. Quarterback James Street capitalized on good fortune again as he guided Texas to another score in four plays. Bertelsen got the initial call and went straight ahead for seven yards. Steve Worster ran for five and Bertelsen carried again for eight. A

roughness penalty on Navy placed the ball at the seven. From the three, Ted Koy, aided by an academy award fake by Worster, burst into the end zone to put Texas ahead by two touchdowns.

Navy soon got on the scoreboard as a Koy fumble was recovered by James Simpson at the Longhorn 42. Nine plays and two pass interference penalties later, Jack Detweiler kicked a 36-yard field goal. Texas now led 14-3.

The Middies then tried an onside kickoff, which was unsuccessful and Texas started from its 48. In the seven-play scoring drive, Bertelsen contributed a 20-yard sweep to the Navy 12. Koy then carried twice, first for 11 yards and then one yard for the score. At the end of the first quarter the Longhorns led 21-3.

Early in the second quarter a Navy punt was short, going only nine yards to the Middie 34. Four running plays carried to the nine. An offsides cost Texas back to the 14. Bertelsen ran to the eight and from there Street faked a handoff, then zig-zagged up the middle to score standing up. With the conversion good Texas led 28-3.

On the next Longhorn possession they rolled up 82 yards of AstroTurf in 13 plays. Eddie Phillips took the quarterback reins and the second unit filled

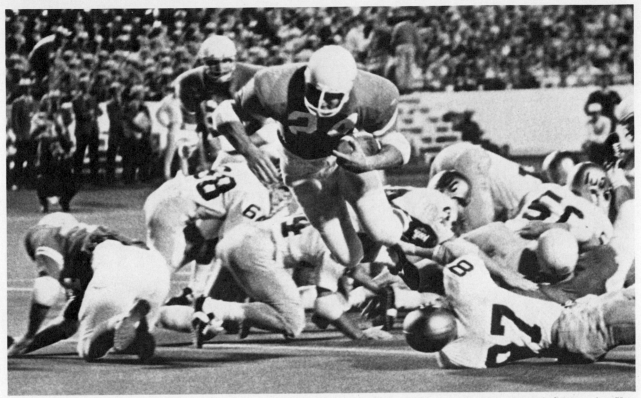

Ted Koy barrels across from three yards out to score touchdown. A great fake by Steve Worster opened the way for Koy.

the other positions. Bobby Callison had the big gainer, a run of 18 yards. He then pulled a "Worster fake" and Terry Collins pell-melled across for the fifth 'Horn TD. The score stood Texas 35-Navy 3.

The next Texas drive was set up on a fumble recovery of a completed Navy pass. Rick Nabors, who tackled the receiver, also recovered the ball. Texas moved to a first down at the Middie 11 with the help of an 18-yard run by Phillips on a keeper. At the two Collins fumbled and a Texas Middie, David Howe, recovered.

The next time the Longhorns hung on to the ball and covered 55 yards in six plays. Phillips, behind a "get out of the way" block by Billy Dale, covered the last 15 yards for the score. With the good extra point Texas led at the half 42-3.

Navy didn't leave their bad luck in the dressing room. On their second play of the second half, Mike Barr fumbled. Paul Kristynik made the hit and Larry Webb recovered for Texas at their 48. In 10 plays the Longhorns scored again. Collins had a 16-yard dash and Phillips scored from the seven. Rob Layne took over the extra point chores and was successful. Texas led 49-3.

As the third quarter curtain was about to descend, Navy quarterback Mike McNallen spied Karl Schwelm fleeing down the sideline. Schwelm caught McNallen's pass at the 25 and went in for the first Navy touchdown. The pass-run covered 62 yards.

Detweiler kicked the point after and Texas now led 49-10.

The Longhorns regrouped and scored again in eleven plays. The drive covered 48 yards and was climaxed by senior Tommy Asaff scoring his first touchdown for Texas. Layne's kick was through the uprights and the 'Horns led 56-10.

Navy then put on its first sustained drive of the game. It covered 63 yards and ended with Jeff Steelman going into the Texas end zone from the four. Detweiler scored the last point of the game with his toe.

A Texas drive died at the Navy one as the game ended. Final score in favor of Texas 56-17.

One of the seven Oklahoma Sooner coaches present, Pat James, summed up the game most accurately. He said, "This is the worst thing that's happened to Navy since Pearl Harbor."

Head for the storm cellar grandma, the Texas-O.U. collision is next.

	Navy	Tex.
First downs	15	32
Rushing yardage	24	523
Passing yardage	254	72
Return yardage	96	3
Passes	17-47-1	7-10-1
Punts	9-39	1-28
Fumbles lost	3	3
Yards penalized	26	82

Navy	3	0	7	7—17
Texas	21	21	7	7—56

Tex — Bertelsen 43 run (Feller kick)

Tex — Koy 3 run (Feller kick)
Navy — FG 36 Detweiler
Tex — Koy 1 run (Feller kick)
Tex — Street 6 run (Feller kick)
Tex — Collins 2 run (Feller kick)
Tex—Phillips 15 run (Feller kick)
Tex — Phillips 7 run (Layne kick)
Navy — Schweim 62 pass from McNallen (Detweiler kick)
Tex — Asaff 1 run (Layne kick)
Navy — Stellman 4 run (Detweiler kick)
Attendance — 63,500.

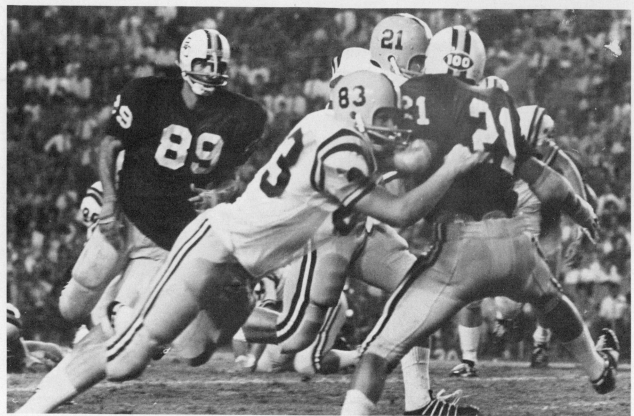

LSU's Randy Toms (83) blocks for Del Walker (21). Bears David Jones (89) and John Miller (21) move in for the tackle.

LSU 63-BAYLOR 8

Baylor was the third Billy Goat Gruff of the Southwest Conference to try to make it over the bridge where the LSU troll lived. But, unlike the fable, Baylor wasn't gruff enough to deal with the Bengals in their Baton Rouge den and another SWC scalp adorns the Tiger's wall. Things were worse for the Bears in 1913 when they lost to Texas 77-0, though.

This win gives the greedy Tigers a grand total of 140 points against their three Southwest Conference opponents. Mercy. It was sort of a homecoming for coach Bill Beall, who had been an assistant under LSU's Charlie McClendon for seven years before leaving to take the top job at Baylor.

Baylor won the toss and elected to receive. Gene Rogers hit left tackle for two, then was dumped for a five-yard loss on his second try. Quarterback Si Southall used a screen pass to Gene Rogers for 11. Ed Marsh punted 41 yards.

LSU returned to the Baylor two in 14 plays, but on second-and-goal tailback Jimmy Gilbert fumbled in the end zone and Bear cornerback Willie Stewart recovered it. That was one of the few times that the

Bengals were denied a score.

It was half way through the first quarter before the Bears managed a first down on an 11-yard run up the middle by fullback Randy Cooper to his own 31. But a 23-yard punt gave LSU the ball on their own 46. Starting quarterback Mike Hillman was replaced by Buddy Lee for the Tigers. It took only eight plays for the Tigers to get their first score, moving ahead 7-0. The tally came after Tommy Reaux, Brian Blessing and Russell Serafin had successfully held back runs by Buddy Lee and Chaille Percy. Allen Shorey made the three, then Jim West took a pitchout around right end for the score.

Later, as Ed Marsh dropped back to punt, he fumbled the snap, recovered it and was downed at the Bear ten. Mike Hillman skirted left end to the two. Eddie Ray made the one, then hit right tackle for the score. Mark Lumpkin's kick made it 14-0.

The Tigers again contained the Bear attack and regained the ball on a punt at the Baylor 40. Once again, it took eight plays to score. A pair of penalties against Baylor helped. Allen Shorey carried the final yard for the score and it was 21-0.

Bear quarterback Si Southall fakes to Gene Rogers (33) as Bengal defensive end Buddy Millican (86) closes in along with Bobby Joe King (61) and Mike Anderson (45).

One of Southall's passes was picked off by Bill Norsworthy on the LSU 36. It only took three plays this time. Now Butch Duhe was at quarterback for the Bengals. Del Walker ran twice, then Duhe passed to Andy Hamilton, who wrestled the ball away from John Miller and scored. Willie Stewart blitzed in to block the extra point, leaving it at 27-0.

With 10:17 left in the half, the Bears started their only productive drive. Si Southall passed for the Bears' second first down to Randy Cooper for 21 yards. Next, he hit Derek Davis on the right sideline to the LSU 20. Cooper carried around right end and Rogers hit left tackle, then Southall hit Jerry Smith for the score. Southall again passed to Smith for two to make it 27-8.

The Bengals hit back for 71 yards in 12 plays with Andy Hamilton turning the corner around the Baylor right side for the three yards needed for another score. Lumpkin's kick added up to a 34-8 mark against the Bears.

On the Bears' first possession of the second half, the snap to punter Ed Marsh sailed over his head on fourth down. The ball ended up in the Baylor end zone with Marsh in possession of it and LSU two points richer, 36-8.

The Tigers took the kickoff 50 yards in seven plays to add to their big sack of points. Hamilton ran for five to score and Butch Duhe added the extra point for a 43-8 margin.

Baylor never offered a scoring threat for the remainder of the night, but the Tigers continued to stomp on the body. Eddie Ray scored from the one, Andy Hamilton ran in from the three and Mike Hillman returned to quarterback to run in the last six points, leaving the Bears on the ropes 63-8. It could have been worse. In 1908, LSU beat Baylor 89-0.

	Baylor	LSU
First downs	16	28
Rushing yardage	20	349
Passing yardage	192	195
Return yardage	0	192
Passes	15-38-3	15-23-0
Punts	8-38	2-48
Fumbles lost	1	3
Yards penalized	48	29

Baylor	0	8	0	0—	8
LSU	14	20	9	20—	63

LSU—West 3 run (Lumpkin kick)
LSU—Ray 1 run (Lumpkin kick)
LSU — Shorey 1 run (Lumpkin kick)
LSU — Hamilton 30 pass from Duhe (kick failed)
Baylor — Smith 15 pass from Southall
LSU — Hamilton 3 run (Lumpkin kick)
LSU—Safety. Marsh covered all in end zone after bad snap from center
LSU—Hamilton 5 run (Duhe kick)
LSU—Ray 1 run (Lumpkin kick)
LSU — Hamilton 3 run (Lumpkin kick)
LSU—Hillman 3 run (kick failed)
Attendance—65,000

Raider quarterback Joe Matulich picks up some of his 53 yards rushing with Johnny Odom (80) escorting. John Little (68) moves in for the tackle.

OKLA. STATE 17 - TEXAS TECH 10

Texas Tech, fresh from their loss to Texas, was still licking its wounds and looking for somewhat kinder treatment from the Oklahoma State Cowboys. Well, the Cowboys were somewhat gentler than the Longhorns, but they proved to be a long way from being tender. The Raiders also got their feet tangled up in a batch of red flags. That put the final hex on Tech's first loss in nine games against Big Eight opponents.

Tech won the toss, though, and elected to receive. Joe Matulich started at quarterback for the Raiders. They looked as though they were going for a rout through the first quarter as Tech monopolized all the fireworks. The first Raider drive was almost totally on the ground and brought seven points at its completion. The longest gain was a 20-yard keeper by Matulich to the OSU 27 on a third and long yardage situation. On the tenth play following that jaunt, Miles Langehennig busted over from the one for the score. Jerry Don Sanders' kick was good for a 7-0 lead.

Raider defensive end Richard Campbell intercepted a Robert Cutburth pass on the Cowboy 28 and returned it to the 19 early in the second quarter. Things looked good for Tech as Jimmy Bennett picked up three more to the 16, then Matulich's pass missed Danny Hardaway. Charles Napper came in at quarterback and was dropped for no gain. The Raiders had to settle for a field goal by Sanders for a 10-0 lead.

Then things started to change drastically. The Cowboys were given a glowing opportunity to score when Raider safety Kevin Ormes was called for pass interference at the Tech two. Bob Cutburth sneaked it over for OSU's first touchdown on the next play. The Cowboy's soccer-style kicker, Uwe Pruss, added the extra point, 10-7.

Early in the third quarter, the Cowboys capitalized on another penalty to tie up the score. OSU had a third-and-four at its own 43. Cutburth dropped back to pass and Larry Lolinaire snatched the pass for the Raiders at the 44 of OSU. Lolinaire returned

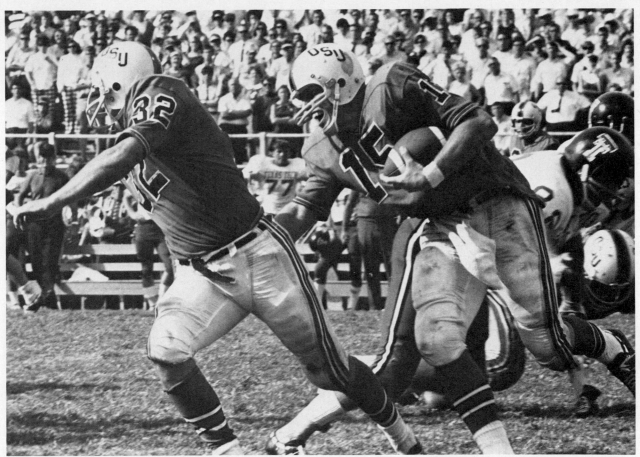

A happy warrior, OSU quarterback Cutburth follows the blocking of Bub Deerinwater (32) as they rush past Raider defensive end Richard Campbell (88).

the ball all the way to the Cowboy 12 before finally being dragged down. But, that fateful red flag had fluttered to the field on a roughing-the-passer call and the Raiders were hauled all the way back to their own 49, with OSU still in possession. Cutburth used his fullback, Bub Deerinwater, to chop up the Raider secondary. He busted for runs of six, eight and eleven yards until the Cowboys reached the Tech 11. The Raider defense stiffened and, after three unsuccessful punches at pay dirt. Pruss trotted in to boot a field goal. His kick from the 24 tied the game at 10-10.

With less than three minutes gone in the fourth quarter, the Raiders had the ball at their own 43. Sanders dropped back in punt formation. He fumbled the snap from center, picked it up, juggled it some more and finally got his kick away. The muffed kick barely got off the ground, wobbled five yards into the Cowboy secondary where OSU tackle John Ward stepped back to field it. All 248 pounds of John Ward rumbled toward the Raider goal. Finally, the gross weight of Tech players on his back managed to bring Ward to the ground on the Tech 22. A face mask penalty did almost as much for OSU,

putting the Cowboys on the Texas Tech 10-yard line.

Deerinwater got three up the middle to the seven. On second down, Cutburth rolled out to his right, but defensive end Richard Campbell was waiting for him. Cutburth spun back in and shoved a pass to tailback Bobby Cole on the goal line. Pruss' kick put the Cowboys ahead 17-10.

Tech could seem to go nowhere without bringing a flag down on them, but the Raiders kept trying and the running of Miles Langehennig at fullback, tailback Danny Hardaway and Joe Matulich's keepers did seem to take its toll on the Cowboy defense.

	Tech	OS
First downs	16	16
Rushing yardage	211	216
Passing yardage	70	125
Return yardage	12	44
Passes	7-20-0	10-27-1
Punts	9-38	8-36
Fumbles lost	0	0
Yards penalized	78	89

Texas Tech	7	3	0	0—10
Okla. State	0	7	3	7—17

Tech—Langenhennig 1 run (Sanders kick)
Tech—FG Sanders 34
OSU—Cutburth 2 run (Pruss kick)
OSU—FG Pruss 24
OSU—Cole 6 pass from Cutburth (Pruss kick)
Attendance—28,500

TOP TEN

1. Ohio State
2. Texas
3. Arkansas
4. Southern Cal
5. Penn State
6. Georgia
7. Missouri
8. Oklahoma
9. Purdue
10. Tennessee

TEAM LEADERS FOR THE SEASON

OFFENSE

Rushing ....Texas 1091 yds.
Passing ....SMU 870 yds.
Total ....Arkansas 1212 yds.

DEFENSE

Rushing ....Texas 193 yds.
Passing ....Texas Tech 232 yds.
Total ....Texas 697 yds.

SWC OFFENSIVE PLAYER OF WEEK

Rocky Self, Quarterback, Texas A & M

SWC DEFENSIVE PLAYER OF WEEK

Andy Durrett, Linebacker, TCU

FRESHMAN GAME RESULTS

Arkansas 20 — SMU 13
Texas A & M 27 — TCU 26

OPEN DATE: SMU

CONFERENCE

	W	L	T
Texas	1	0	0
Arkansas	1	0	0
Rice	0	0	0
Texas A & M	0	0	0
Baylor	0	0	0
SMU	0	0	0
TCU	0	1	0
Texas Tech	0	1	0

SEASON RECORDS

	W	L	T
Texas	3	0	0
Arkansas	3	0	0
Rice	1	2	0
Texas Tech	1	2	0
Texas A & M	1	2	0
TCU	0	3	0
SMU	0	3	0
Baylor	0	3	0

Fourth Week
October 10, 11

Gordon Utgard (41) scores Baylor's tying touchdown from the one after taking handoff from quarterback Si Southall.

ARKANSAS 21-BAYLOR 7

The Hogs came to Bear country and almost fell into their own Bear-trap. With 30,000 spectators looking on the Baylor Bruins ignored the odds, point-spread and Arkansas' high national ranking to battle the Fayetteville boys to a standoff after three quarters. Both teams were displaying a hit 'em in the gut ground game until a long pass broke up the standoff.

Arkansas kicked off and Baylor started play on their 20. Falling just short of a first down after three tries, the Bears punted out of bounds at the Arkansas 39. On fourth and 11 the Razorbacks punted into the Baylor end zone. The Bears moved the ball to the Hog 41 before running out of downs and punting to the Arkansas 11. The Razorbacks possession was brief and on fourth and 15, Cary Stockdell punted to the Arkansas 48. The Bruins couldn't come up with the necessary 10 yards for ball retention and Ed Marsh punted beyond the goal line. The Arkansas offensive troops then moved the pigskin for the first time, starting with fullback Bruce Maxwell's 10-yard run around left end. After an incompletion, quarterback Bill Montgomery passed to split end Chuck Dicus for 39 yards to the Baylor 31. The Hogs were to be denied though as on second down,

Russell Serafin intercepted a Montgomery pass at the 15 and returned to the Baylor 21. The Bears reached their 35 as the first quarter ended, with both teams frustrated in their efforts to get on the scoreboard.

As the second quarter opened the Bears again came up a yard short of a first down. Marsh's punt went into the end zone. From their 20, Arkansas started moving the ball. Bill Burnett ran for five and seven yards. Two quarterback keepers gained only one before Montgomery completed a 17-yard pass to Dicus at the 50. A screen pass to Burnett was good for eight and a Burnett run of two produced a first down at the Baylor 40. On third and 10, Dennis Watson and Gary Sutton dumped Montgomery for a six-yard loss. Stockdell punted to the Baylor two. The Bears, unable to move, punted to the Arkansas 49. Dennis Berner fumbled the fair catch, but Jerry Moore retained possession for the Razorbacks. On second down Montgomery was intercepted again, this time by John Miller at the Baylor 18. Stymied by a half-the-distance penalty, the Bears punted to the Arkansas 38.

The Razorbacks put the ball in play at their 45 as the fumbled punt bounced upfield seven yards be-

Bill Burnett makes the tie-breaker touchdown from the two. Brian Blessing (44) arrives too late. Fullback Bruce Maxwell (34) led the play.

fore Arkansas recovered the ball. Following a 21-yard Montgomery pass to Dicus, Burnett did a one-man-gang act from the Bear 32. He carried seven straight times to wipe out the 32 yards and score the Razorbacks' first touchdown. Bill McClard kicked the extra point and Arkansas led 7-0.

Baylor took the kickoff and hammered its way to the Hog 49. From there quarterback Si Southall threw four incompletions to wind up first half action. At the break the Bears were down by seven points.

After the Bruins kicked off to open the second half, Maxwell fumbled on a sweep and David Jones recovered for Baylor at the Arkansas 27. Following a first down at the 17, Gordon Utgard showed his iron man capabilities as he carried four straight times to score Baylor's tying touchdown. Terry Cozby's kick put it all even at 7-7.

The two teams spent the rest of the third quarter exchanging punts as bruising defensive play dominated the game. The Baylor defensive unit received standing ovations as they forced punt after punt. As the fourth quarter opened, Arkansas had moved from their seven out to their 48. All but three yards of the 41 was gained by a rampaging Burnett.

The Razorbacks moved to score the tie-breaker in six plays. The key play coming after Montgomery had been dropped for an eight-yard loss. Facing third and 16, Montgomery fired to Dicus who caught

the ball at the Baylor two. Burnett went over on the next play and McClard added the extra point to put Arkansas ahead 14-7.

Baylor received the kickoff, and after an exchange of punts, put the ball in play at their own 17. On third and nine Southall passed to Derek Davis for 10 yards. Davis fumbled the ball after the catch and Moore recovered for Arkansas at the Bear 27.

Burnett ran for two, Steve Hockersmith caught a pass for eight and Maxwell made five over left tackle. From the 12 Mr. Burnett took over and scored on his fourth carry. McClard's conversion closed out the scoring. Arkansas led 21-7.

Baylor did come back, but after reaching the Hog 15 ran into penalty trouble, surrendering the ball at the Arkansas 37. Baylor's hopes and the game both ended. Final Arkansas 21 — Baylor 7.

Although they lost, the Bruins became the first team to score a touchdown on Arkansas in four games. Naturally that is little solace for the short end of a bruising football game.

	Ark.	Bay.
First downs	17	13
Yards rushing	213	116
Yards passing	133	87
Return yardage	6	56
Passes	7-14-2	8-24-1
Punts	7-43	10-48
Fumbles lost	2	0
Yards penalized	52	74

Arkansas	0	7	0	14—21
Baylor	0	0	7	0— 7

Ark — Burnett 1 run (McClard kick)
Bay — Utgard 1 run (Cozby kick)
Ark — Burnett 2 run (McClard kick)
Ark — Burnett 3 run (McClard kick)
Attendance — 30,000

Here's Pony quarterback Chuck Hixson as he turned in an unusual amount of running for the night. Larry Wright (22) and Bob Schobel (74) play defense for the Frogs.

SMU 19-TCU 17

It looked like TCU was going to win their first ball game of the season in the Cotton Bowl on this windy Friday night. They even had a record-shattering pass by quarterback Steve Judy to start them on their way. But it finally turned out to be just close as the Mustangs stuck to the somewhat unfamiliar turf to edge out the Frogs. Mustang quarterback Chuck Hixson set a record, too. It was a personal one as he hit 14 of 22 passes for only 145 yards . . . the lowest of his career. So, the Ponies made it on the ground with a total of 316 yards rushing. Some of that running was done by Hixson . . . 41 yards of it, to be exact.

Steve Judy, the scrambling quarterback from Longview, didn't wait long to drop his first bomb on the Ponies. On the Frogs' second possession, Linzy Cole slipped behind SMU safety Danny Gordon to take Judy's pass at the Mustang 44. Judy had thrown the pass from his own 22 and Cole took it in for the first Frog score. Wayne Merritt's kick put the

Horned Frogs ahead 7-0. Judy's pass was the longest completion in TCU history. Even Sammy Baugh and Davy O'Brien never equalled it in their TCU careers.

With 2:51 left in the first quarter, the Frogs' drive stalled at the Pony 26. Busty Underwood came in to kick the first field goal of his career from 40 yards out, putting the Frogs ahead 10-0.

With 7:32 left in the half, the Mustangs finally managed a scoring drive. Beginning on the TCU 47-yard line, the Ponies managed to get on the scoreboard in just seven plays. It was Gary Hammond, playing at tailback for the first time, who managed to get the score with his five-yard drive off right tackle. Bicky Lesser's kick closed the gap to 10-7.

But the first half belonged to the Frogs and, with 3:21 remaining, it was Cole again who got a step on Joe Stutts and Pat Curry. Judy passed complete to Cole from the Mustang 17 and the speedy flanker raced over the goal line untouched. Merritt added

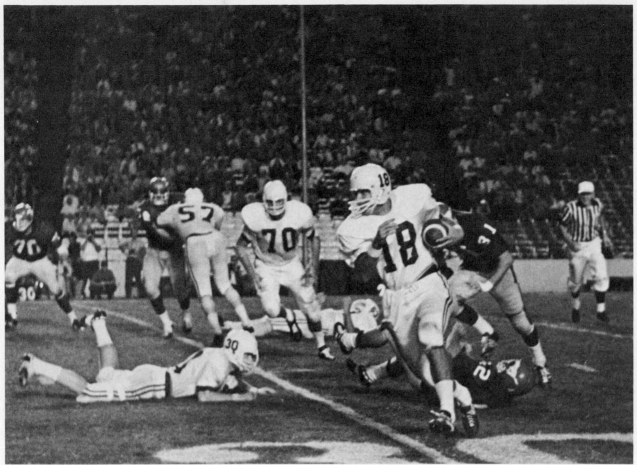

Quaterback Steve Judy did a lot of running, too. Here, he upsets Danny Gordon (42) and Joe Stutts (31). Frog escorts are Sammy Rabb (30), John Ruthstrom (57) and Gerald Kirby (70).

another point to put TCU in the lead 17-7.

Shortly after that, the Mustangs were knocking at the Frog door again, but the TCU defense shut them down at the Frog 23. The fourth down situation called for the talented toe of Lesser. His kick again narrowed TCU's lead 17-10.

The Frogs continued to threaten early in the second half, but Mike Nekuzza's interception of a Judy pass killed one promising drive. Mustang defensive back Pat Curry caused Judy's pass to go astray when he tipped it. Mike Nekuza was in the right place at the right time and intercepted for the Mustangs.

On a third down pass, TCU split end Jerry Miller made a spectacular reception of a desperation pass thrown by Judy. The Frogs were in business on the SMU 28, but that was as far as it went. A final attempt at a score was made by Underwood, kicking from the 43, but it was into a stiff south breeze and the boot fell short and to the left.

The Mustangs came alive in the second half and it was time. Exactly 6:09 remained in the third period when the Mustangs scored. This time, they had to go 72 yards from their own 28 to get the six

points. It took them only eleven plays, the score coming on a spectacular run by halfback Gordon Gilder for 25 yards. Lesser's kick was blocked by Frog tackle Terry Shackelford and the Mustangs still trailed TCU 17-16.

The back-breaker for the Frogs finally came when the Mustangs started their final drive on the SMU 30. It was another ground attack that rolled 71 yards to the Horned Frogs' nine. It was the fifteenth play of the drive and the Ponies faced a fourth-and-goal. This time, it was soph kicker Chipper Johnson who came in at Lesser's familiar spot. Hammond took a rather high snap, planted it and Johnson kicked the Mustangs ahead 19-17.

	TCU	SMU
First downs	14	27
Rushing yardage	138	316
Passing yardage	225	145
Return yardage	17	45
Passes	12-27-2	14-23-1
Punts	5-31	4-37
Fumbles lost	0	0
Yards penalized	32	29

TCU	10	7	0	0—17
SMU	0	10	6	3—19

TCU — Cole 78 pass from Judy (Merritt kick)
TCU — FG Underwood 40
SMU — Hammond 5 run (Lesser kick)
TCU — Cole 17 pass from Judy (Merritt kick)
SMU — FG Lesser 37
SMU — Gilder 25 run (kick failed)
SMU — FG Johnson 26
Attendance — 31,575

Oklahoma tailback Steve Owens goes airborne to score the Sooner's second touchdown. During the game Owens broke Gayle Sayers' Big Eight career rushing record.

TEXAS 27-OKLAHOMA 17

The Sooners head south and the Longhorns north and the twain meet in the Cotton Bowl. The collision is heard around the country. All the talking and bragging time has run out. Today performance, not the spoken word, will tell the story. For the 24th straight year the game is a sellout. There is no settling down in your seats for this one, it's a grabber all the way.

Oklahoma won the toss and elected the wind at their backs. Texas chose to receive. The Longhorns couldn't move and punted. OU put the ball in play at the Texas 41. Staying on the ground, Steve Owens and Roy Bell tore through the Longhorn line to reach the Texas nine. Bell then turned blocker for quarterback Jack Mildren as he skirted left side to score. Bruce Derr added the point after and the Sooners led 7-0.

Texas received the kickoff, made one first down, then had to punt. Oklahoma made a first and then also punted. The Longhorns were in possession on their 16. Quarterback James Street was intercepted on a pass intended for Tom Woodward. Steve Aycock made the interception and ran it back to the Texas 17. Owens made seven and Bell got a first down just inside the seven-yard line. On third down Owens dove over for the second Sooner touchdown.

OU, with Derr's boot, led 14-0.

The stands on both sides were stunned as Texas awaited the third OU kickoff in the first quarter. Jim Bertelsen ran the ball back to the Texas 42. With the triple-option unable to move against OU's eight-man front, Street took to the air. He passed 35 yards to Cotton Speyrer at the Sooner 23. A running play lost a yard before Street passed to Speyrer again. The wind held the ball aloft and Speyrer made a pop-fly catch in the left corner of the end zone. Happy Feller kicked the conversion and Texas trailed 7-14.

OU took the kickoff and started their next series at their 18. They reeled off successive first downs at their 32, 45 and Texas 44 as play moved into the second quarter. Owens, on a fourth and one, made another first down before Texas held. OU punted into the end zone and the 'Horns started at their 20.

Texas took to the air again and a Street to Bertelsen pass carried 55 yards to the Big Red 25. A pass to Speyrer gained six and a five-yard offside penalty against OU gave a first down at the 13. Another offside penalty moved the ball to the eight. On fourth down and a foot, Steve Worster made three to the one. Bertelsen took a wide pitchout and submarined around right end for the score. Feller tied up the game at 14-14.

Bruce DeLoney (88), Sooner defensive end, has Longhorns Jim Bertelsen and Steve Worster covered, but behind him is one that got away. Cotton Speyrer makes the reception for Texas.

Texas chose the wind to start the second half and kicked off. OU made a first down then had to punt. Texas, at their 36, moved to a first and ten at their 47. Their next first down was the courtesy of an OU offside. Then Street was stopped short of a first down, on third down, but the Sooners were penalized 15 yards for grabbing the face mask. From the 17 the Longhorns reached the 10, then called on Feller, who responded with a 27-yard field goal. Texas went ahead 17-14.

On the Sooners' next possession, Fred Steinmark intercepted a Mildren pass to set Texas up on the OU 49. Soon after that Vince LaRosa picked off a Street aerial, lateraled to Joe Pearce who ran to the Texas 24. Owens made 10 yards to the 14, but the 'Horns held after that and Derr tied up the game with a 22-yard field goal.

Texas took the kickoff and started at their 32. Speyrer caught a Street pass and looked like he would go all the way, but his tear away jersey didn't tear away. Bruce Stensrud hung on for dear life and brought Speyrer down at the OU 19. Ted Koy scored from the nine, but it was nullified by a 5-yard penalty. After a first down at the seven, OU was penalized half the distance, but held and Feller kicked a field goal to put Texas back on top 20-17.

OU, on their next possession, made it to the Texas 34. Owens made a first down, but it was called back and OU penalized five yards. Derr just missed on a field goal try. Texas took over at their 20 and Pearce intercepted a Street pass at the Sooner 44. Another penalty of five yards and the Sooners failed for the first and only time in the game to pick up at least one first down on a possession. OU punted and held Texas, but Glenn King fumbled the Longhorn punt and Bob McKay recovered for Texas at the Sooner 23. Worster scored from one yard out, on the fifth play, to put Texas ahead 27-17, Feller's point included.

OU got one first down before Tom Campbell picked off a Mildren pass at the Big Red 33. The Sooners held at their one to take possession. Mildren threw a sideways pass to Owens in the end zone and Owens ran it out to the 12 for a first down. Mildren was dropped for a loss as the game ended. Texas wins 27-17.

What will Texas do when someone stops their running game? Street will pass to Speyrer as the Sooners, sadder but wiser, found out.

	Oklahoma	Texas
First downs	20	18
Yards rushing	198	158
Yards passing	84	215
Return yardage	63	26
Passes	9-15-2	9-18-3
Punts	5-38	4-38
Fumbles lost	1	0
Yards penalized	42	5

Oklahoma	14	0	3	0—17
Texas	7	7	6	7—27

OU — Mildren 9 run (Derr kick)
OU — Owens 2 run (Derr kick)
UT—Speyrer 24 pass from Street (Feller kick)
UT—Bertelsen 1 run (Feller kick)
UT — FG Feller 27
OU — FG Derr 22
UT — FG Feller 21
UT — Worster 1 run (Feller kick)
Attendance — 71,938

The opening kickoff return by Tech's John Kleinert behind Tom Newton (60) and Mike Holladay (79). Pursuing Aggies are: David Hoot (26), Gary Armbrister (48) and Mike Bellar (19).

TEXAS TECH 13-TEXAS A&M 9

The temperature got colder, but the game got hotter right up to the finish in Tech's Jones Stadium. The mercury dropped 15 degrees from 62 at the kickoff to 47 at the finish, but the Raiders and Aggies waited until the last eight minutes to get hot. The neck-and-neck finish has become almost a permanent part of the Tech-A&M football games. This was the fifth of the last six of their games to be decided by less than a five-point spread.

Tech took the kickoff by A&M's Mike Bellar. Tech halfback John Kleinert fielded the ball on his 18 and darted through the Aggies to the Tech 39. On the first play from scrimmage, Danny Hardaway was stopped for a one-yard loss, but a personal foul call against A&M gave the Raiders a first down on the Aggie 47. The Red Raiders smelled blood, driving 41 yards in five plays to the Army six. But the Cadet defense held and on fourth down, the Raiders were still five yards from pay dirt. So, Jerry Sanders was called on for a field goal. His 22-yard boot put Tech on the scoreboard 3-0.

The rest of the half was mostly a pie-in-the-face sort of affair with lots of wild breaks, but no scores. The Aggies were stalled on their first possession and punted. Tech gave the ball back to the Aggies when

Ag defensive guard Van Odom intercepted a Joe Matulich pass on the A&M 40. The pie flew as Larry Stegent, on first down, was hit hard and the ball squirted to the Tech 30. Raider defensive guard Pete Norwood recovered for Tech.

It was Tech's turn to punt and intercept, this time. On second down, Aggie quarterback Rocky Self was rushed hard and flung a sideline pass without noticing Raider cornerback Denton Fox in the area. But, Fox noticed the ball and intercepted it at the Aggie 48.

More custard hit the air as Kleinert hit the line, bounced off a closed hole, rolled left and tried a pass. It was short of his intended receiver, but not too short for Aggie safety, Dave Elmendorf. He picked it off, but the A&M offense couldn't generate a first down. That didn't matter, because the ensuing punt was fumbled by Tech safety Bruce Bushong. The Aggies recovered at the Raider 40.

For a minute, things looked like the game had finally gotten serious as A&M made three first downs to the Raider nine. Tech's defense would allow no more and Mike Bellar tried a field goal from the 23. It was wide to the right.

The Aggies took the kickoff to begin the second

A&M's Rocky Self takes aim at fullback Marc Black (41) as Raiders Pete Norwood (67), Jim Dyer (75), Larry Molinaire (52) and Bruce Dowdy (91) close in.

half. They gained their own 37 and stalled. Then, Sheffield came in to punt. He blasted a 58-yarder, putting the Raiders on their ten with their backs to the wall. It didn't seem to bother them much. They ran like crazy, piling up four first downs in seven plays on a 62-yard march. This brought up a first-and-ten at the Aggie 28, but that was it. On a fourth-and-three at the 21, Sanders came in to put a 39-yard field goal over, making the score 6-0.

Beginning their drive on the A&M 20, the Aggies likewise stayed on the ground, depending on the powerful running of Larry Stegent and Marc Black. They rolled 56 yards to the Tech 24, then drew an offside penalty, giving A&M a first-and-fifteen at the Tech 29. The Aggie drive mired down with a third-and-eight when Self fell down. However, an over-zealous Raider hit him late and the red flag gave A&M a first down on the Tech 12.

Self ran a keeper for no gain. The next play was an option that put the Aggies on the scoreboard when Self kept inside end for the TD. It looked as if the Cadets were pulling ahead until Raider corner-back Jerry Watson busted in to partially block Mike Bellar's kick, forcing it off to the right. And the score was tied 6-6.

The defenses tightened their grip and both offenses became unproductive until four minutes deep in the fourth quarter. Stegent fielded a Tech punt on

the A&M 45. On third-and-three, Stegent took a pass from Self for a first down at the Raider 42. It was Stegent again on a draw play to the 24. On third-and-five, Self's pitchout was almost picked off by a Tech lineman, but it bounced out of his hands and Stegent recovered. Bellar kicked from the 37 to put A&M ahead 9-6.

Kleinert ran the kickoff back to the Tech 31, but the Raiders lost three on the next two downs. Matulich went for the bomb on third-and-thirteen. Hardaway couldn't quite hang onto the ball at the A&M 29, but safety Mike Bunger was called for interference. On fourth-and-one on the 19, Hardaway barely got it. On third-and-two from the ten, Hardaway drove to the six. Hardaway carried three more shots into the tough Aggie middle to the six-inch line and Matulich called time out with 1:19 left. On the twelfth play of the drive, Hardaway made his ninth carry for the score and Tech led 13-9 with 1:16 remaining.

	A&M	Texas Tech
First downs	17	16
Yards rushing	200	152
Yards passing	48	56
Return yardage	28	64
Passes	5-16-3	6-14-2
Punts	6-45	6-36
Fumbles lost	1	1
Yards penalized	103	73

Texas A&M	0	0	6	3— 9
Texas Tech	3	0	3	7—13

Tech — FG 22 Sanders
Tech — FG 39 Sanders
A&M — Self 12 run (kick failed)
A&M — FG 37 Bellar
Tech — Hardaway 1 run (Sanders kick)
Attendance — 49,000

SYNOPSIS

TOP TEN

1. Ohio State
2. Texas
3. Southern Cal
4. Arkansas
5. Penn State
6. Missouri
7. Tennessee
8. UCLA
9. LSU
10. Florida

TEAM LEADERS FOR THE SEASON

OFFENSE

Rushing .Texas 1249 yds.
Passing . . . . .SMU 1015 yds.
Total . . . . .Texas 1583 yds.

DEFENSE

Rushing . . . . .Arkansas 384 yds.
Passing . . . . .Texas Tech 280 yds.
Total .Arkansas 926 yds.

SWC OFFENSIVE PLAYER OF WEEK

Charles Speyrer, Split End, Texas

SWC DEFENSIVE PLAYER OF WEEK

Scott Henderson, Linebacker, Texas

FRESHMAN GAME RESULTS

TCU 27 — North Texas State 7
Arkansas 23 — Texas Tech 22
Texas 34 — Baylor 28

OPEN DATE: Rice

CONFERENCE

	W	L	T
Arkansas	2	0	0
Texas	1	0	0
SMU	1	0	0
Texas Tech	1	1	0
Rice	0	0	0
Baylor	0	1	0
Texas A & M	0	1	0
TCU	0	2	0

SEASON RECORDS

	W	L	T
Texas	4	0	0
Arkansas	4	0	0
Texas Tech	2	2	0
Rice	1	2	0
SMU	1	3	0
Texas A & M	1	3	0
TCU	0	4	0
Baylor	0	4	0

Fifth Week
October 18

Tech's Bob Mooney (69) uses his head on State fullback Don Dudley while Wayne McDermand (77) ties up his feet. Mississippi State blockers are Ronnie Gray (51), Freddie Russell (76) and Joe Edwards (71).

MISS. STATE 30-TEXAS TECH 26

Joe Reed, a transfer from Baylor, returned to Texas as a replacement for Mississippi State's injured quarterback Tommy Pharr. But, it wasn't Old Home Week as far as Reed was concerned.

It only took Reed nine plays to show the Raiders that he meant business. It was a 56-yard march, ending with a 23-yard romp into the end zone by tailback Steve Whaley. He first tried left tackle, then rolled outside to streak for the score. Chuck Jordan's kick put MSU ahead 7-0.

State got a break little more than three minutes later when Raider end Ronnie Ross fumbled to the Bulldogs on the Tech 33. The Raider defense held their ground inside the 20, but Jordan's kick added another three points from the 33 and the Bulldogs led 10-0.

The Raiders came alive late in the first quarter when Tech's defensive right end Richard Campbell caught Reed in the MSU end zone for a safety, cutting the Bulldog lead to 10-2. Tech was warming to the game, now, and on their next possession, they ran clear out of the first quarter and into eight points to begin the second. The first quarter ended after the Raiders, under quarterback Joe Matulich, drove 46 yards in nine plays. Beginning the second quar-

ter with the wind at their backs, Tech took six plays to score on a one-yard run by Danny Hardaway. Hardaway's number was called again on the conversion as he took a swing pass for two points, bringing the Raiders even, 10-10.

The half was not destined to end in a tie, however. The Bulldogs did make a deep penetration into Tech territory, stalled, tried a field goal from the 30, but cornerback Jerry Watson smacked in to block it. Then, with 1:45 left in the half and MSU on third-and-seventeen at the Tech 45, split end Sammy Milner ran a post pattern, made a fine catch of Reed's pass at the 25, and blazed into the end zone. Jordan missed the extra point and the half ended with MSU leading 16-10.

Joe Matulich appeared again to start the second half after being relieved late in the second quarter by Charles Napper. He made a first down on the Tech 35. Passing into the wind, he threw incomplete. On second down, Matulich was rushed hard as he dropped back to pass. His hurried throw was intercepted by Buddy Newsom on the Tech 37.

On first down, Reed connected with Dave Smith at the Raider 17. It was second-and-eight when fullback Don Dudley, another Texan, took the screen

Joe Reed throws over Raider defenders Wayne McDermand (77), Dicky Grigg (56) and Eddy Windom (85). Pocket is formed by Joe Edwards (71), Tate Marsh (77) and Terry Smithart (26).

pass for fifteen yards to score. Jordan's kick was good enough to move the score to 23-10.

The Bulldogs started the fourth quarter with another score. It took an eighty-yard drive this time. But it only took ten plays and a 15-yard penalty. With a first down on the Tech 24, Reed passed to Sammy Milner at the eight and tailback Steve Whaley rammed through right tackle for another TD. Again, Jordan swung his foot and the score jumped to 30-10.

Napper reappeared at quarterback for Tech, but was unable to move the Raiders on his first series. Then Conn Canale punted short into the wind for MSU, rolling dead on the Bulldog 36. Mile Langehennig blasted to the eleven on the first play. Hardaway bucked to the seven, then Napper kept for the touchdown. Jerry Don Sanders came in to make good his first extra point of the game for a 17-30 score.

Dickie Grigg dumped Reed at his 29 for a six-yard loss on a first down play. Reed managed to connect with Milner on third-and-15, but Jerry Watson hit him hard and he dropped the pass. On fourth down, the combination of a fierce Raider rush and a headwind caused Canale to punt out-of-bounds at the Bulldog 38.

Napper covered the distance in seven plays. Hardaway took a pass for a first down at the 28 and

Robbie Best snagged another toss for a first down at the three. Jimmy Bennett took a pitch around left end for the score and Sanders' kick moved the Raiders within striking distance at 24-30.

Tech was driving again, but a penalty stalled them, turning the ball over to the Bulldogs at their own ten. Dicky Grigg dumped Reed at the seven and State was soon facing fourth-and-eleven on their nine. Then came the strategy. Canale dropped back to punt. The clock showed 1:24 as Canale took the snap, ran toward the wide side of the field, using up time and running through the end zone. Eddie Windom chased him out for a safety and two points. The Bulldogs took the option of a placement rather than a free punt from the 20. Ken Perkins took the kick on the Tech 39 and returned it to the 49. It was too far to come back.

	Miss State	Texas Tech	
First downs	17	20	MSU — Whaley 23 run (Jordan kick)
Rushing yardage	124	181	MSU — FG Jordan 33
Passing yardage	190	150	TT—Safety (Reed tackled in end zone) (kick failed)
Return yardage	11	70	TT — Hardaway 1 run (Hardaway pass from Matulich)
Passes	12-19-0	18-37-1	MSU—Milner 45 pass from Reed (kick failed)
Punts	7-38	6-43	MSU—Dudley 15 pass from Reed (Jordan kick)
Fumbles lost	0	2	MSU—Whaley 8 run (Jordan kick)
Penalties	64	25	TT—Napper 11 run (Sanders kick)
Miss. State 10	6 7	7—30	TT—Bennett 4 run (Sanders kick)
Texas Tech 2	8 0	16—26	TT — Safety (Canale tackled in end zone) (kick failed)
Attendance — 34,000			

Up goes quarterback Rocky Self and over Ag teammate Andy Philley to pick up nine to the TCU 45. Ross Brupbacher (80) blocks as Clay Mitchell (72) and Bob Creech (78) try to close the gap.

TCU 16-TEXAS A&M 6

Well, the Frogs finally won one. Lady Luck, who hadn't been too kind to either team in the past, had to pick a favorite and the Aggies came out second in Fort Worth.

There was a strong breeze blowing. The Aggies won the toss, elected to go with the wind and kicked to the Frogs. TCU revealed a strong running game

right from the start. Running back Marty Whelan was responsible for much of it. He smashed into the Aggie line nine times for 43 yards. The drive was stalled temporarily when the Frogs caught a 15-yard penalty for having an illegal receiver downfield. Facing a first-and-25, Judy threw to end Jerry Miller on the sideline to the Aggie ten. Whelan crunched down

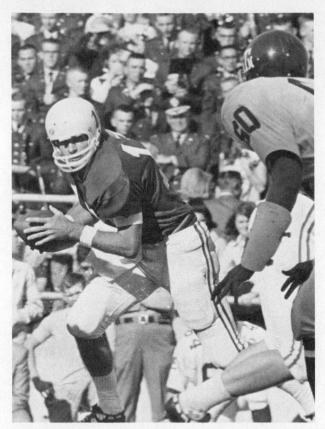

Frog quarterback Steve Judy picks up twelve yards on a keeper in the fourth quarter. Aggie linebacker Buster Adami (60) comes up to cut him off.

fight, holding for three downs at the 12. But, on fourth-and-one, Whelan would not be denied and battled to the ten for a first down. One big jump covered the last ten this time. Linzy Cole broke open in the middle of the end zone to take Judy's pass for the TD. Wayne Merritt's kick for the extra point was blocked by linebacker Mike Lord and TCU led 13-0.

The Frogs had thoroughly dominated the first half. Facing the wind in the first quarter, TCU gained six first downs and 91 yards in total offense. Running with the wind in the second quarter, the Frogs moved to seven first downs and 114 yards while holding the Aggies to one first down and a net offense of 17 yards.

Late in the third quarter, Judy flung a pass from his 36 straight down the middle to end John Beilue at the A&M 30. Beilue again took a third down pass to the 17. Penalties sent them back to the 37, then Judy passed to Jerry Miller at the 27. Busty Underwood booted the field goal from 44 yards and TCU pulled ahead 16-0.

The Aggies finally found the gas pedal with 13:29 left in the game. Marty Whelan had sliced a punt for only nine yards, giving the Maroon the ball on the TCU 39. Jimmy Sheffield had replaced Rocky Self to begin the second half, but Self returned to guide this attack. He passed to Barney Harris for 12, then a clipping penalty wiped out a 17-yard completion to Marc Black. It was second-and-17 on the TCU 34 when Self again called Black's number for an 18-yard pass completion and a first down. Black ran for one yard. On second-and-nine, Self hit Brupbacher on the sideline for the remaining 15 yards to score. Self tried for two points, but found his receivers covered. He scrambled up the middle, but was stopped inches short of the goal by Eddie Matthews and Jimmy Tidwell and it was 16-6.

The Aggies made one strong effort before they died. They forced the Frogs to punt. It went only 24 yards to the A&M 33. Self connected with Ross Brupbacher who broke to the TCU 25, then he fumbled. There was a scramble for the ball as it rolled toward the Frog goal. James Vanderslice recovered for TCU. The clock showed 11:34 and the Aggies never touched that precious ball again.

to the one in three tries, then Judy kept for the score. Wayne Merritt's kick was good and the Frogs led 7-0.

The Aggies nearly got on the board in the first quarter. They had driven to the TCU 25 and, on fourth down, with the wind at their backs and 23 seconds left in the quarter . . . nobody called for the snap. Time ran out and the Aggies were marched to the other end of the field. Once again on the 25, kicker on the 42, but with the wind in their faces, Mike Bellar's kick was straight but about 15 yards short.

The Frogs were ready to drive again. With the wind at their backs, TCU took a Jimmy Sheffield punt at their own 45. Whelan ran and Judy passed; one for eighteen yards to Jerry Miller at the A&M 21. The entire drive covered 55 yards in 11 plays for the score. The Aggies put up a good defensive

	A&M	TCU
First downs	9	24
Rushing yardage	41	214
Passing yardage	187	183
Passes	11-24-1	13-20-0
Return	2	8
Punts	8-34	8-37
Fumbles lost	1	1
Yards penalized	55	52

Texas A&M	0	0	0	6—	6
TCU	7	6	3	0—	16

TCU — Judy 1 run (Merritt kick)
TCU — Cole 10 pass from Judy (kick failed)
TCU — FG Underwood 14
A&M — Brupbacher (run failed)
Attendance — 38,123

SMU's Daryl Doggett pile drives ahead for the second of his three touchdowns. Owl defenders are Dale Grounds (34), Steve Bradshaw (70) and Joe Barron (74).

SMU 34-RICE 14

The Mustangs brought their flying circus to Rice Stadium but back Daryl Doggett used a ground attack to rush for 120 yards and score three touchdowns. There were 30,000 on hand to watch the Owls' conference opener. The air-minded Mustangs scored all of their touchdowns on the ground.

On their first possession, SMU moved 63 yards to score. This was their longest drive of the night. Quarterback Chuck Hixson passed for three completions in the 11-play drive. The big gainer was a pass to Gary Hammond, good for 20 yards to the Rice 15. Doggett took the ball to the one on four straight carries. From there Hixson scored on a keeper. Chipper Johnson kicked the seventh point and SMU led 7-0.

The Mustangs kicked off and quarterback Phillip Wood fumbled on the first play. Joe White recovered for SMU on the Rice 31. Hixson passed to Bicky Lesser for 17 yards but holding on the next play rubbed out most of that gain. Undaunted, Hixson hit Hammond on a pass to the Owl three. Doggett scored on fourth down from the one. Johnson's point after put SMU ahead 14-0.

Rice got untracked in the second quarter and put together a 51-yard drive in 10 plays. It was all via the ground. The drive seemed stalled as the Owls faced a fourth and four at the SMU 27. Dale Bernauer took a wide pitch from Wood and sprinted 19 yards to the Mustang eight. Wood faked and kept on third down to score from the four. Tim Davis booted the conversion point and Rice trailed by a 7-14 count.

With just over three minutes left in the first half, the Mustangs scored again on a 57-yard drive. Sam Holden and Hammond each caught passes for 13 yards. From the 17, Gordon Gilder blew through on a halfback draw to score SMU's third touchdown. Johnson's kick was good and the Mustangs led 21-7.

SMU came back to try for another TD with a fake field goal attempt. Hammond, who was holding, ran 11 yards to the Rice 13 before being tackled out of bounds. This left two seconds on the clock. Johnson then tried a field goal which Monte Hutchinson blocked. Randy Lee picked up the ball and ran.

The irresistible force meets the immovable object as Rice's Larry Caldwell (44) meets SMU's Rufus Cormier (56) head on.

Lee's run and the first half both ended at the 50.

Neither team scored in the third quarter, although late in that period Johnson tried for an SMU field goal from 47 yards out. The kick was off to the left and Rice took over at their 20. Wood was thrown for a loss of 11 yards and Mike Kramer entered the game at quarterback. The Owls' starting quarterback, Stahle Vincent, was hurt late in the first quarter and was not to get back into the game. Kramer received a rude reception as Bill Wright dumped him for an eight-yard loss. Bucky Allshouse punted from the end zone, on fourth down, out to the Rice 39.

Just over 12 minutes remained in the game as SMU scored its fourth touchdown. The Owls almost stopped the scoring drive at their 28. Facing a third and 10, Hixson passed to Fred Stringer who juggled the ball, but hung on before being downed at the 15. Doggett crunched over from the one for the score to put SMU ahead 27-7. Johnson's kick was no good.

Rice scored again late in the game with breaks playing a big part. First, Danny Gordon fumbled a punt and Mike Phillips recovered for Rice at the Mustang 42. Second, Larry Tunnell intercepted a Kramer pass in the end zone, but SMU was offside and Rice retained possession. Third, pass interference was called on SMU at the eight which placed the ball on the one. On third down, Larry Caldwell got the ball over and with Davis' good kick the Owls trailed 14-27.

When Rice again got the ball, the Mustangs had used up all but 1:15 on the clock. They didn't have it long as Tunnell intercepted a Kramer pass at the Owl 16 and returned to the four-yard line. With only 41 seconds remaining the Mustangs went the four yards in two plays. The game ended with SMU winning 34-14.

The Owls tossed Hixson for 35 yards in losses, but the pass rush left receivers open when he wasn't reached in time. Hixson, after two games against the Owls, has yet to score on them through the air.

		SMU	Rice
First downs		22	12
Rushing yardage		168	95
Passing yardage		27	50
Return yardage		27	50
Passes		22-32-0	6-18-3
Punts		5-38	6-35
Fumbles lost		2	2
Penalties		96	37
SMU	14	7	0	13—34
Rice	0	7	0	7—14

SMU — Hixson 1 run (Johnson kick)

SMU — Doggett 1 run (Johnson kick)

Rice — Wood 4 run (Davis kick)

SMU — Gilder 17 run (Johnson kick)

SMU—Doggett 1 run (kick failed)

Rice—Caldwell 1 run (Davis kick)

SMU — Doggett 3 run (Johnson kick)

Attendance — 30,000

SYNOPSIS

TOP TEN

1. Ohio State
2. Texas
3. Tennessee
4. Arkansas
5. Missouri
6. UCLA
7. Southern Cal
8. Penn State
9. LSU
10. Florida

TEAM LEADERS FOR THE SEASON

OFFENSE

Rushing .... Texas 1249 yds.
Passing .... SMU 1270 yds.
Total .... SMU 1862 yds.

DEFENSE

Rushing .... Arkansas 384 yds.
Passing .... Texas Tech 470 yds.
Total .... Arkansas 926 yds.

SWC OFFENSIVE PLAYER OF WEEK

Chuck Hixson, Quarterback, SMU

SWC DEFENSIVE PLAYER OF WEEK

Greg Webb, Defensive Back, TCU

FRESHMAN GAME RESULTS

Texas A & M 16 — Baylor 6
Rice 13 — SMU 12
Arkansas 34 — Oklahoma State 15

OPEN DATE: Texas, Arkansas, Baylor

CONFERENCE

	W	L	T
Arkansas	2	0	0
SMU	2	0	0
Texas	1	0	0
Texas Tech	1	1	0
TCU	1	2	0
Rice	0	1	0
Baylor	0	1	0
Texas A & M	0	2	0

SEASON RECORDS

	W	L	T
Texas	4	0	0
Arkansas	4	0	0
SMU	2	3	0
Texas Tech	2	3	0
Rice	1	3	0
TCU	1	4	0
Texas A & M	1	4	0
Baylor	0	4	0

Sixth Week
October 24,25

After picking up five yards on a keeper, James Street is bear-hugged by Rodrigo Barnes. Monte Hutchinson grabs a leg and Cliff Hammond (86) is help on the way.

TEXAS 31-RICE 0

Because of remodeling at Memorial Stadium, the lights had been removed. Therefore the Steers and Owls were meeting in broad daylight. If the sun plays favorites, then it shone on Texas. Before a capacity crowd the Longhorns proceeded to win their fourteenth game in a row.

Early in the first quarter Rice quarterback Stahle Vincent fumbled when hit and Leo Brooks recovered for Texas at the Rice 15. The Owl defense defensed the Longhorns and took over at their nine-yard line.

Soon the Owls were in trouble again. A Vincent pass was tipped by Fred Steinmark and caught for Texas by Mack McKinney. McKinney returned four yards to the Rice 32. Ted Koy ran for two, then quarterback James Street hit Cotton Speyrer with a pass for 19 yards. Street kept, on the next play, to the one-yard line. Steve Worster carried the ball and Bucky Allshouse, Rice defender, over the goal for the Longhorn's first touchdown. Happy Feller kicked the extra point and Texas led 7-0.

Texas headed for the Rice end zone again on the battering runs of Worster. They reached the end zone only they didn't have the ball. From the one Street missed a handoff and the ball bounced into the end zone. Mike Tyler pounced on the pigskin for Rice and the Owls had a touchback and the Longhorns had nothing.

Rice moved to the Texas 48 as play entered the second quarter. From there they were forced to punt. Danny Lester fielded the kick at the Texas 30 running at full steam. Up the sideline went Lester as he burst through a wave of Rice defenders. Tony Conley finally caught Lester and dropped him at the Rice four. The runback covered 66 yards. Jim Bertelsen went through the left side for four yards and a Texas touchdown. Feller again kicked good and Texas led 14-0.

As the half approached Roger Roitsch recovered Worster's screen pass fumble at the Texas 48. On the Owl's first play, David Arledge caused quarterback Mike Kramer to lose the ball. Brooks recovered his second fumble for the Longhorns at the Rice 46. Texas scored in six plays. The big gainers were a 22-yard pass to Worster and a 16-yard run by Koy. With 2:02 left, Billy Dale skirted the left side

Phillip Wood (11) is thrown for eight yard loss by David Arledge (89). Kim Malone (32) leans one way and Bill Zapalac (80) the other.

for the score. Feller added the 21st point and that was the first half scoring as time ran out with Texas holding a 21-0 advantage.

Texas received to open second half action and moved 71 yards in 12 plays for their final touchdown. Eddie Phillips took over the quarterbacking chores and engineered the drive. Besides picking up 45 yards on five carries, Phillips also passed to Randy Peschal for 14 yards. Dale dove over left tackle from the one. He fumbled and the Rice players argued that the ball was lost before crossing the goal. The protest did not change the result and with Feller's kick, Texas led 28-0.

Following the kickoff Rice almost went all the way. With Kramer passing and Phillip Woods running, the Owls reached the 'Horn 11-yard line. The Texas defense stiffened at this point and Rice ended its threat on the 20.

As the third quarter was coming to a close, Kim Malone was hit hard by Jim Williamson and Lester recovered the lost ball at the Rice 28. Feller tried a 50-yard field goal which failed, but got a second chance moments later. Mike Campbell intercepted a Wood pass and returned to the Rice 11. On fourth down Feller made good on a 24-yard field goal and Texas led 31-0 with play now into the final quarter.

Rice had one last chance to get on the scoreboard as Don Hayward recovered Bobby Callison's fumble at the Owl 46. Wood and Larry Caldwell spearheaded the running attack and moved the ball to the 15. Sam Reed caught a pass at the five. The bubble burst though as David Richardson intercepted a Wood pass with 20 seconds left. Two plays later a Texas pass was intercepted, but there was no time left on the scoreboard clock. The final score showed Texas winning 31-0.

The Owls again lost their starting quarterback, Vincent, early in the game. Rodrigo Barnes, who replaced the injured Dale Grounds at linebacker drew praise from Coach Darrell Royal who said, "I guarantee you that linebacker was a fine one." Barnes returned the compliment by saying that Texas has the three best backs on one team.

	Rice	Texas
First downs	21	20
Yards rushing	47	291
Yards passing	91	156
Return yardage	3	93
Passes	9-29-2	9-16-1
Punts	10-38	5-40
Fumbles lost	3	3
Yards penalized	25	100

Rice	0	0	0	0— 0
Texas	7	14	7	3—31

Texas — Worster 2 run (Feller kick)

Texas — Bertelsen 4 run (Feller kick)

Texas — Dale 4 run (Feller kick)

Texas — Dale 1 run (Feller kick)

Texas — FG Feller 24

Attendance — 61,500

TCU's Marty Whelan finds crowded quarters at the end of his six-yard run. Horned Frog blockers include Sammy Rabb (30), James Ray (63) and Danny Lamb (60).

MIAMI 14-TCU 9

The Horned Frogs traveled to the Orange Bowl Friday night to the Miami Hurricanes. With a crowd of only 21,195 on hand, business manager Frank Windegger figured the team cleared 86 cents on the trip. They also came in on the short end of the score. Breezes gusted up to 30 miles an hour during the game. It was an ill wind for TCU as mistakes continually blunted their offense and led to both of Miami's touchdowns.

The game started out favoring the Horned Frogs as 240-pound fullback Steve Schaap fumbled at the Miami 37. Jimmy Tidwell recovered the ball for TCU. Quarterback Steve Judy guided the Frogs to the Hurricane 12-yard line. There a fourth and one confronted the Texans and a field goal attempt, if entertained, was quickly discarded. Marty Whelen got the call and responded with a first and goal at the 10. Three plays later Whelan pounded through the right side for the touchdown. Wayne Merritt missed the extra point and the score stood TCU 6 — Miami 0.

The missed extra point may have been an omen for things to come. Late in the first quarter the Horned Frogs were operating from deep in their own end of the field. Judy dropped back to pass from the eight. Al Palewicz approached Judy from the blind side and the impact sent Judy one way and the ball the other. Jim Seely recovered for the Hurricane at the TCU four-yard line. Vince Opalsky cracked down to the one, then bulled over on the next play. Jim Huff broke the tie with a successful conversion. Miami led 7-6.

With two minutes left in the first quarter after the Hurricane touchdown, the two teams could not get the ball across the goal again in the first half. With two goose eggs the only thing on the second quarter scoreboard, the teams took to their dressing rooms with Miami's one point lead looming larger.

The two teams seemed to be hung on the goose eggs as they repeated the act in the third quarter. Neither side could get untracked as their offense was ineffectual. Mistakes plagued both teams al-

Miami's Bobby Best (40) makes five yards to TCU four. Run set up the Hurricane's second touchdown. Bringing down Best is Doug McKinnon (31).

though none led to points on the board.

As play moved into the fourth quarter another mistake caused the scoring drouth to be broken. Billy Fondren dropped back to punt for the Horned Frogs and linebacker Lou Erwin slipped through the TCU blockers to deflect the kick. Miami took over at the Horned Frog 35. Quarterback Kelly Cochrane didn't let this opportunity pass by as he directed the Hurricane assault troops in for the score. Opalsky again went over from the one and Huff again kicked the extra point. Miami breathed easier at 14-6.

With time increasingly becoming a large factor, TCU tried to move off dead center. Mistakes still haunted them as dropped passes and penalties at crucial times blunted any promising drive. A field goal by Merritt, from 28 yards out was the only reward for their efforts. This left them with a five-point deficit which proved to be an insurmountable obstacle. The game ended with no change and the Hurricane turned off the wind machine and snuck out of the Orange Bowl with a 14-9 victory.

TCU coach Fred Taylor described the ball game as the lousiest, stinkingest the Horned Frogs had played in a long time. "Our offense was poor. Our defense was about the same. If we play the way we did against Miami we won't win another game. We were awful. Terrible. Lousy," said Taylor as he bitterly reviewed the game.

Statistically the game was about even. TCU had 17 first downs and 300 total yards while Miami gained 15 first downs and 289 yards. Despite the wind, Judy completed 18 of 36 passes, but some that might have changed the game around were dropped. Schaap, who fumbled to set up the Frog touchdown, did his part to keep the breaks even. He also lost the ball at the TCU goal line, which took away another Miami touchdown.

The Horned Frogs now return to finish out the season in the SWC trenches. Maybe things will get better, they couldn't get any worse.

	TCU	Miami
First downs	17	15
Rushing yardage	136	179
Passing yardage	164	110
Return yardage	50	111
Passes	18-36-2	11-18-0
Punts	4-36	4-40
Fumbles lost	1	3
Yards penalized	33	40

TCU	6	0	0	3— 9
Miami	7	0	0	7—14

TCU—Whelan 1 run (kick failed)
Mia—Opalsky 1 run (Huff kick)
Mia—Opalsky 1 run (Huff kick)
TCU—FG Merritt 28
Attendance—21,195

Mustang fullback Walter Haynes fights for yardage against Raider defensive left end Eddy Windom (85), linebacker Larry Molinaire (52) and an unidentified pair of legs.

TEXAS TECH 27-SMU 24

Texas Tech head coach J. T. King said he started senior quarterback Joe Matulich to give his soph star, Charles Napper, time to quiet his nerves. But it was another one of those games that gave no consideration to the nerves of the fans. Both Tech and SMU are famous for that. So, 27,465 Cotton Bowl patrons hung by their thumbs until the final gun in Dallas.

Matulich seemed to have no nervous problems as he ripped the Mustangs in four plays from his own 35 to a first down at the SMU 19. Then Pony cornerback Pat Curry intercepted a pass bound for Tech end Charles Evans. He returned it to the 27, but a clipping penalty gave SMU the ball on their own 12. Tech was not to be denied, though. Denton Fox grabbed off Hixson's first pass at the 24 and returned it to the SMU eight. Danny Hardaway punched to the two, then carried again for the TD. Jerry Don Sanders' kick put the Raiders ahead 7-0. The clock said 11:29.

By the time the clock had gotten around to 6:00 left in the first quarter, the Ponies tied it. They covered 64 yards in twelve plays. The scoring play came with an end-around by Gary Hammond, sprinting from wide right around left end, socking heads

with Raider Jerry Watson on the goal line and rolling over for the six points. Chipper Johnson kicked to tie it up 7-7.

Napper stepped in at quarterback and took the Raiders to the Mustang 15-yard line before having to rely on the toe of Sanders for a 32-yard field goal. The first quarter had 57 seconds left and the Raiders led 10-7.

It was Daryl Doggett who turned in some large chunks of ground for the Ponies on the next series. On the first play, he broke up the middle for 47 yards from his own 20 to the SMU 33. It took seven plays to gain the Tech 12. On third-and-three, Doggett made it all the way on a bruising run. Johnson kicked and the Ponies took the lead 14-10.

Hixson's throwing began to click as he threw complete to Hammond on third-and-eight to put the Mustangs in business on the Raider 34. Two offside penalties put a bad dent in the Tech defense, since one of them nullified Dicky Grigg's recovery of a Hixson fumble. But, with a Mustang first down on the Tech one, the Raiders, thanks to Walter Yarbrough and Larry Molinaire, held the Ponies out. In fact, they ended up on the nine.

Then Napper came in to take his scrappy bunch

Tech's Tony Butler leans into a Pony tackler as Mustang defensive tackle Bill Wright (56) and rover Mike Shelton (92) hurry to lend aid. David Browning (76) sits this one out.

81 yards in four plays for the TD. The biggest gainer was a 77-yard pass to soph end Johnny Odom. Odom took the bomb on the SMU 47 and nobody could catch him. That seesawed Tech back in front 17-14 after Sanders' kick.

The scoreboard was allowed to rest until the fourth quarter. That's when Hixson usually cuts loose with a wild aerial attack. And, he did. On their first possession of the quarter, Hixson borrowed Tech's plans for their 77-yard bomb and built one of his own. The receiver was Gary Hammond and he outran the Raider defense to put the Mustangs ahead 21-17.

Napper's luck slipped a little on the first play after the kickoff. So did the ball. SMU tackle John Jordan belted him, he fumbled and Pat O'Connell snagged the ball in mid-air, returning it to the Tech 15. But, the Raiders held again, safety Dale Rebold breaking up one pass to Hammond at the goal line, and Johnson came in to add three points from the 30. That shot put the Ponies ahead 24-17.

John Kleinert returned the Mustang kickoff to the Tech 33, then Napper started the Raiders rolling again. Things got tight at the SMU 43 on third-and-nine, but Napper passed to David May for a first down on the 19. Hardaway carried four times in the next five plays. His last carry was into pay dirt from the four. Coach King decided to kick to tie the game

at 24 all. Sanders' boot was good.

The Mustangs had second-and-eight at their own 20. Hixson dropped back to pass and Hammond was open. He made a fine catch at the 50, but Tech's John Howard got a clothesline on him from behind and laid him out on his back. Hammond was out cold, the ball bounced free and Dale Rebold recovered on the Raider 43.

Napper was thrown for a seven-yard loss by Bill Wright with 1:39 left to play. His pass to Robbie Best made the 48, then Hardaway ran to the SMU 45. Johnny Odom caught the next pass to the 39 and Napper ran a keeper to the Mustang 20. Sanders' toe then snuffed out Pony hopes from the 36.

	Tech	SMU
First downs	19	18
Rushing yardage	181	154
Passing yardage	187	256
Return yardage	57	56
Passes	9-23-3	19-34-2
Punts	5-41.8	6-42
Fumbles lost	1	1
Yards penalized	53	60

Texas Tech	10	7	0	10—27
SMU	7	7	0	10—24

Tech — Hardaway 1 run (Sanders kick)
SMU—Hammond 13 run (Johnson kick)
Tech—FG Sanders 32
SMU — Doggett 12 run (Johnson kick)
Tech—Odom 77 pass from Napper (Sanders kick)
SMU — Hammond 77 pass from Hixson (Johnson kick)
SMU—FG Johnson 30
Tech — Hardaway 4 run (Sanders kick)
Tech—FG Sanders 36
Attendance—27,465

The scoreboard tells the story as Baylor right cornerback Russell Serafin bats away a sure TD strike from the wating hands of Aggie wingback Barney Harris.

TEXAS A&M 24-BAYLOR 0

After five games on the road, the Aggies finally opened their first home stand at Kyle Field. And, they played like they were glad to be home. For the Baylor Bears, it was just another lost weekend.

The Bears had possession of the ball five times in the first quarter and failed to make a first down. The Aggies did more with their opportunities. On their second possession of the game, the Aggies began a 45-yard march to pay dirt in ten plays. The Bears had punted, A&M's Dave Elmendorf made a 19-yard return to the Baylor 45. Guard Lynn Odom threw a block that sprung Elmendorf loose. Aggie tailback Larry Stegent busted the Bear line three times in a row for a first down. Another first was gained on a Rock Self-to-Barney Harris pass to the Baylor 21. From there, Stegent carried three times and fullback Marc Black carried once to put the ball on the two. Stegent made a flying leap over the Bear line to pick up the first score of the game. Mike Bellar's extra point was good enough to put the Aggies ahead 7-0.

The Bears' total offense for the first quarter amounted to 28 yards as the Aggie defense teamed with Jimmy Sheffield's punting to keep the Bruins caged. In fact, punting and defense of both clubs kept the scoreboard quiet for all but the last five minutes of the half. Baylor's Ed Marsh stuck the Aggies deep in their own territory twice with a couple of booming punts.

Late in the second quarter, it was Dave Elmendorf, again, who returned a Marsh punt ten yards to the Aggie 29 to start another drive. The Cadets got nowhere on the ground, but on third-and-eleven, Self hit Barney Harris on the 40 for a first down. Army was able to pick up three more on the ground to the 43. Jimmy Adams had replaced Harris at wingback. Self threw to Adams on the right sideline. It was good for 37 yards and a first down on the Bear 20. Self ran a keeper into the left side for five, then let Stegent do the work for the next four carries. He picked up another first down, but could go only two yards more on two more tries. Self went for Ross Brupbacher in the end zone, but it was incomplete. The only thing left to do was call in Bellar. His kick was good from 25 yards out and the Aggies led 10-0.

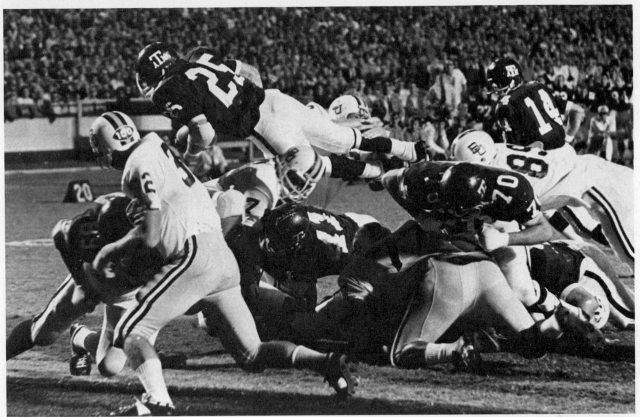

Larry Stegent goes over for the first quarter TD with Mike DeNiro (89), Marc Black (41) and Randy Maddox (70) blocking. QB Rocky Self (14) watches Bear defenders Tom Bambrick (32), Gary Sutton (79) and David Jones (89).

With nine seconds left in the half, the Bears had driven to the Aggie 44 after picking up a pair of first downs. But Dave Elmendorf was there with an interception to send the Bears to the lockers scoreless for the half.

It took the Aggies some time to warm up after the second half kickoff. It was late in the third period before the Ags began to roll. Starting at the Bear 41, Stegent rammed to the 38, then Self, finding no receivers open on a pass play, picked up some blocking, tore loose from a couple of Bruin tacklers on the way and was finally brought down on the Baylor three. The Bruins dug in and it took Stegent three blasts into the line before he hit the end zone. Bellar's kick moved the Aggie lead to 17-0.

On a second-and-eleven, Bear quarterback Laney Cook threw to Jerry Smith. The ball shot through his hands and into those of Ed Ebrom at the Bear 44. The Aggie cornerback took off down the left sideline, broke a Bear tackle at the two, and scored standing up. With 2:57 left in the third quarter, Beller's kick pushed the score to 24-0.

Baylor managed its deepest penetration of the game after receiving the A&M kickoff. It took them seven plays and they earned four first downs to reach the Army 27. But, Ebrom was there again to intercept a pass in the end zone and downing it there.

The Aggies weren't able to turn the possession into anything and had to punt. It didn't take long to put the ball back into Cadet hands, though. On first down, Steve Luebbehusen stole another Bear pass for the Aggies, returning it 14 yards to the Baylor 45. A pass interference call gave the Aggies a first down on the Bear seven, but they could make only one yard in three plays. They decided to go for the six points, but Self's pass was knocked down in the end zone.

The Bruins appeared to finally have scratched the scoring column when tailback Gene Rogers broke loose for a 57-yard touchdown run near the end of the game, but a holding penalty nullified the score. So, the Bears went home empty-pawed.

	Baylor	A&M
First downs	7	18
Yards rushing	123	235
Yards passing	64	103
Return yardage	46	138
Passes	7-23-4	8-23-0
Punts	0.2-45	9-40
Fumbles lost	0	2
Yards penalized	101	50

Baylor	0	0	0	0—	0
A&M	7	3	14	0—	24

A&M—Stegent 2 run (Bellar kick)
A&M—FG Bellar 25
A&M—Stegent 1 run (Bellar kick)
A&M—Ebrom 44 pass interception (Bellar kick)
Attendance—37,190

Bruce Maxwell turns blocker as Bill Burnett (33) carries the ball in this first quarter action. Keith Morrison (77) is the recipient of Maxwell's fury.

ARKANSAS 52-WICHITA STATE 14

The Wheatshockers of Wichita came to Little Rock and the Razorbacks gathered a harvest. With a crowd of 36,100 looking on, Senior John Eichler replaced the injured Bill Montgomery at quarterback and proceeded to set an Arkansas record for pass completions as he hit on 23 of 41 attempts.

Wichita kicked off and Arkansas wasted no time in visiting the Wheatshockers end zone. Eichler completed three passes to David Cox and Bill Burnett, and Bruce Maxwell handled the ground attack. On the 13th play Burnett cracked over from the four for the score. Bill McClard kicked the point and Arkansas led 7-0.

The Razorbacks mounted another scoring drive in the first quarter which was halted when Burnett fumbled, after a nine-yard gain, and lost the ball at the Wichita 20.

As the second quarter opened Arkansas had possession on the Wichita 24. Denied a touchdown, McClard came in for a field goal try. The snap was high and holder Gus Rusher passed to Maxwell for a three yard loss. Wichita was unable to move and punted to their own 39. Arkansas reached the Shockers five, but Wichita held and McClard came on for another field goal attempt. His kick went 23

yards and split the uprights. Arkansas led 10-0.

Wichita received the kickoff and fumbled on the second play. Dick Bumpas recovered for the Razorbacks at the Wichita 22. An Eichler pass to Cox was good for 18 yards and Burnett ran for two and then two more for the touchdown. McClard's kick was successful and Arkansas led 17-0.

After an exchange of punts, Wichita owned the ball on the Razorback 40. On two runs and a pass the Shockers reached the 24. From there quarterback Bob Renner passed complete to Gene Robinson for a Wichita touchdown. Ray Kinkaid kicked the conversion point and Arkansas' lead was cut to 17-7.

Arkansas received the kickoff and started from their 31. On the first play Maxwell ran for 27 yards around left end, to the Shocker 42. Eichler lost 11 yards attempting to pass then passed complete to John Rees for 13 yards. Two more completions, one to Pat Morrison for 16 yards and one to Rees for 14, set the ball on the Wichita 10. Eichler then passed to Morrison for the touchdown. McClard kicked the 24th point to give the Razorbacks a 17-point lead. The first half ended 24 seconds later.

Wichita took the second half kickoff and moved

Senior quarterback John Eichler received fine pass protection all day from the Hog offensive line. Here Keith Morrison (77) is blocked and Lynn Duncan (75) leaps to no avail.

to their 49 before punting out of bounds at the Razorback 16. After Maxwell gained nine yards on two carries, Eichler passed complete to Morrison for 37 yards to the Shocker 38. Maxwell ran for 11 more yards and when an end around gained nothing, Eichler tossed a pass to Burnett for seven yards. Maxwell gained three more and a pass to Rees put the ball at the Wichita 10-yard line. Maxwell carried four straight times to erase the 10 yards and score another Razorback touchdown. McClard's kick was good and Arkansas led 31-7

After kicking off and then receiving Wichita's punt, Eichler moved the second unit into field goal position. Another high snap from center was recovered by Rusher for a 16-yard loss. After one first down the Wheatshockers were forced to punt. Terry Stewart received the ball on his 10 and returned 90 yards for a touchdown. Add the point by McClard and Arkansas was on top 38-7.

Soon after the kickoff play moved into the final quarter. The Razorbacks rode the passing arm of Eichler for another score after forcing a Wichita punt. Russ Garber scored from the one, but the play was nullified and Arkansas penalized 5 yards for illegal procedure. Eichler passed to Bob Nichols for the touchdown and this one counted. McClard kicked the PAT and Arkansas led 45-7.

Following the kickoff a Wichita fourth down punt was partially blocked by Ronnie Jones and Arkansas had possession on the Shocker 32. Steve Walters ran right end for the six points. McClard made it seven and the Razorbacks now lead 52-7.

The Shockers pulled a shocker on the second play after the kickoff. Fullback Randy Jackson got outside right end and went 78 yards for a touchdown. Kinkaid added the extra point and Wichita trailed 14-52.

Wichita kicked off with 5:43 left and never got possession of the ball again. The Razorback subs drove from their 30 to the Wichita three. An offside penalty moved them back to the eight from where the game ended on an incomplete pass. Final score read Arkansas 52 — Wichita 14.

All was not lost for Wichita State. They defeated Arkansas in a cross country track duel Saturday morning.

	Wich.	Ark.
First downs		32
Rushing yardage	41	232
Passing yardage	66	299
Return yardage	12	159
Passes	8-19-0	26-47-0
Punts	10-33	3-37
Fumbles lost	1	1
Yards penalized	0	64

Wichita	0	7	0	7—14
Arkansas	7	17	14	14—52

Ark—Burnett 4 run (McClard kick)
Ark—McClard FG 22
Ark—Burnett 2 run (McClard kick)

WS — Robinson 24 pass from Renner (Kinkaid kick)
Ark—Morrison 10 pass from Eichler (McClard kick)
Ark — Maxwell 1 run (McClard kick)
Ark—Stewart 90 punt return (McClard kick)
Ark—Nichols 6 pass from Eichler (McClard kick)
Ark—Walters 6 run (McClard kick)
WS — Jackson 78 run (Kinkaid kick)
Attendance—36,000

SYNOPSIS

6

TOP TEN

1. Ohio State
2. Texas
3. Tennessee
4. Arkansas
5. Penn State
6. Southern Cal
7. Florida
8. LSU
9. UCLA
10. Notre Dame

TEAM LEADERS FOR THE SEASON

OFFENSE

Rushing ....Texas 1540 yds.
Passing ....SMU 1526 yds.
Total ....Arkansas 2103 yds.

DEFENSE

Rushing ....Texas 438 yds.
Passing ....Arkansas 608 yds.
Total ....Texas 1117 yds.

OFFENSIVE PLAYER OF WEEK

Charles Napper, Quarterback, Texas Tech

DEFENSIVE PLAYER OF WEEK

David Arledge, Defensive End, Texas

FRESHMAN GAME RESULTS:

TCU 16 — Baylor 14
Texas Tech 31 — UT-Arlington 14
Texas 28 — Rice 8

CONFERENCE

	W	L	T
Texas	2	0	0
Arkansas	2	0	0
SMU	2	1	0
Texas Tech	2	1	0
TCU	1	2	0
Texas A & M	1	2	0
Baylor	0	2	0
Rice	0	2	0

SEASON RECORDS

	W	L	T
Texas	5	0	0
Arkansas	5	0	0
Texas Tech	3	3	0
SMU	2	4	0
Texas A & M	2	4	0
Rice	1	4	0
TCU	1	5	0
Baylor	0	5	0

Seventh Week
November 1

SMU's Bicky Lesser at the Texas 18 on his way to the Mustang's only touchdown. The pass from Chuck Hixson covered 29 yards. Bill Zapalac (80) chases Lesser across goal.

TEXAS 45-SMU 14

The Longhorns visited the Cotton Bowl for the third time this year. Before a crowd of 55,287 they gained their third victory. With 8:13 left in the third quarter and owning only a four-point lead, Texas unleashed their "Doomsday Offense" and overwhelmed the Mustangs.

Texas took the opening kickoff and using their ground shock troops marched 80 yards in 12 plays. Jim Bertelsen, who was to tie Bobby Layne's school record of four touchdowns in one game, scored the Longhorns' initial touchdown from seven yards out. Happy Feller kicked the first of six successful conversions. Texas led 7-0.

SMU's stunting defense didn't let this dampen their spirits and for the rest of the first half they kept Texas bottled up from their own mistakes. Bertelsen fumbled the ball at the Texas 27 and the SMU 31. The Mustangs recovered both times. Joe Stutts turned thief and stole the ball from quarterback James Street as he retreated to pass.

Although Texas gained 199 yards rushing and 55 passing, the remainder of the first half, they only got into SMU's end zone once more before the half. This came about through the air as Feller kicked a 32-yard field goal with 11 seconds remaining until intermission. This successful effort took place four and a

half minutes after Chip Johnson had toed a three pointer through the uprights from the same distance for SMU. At the half Texas led 10-3.

The Mustangs took the second half kickoff and through the passing of quarterback Chuck Hixson, moved 78 yards to a first and goal at the Texas three. Daryl Doggett carried three straight times and was only able to reach the one-half yard line. On fourth down, amid a chorus of boos from the stands, Johnson came in to kick a 17-yard field goal. This closed the gap to four points, followed closely by the avalanche.

The Longhorns took the kickoff and marched 67 yards in eight plays. One play that was nullified by a motion penalty was a 57-yard scamper by Bertelsen. Street made up most of this setback by keeping for a run of 44 yards. Steve Worster scored the touchdown from the one. Texas led 17-6.

The rampaging 'Horns then scored on their next four possession as they resembled the famous German Blietzkrieg of World War II. First, they went 35 yards in two plays. Bertelsen scored through a huge hole at right tackle, going 26 yards. Texas 24—SMU 6.

Then, on their next series, they went 68 yards in four plays. Ted Koy earning the six points on a 40-

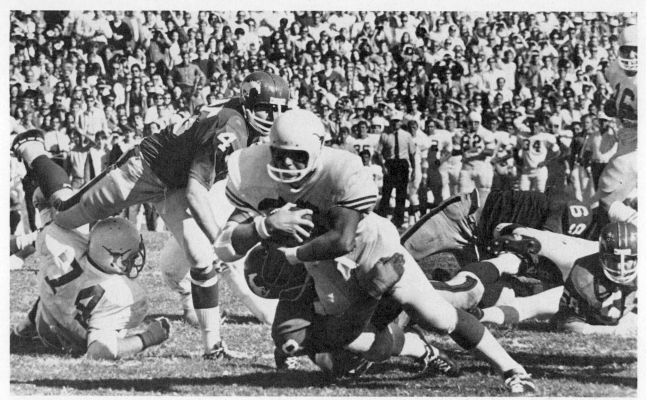

Jim Bertelsen scores the first Texas touchdown with Bruce Portillo hanging on. The Mustangs' Mike Nekuza (45) steps over Randy Stout (74) but arrives too late.

yard cannon shot through left tackle. Texas 31 — SMU 6.

When Texas got the ball again, play had moved into the fourth quarter. A 44-yard drive was put to rest as Bertelsen scored from the three. Texas 38 — SMU 6.

To beak the monotony, SMU put on a touchdown drive of their own, before Texas got possession again. The Mustangs scored on a Hixson to Bicky Lesser pass good for 29 yards. This capped a nine-play 69-yard march. Hixson then passed to Sam Holden for a two-point conversion. Texas now led 38-14.

Unfortunately, after scoring, they had to give Texas the ball again. The Longhorns started from their 20 and alternating Worster, Koy and Bertelsen, moved 80 yards to score. Koy had a 17-yarder. Worster ran for 11, 15 and 28 yards. Bertelsen scored his record tying touchdown on a run of 13 yards. Texas 45 — SMU 14.

On their next possession the Texas second unit moved from their 23 to the Mustang six. Penalties, the bugaboos of overeager second units, then blunted the drive. The game ended with no more scoring.

The victory was a costly one for the Longhorns as their fine tackle Leo Brooks suffered torn ligaments in his right knee and will be lost for the remainder of the season. Center Forrest Wiegand also

suffered a knee injury that might cause him to miss one or two games.

Texas wound up with 611 yards rushing which broke the record of 594 yards Arkansas ran up on Kansas State Teachers in 1936. Each member of the starting backfield rushed for over 100 yards. Bertelsen and Worster each had 137 yards. Koy had 111 yards and Street added 121 yards.

Not to be overlooked in the carnage is the record Hixson set with an 11-yard pass to Holden in the second quarter. This pass broke the SWC all-time career pass completion record set by Texas A & M's Edd Hargett last year. Hixson has the rest of this season and all of next year to improve on his record which now stands at 416 completions.

SMU coach Hayden Fry paid tribute to the Longhorns by saying, "Texas has got the greatest college team I have ever seen and probably ever will." Some folks around Fayetteville may not go along with that appraisal just yet.

	Texas	SMU
First downs	34	15
Yards rushing	611	73
Yards passing	65	223
Return yardage	52	46
Passes	4-10-0	20-38-2
Punts	3-29	5-39
Fumbles lost	3	2
Yards penalized	124	108

Texas	7	3	21	14—45
SMU	0	3	3	8—14

Attendance—55,287

Tex—Bertelsen 7 run (Feller kick)
SMU—FG Johnson 32
Tex—FG Feller 32
SMU—FG Johnson 17
Tex—Worster 1 run (Feller kick)
Tex—Bertelsen 26 run (Feller kick)
Tex—Bertelsen 3 run (Feller kick)
SMU—Lesser 29 pass from Hixson (Hixson pass to Holden)
Tex—Bertelsen 13 run (Feller kick)

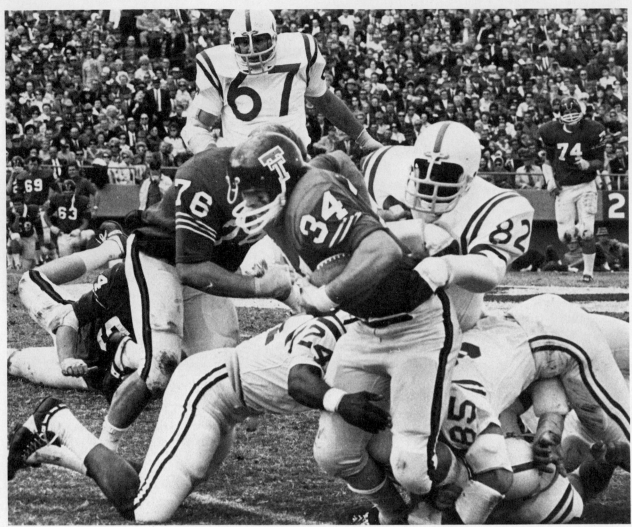

Tech's Miles Langehenning is swarmed under by a host of Owls. Mike Taylor (24), Rodrigo Barnes (82) and Roger Collins (85) each got a piece of Miles. Tech's David Browning (76) and Rice's Roger Roitsch (67) arrive late.

TEXAS TECH 24-RICE 14

The Rice Owls came to Jones Stadium in Lubbock, not only to break a four game losing streak, but to ruin Tech's homecoming before 38,500 who came home. The first half was all Rice, until 10 seconds before the break. Tech not only scored in that short space of time, but in doing so shifted the momentum to their side for the second half.

The Owls scored on their first possession of the game. They went 54 yards in eight plays. Quarterback Stahle Vincent's passing opened up the Tech defense as he hit Sam Reed for 13 yards and Joe Henderson for 12 and 11 yards. The 11-yarder was for the touchdown. Tim Davis added the extra point and Rice led 7-0.

About midway through the second quarter Rodrigo Barnes set up Rice's second touchdown. He intercepted Tech quarterback Charles Napper's pass

and returned eight yards to the Red Raider 46. The Owls moved to the Tech 22, mainly on Vincent passes to Cliff Crabtree for seven yards and to Bob Brown for eight more. A high pitch caused Crabtree to lose seven yards. Jimmy Davis, a red-shirt playing his first varsity game, took over at quarterback and was dropped for a three-yard loss. He was dropped a little too hard and Tech drew an unnecessary roughness penalty. This brought up a fourth and three at the 17. Vincent replaced Davis and kept around left end for all 17. Jim Davis' kick put Rice two TD's up, 14-0.

In the fading moments of the first half Tech took over, after an Owl punt, at the Rice 39. Joe Matulich replaced Napper at quarterback. Two passes, a 21-yarder to Robbie Best and a 12-yarder to David May, served up Tech with a first and goal at the

110

Flanker David May leaps high to make a Red Raider pass reception in front of Rice defender Bucky Allshouse.

Owl six. Miles Langehenning ran for four and Matulich kept for one more. On third and one Danny Hardaway was stopped cold. The officials then stopped the clock with 10 seconds remaining, saying the Owls were not unpiling fast enough. This was a break for Tech as they had no time-outs left. On fourth and goal, Hardaway was stopped again as time ran out. The Owls then had an offside penalty called on them which gave Hardaway one more chance. This time he made it. Jerry Don Sanders kicked the point and at the half Rice led 14-7.

The Red Raiders scored on their first possession in the second half. The important gainers on the 10 play 61-yard drive were Matulich passes to Ronnie Ross for 23 yards, to Charles Evans for 14 yards, and back to Ross again for 11 yards. Jimmy Bennett scored from the one and with Sanders' good PAT the score was a standoff, 14-14.

The score hadn't changed as Tech took over at their 47 early in the fourth quarter. Bennett ran nine yards on a draw play, but Hardaway lost a yard on second down. Matulich faked inside, then passed down the middle to Evans, who was bought down at the Rice 19. Hardaway ran for four. On the next play a scrambling Matulich found Johnny Odom in the end zone and hit him with a picture pass. Sanders converted and the Red Raiders led for the first time, 21-14.

With just over five minutes left in the game, Jerry Watson intercepted a Jimmy Davis pass to give Tech possession on the Rice 32. Matulich kept twice to run for a first down at the 18. From there Rice stopped the time-consuming ground game and on fourth and two, Sanders came in and kicked a 27-yard field goal. This enlarged Tech's lead to 10 points and with 3:42 left it could have been a very big three points. It definitely left Rice with the problem of scoring, getting the ball back, and then scoring again.

The game soon ended without any of this happening. The Red Raiders had won their fourth game of the year 24-14. The win kept alive the hopes of a conference championship for Tech. The loss, for Rice, just makes the next game that much more important.

	Rice	Texas Tech
First downs	10	12
Yards rushing	36	113
Yards passing	104	172
Return yardage	10	23
Passes	11-22-1	12-23-2
Punts	12-38	10-40
Fumbles lost	0	2
Yards penalized	41	20

Rice	7	7	0	0—14
Texas Tech	0	7	7	10—24

Rice — Henderson 11 pass from Vincent 17 run (Davis kick)
Rice—Vincent 17 run (Davis kick)
Tech — Hardaway 1 run (Sanders kick)
Tech — Bennett 1 run (Sanders kick)
Tech—Odom 15 pass from Matulich (Sanders kick)
Tech—FG Sanders 27
Attendance—38,500

Marty Whelan grinds out yardage over center (John Ruthstrom to be exact). Frog blockers Jerry Cooper (69), James Ray (63) and Gerald Kirby tangle with Bears Dennis Watson (86), Brian Blessing (44), Tom Reaux (77) and Gary Sutton (79).

TCU 31-BAYLOR 14

The Horned Frogs made it six in a row over the staggering Bears before the homecoming crowd at Baylor Stadium in Waco. TCU's sophomore quarterback Steve Judy was making yards running when he wasn't making yards passing. Generally, he was making life miserable for the already sorrowful Bears. Judy's personal offensive toll against Baylor amounted to 364 yards; the second best one-man offense mark in TCU history. Emery Nix busted the Bears for 398 yards in 1941.

However, the Bears had their moments, too. Laney Cook took over the quarterback spot early in the second quarter and piled up 175 yards in total offense. He rushed for 87 yards, averaging 5.5 yards per carry.

TCU cashed in on their first possession of the ball game. Running back Marty Whelan churned through the Bears on six straight carries, moving from the Frog 40 to the Baylor 32. With fourth down coming up at the Baylor 27, an offside penalty against the Bears gave TCU a first-and-ten on the 22. It was Whelan again to the 17, then Judy carried to the eight. Judy scrambled again to the five

and Whelan banged for one. Along came Judy's first pass as he rolled left and tossed to split end Jerry Miller in the end zone. Wayne Merritt kicked and the Frogs led 7-0. That was Miller's first varsity score.

The Bears muffed a scoring opportunity when left linebacker David Jones made an interception at the Bruin 43, but the field goal attempt missed. Starting quarterback Steve Stuart was replaced by Cook.

The Frogs had their low moments, too. Judy fumbled at the end of a 17-yard sweep, stopping a TCU drive at the Bruin 21. And, as the half was drawing to a close, the Frogs marched from their 32 to the Baylor 18. The drive stalled and they tried a field goal which was wide.

On the second play of the third quarter, Cook fumbled the snap. Frog defensive left tackle Clay Mitchell wrestled Cook for it and won, giving TCU the ball on the Bear 22. Acting on the old axiom to hit 'em when they're shook, Judy went for blood on the first down with a pass to Jerry Miller in the end zone. He was covered by two defenders, but outjumped them for the score. Merritt's kick moved

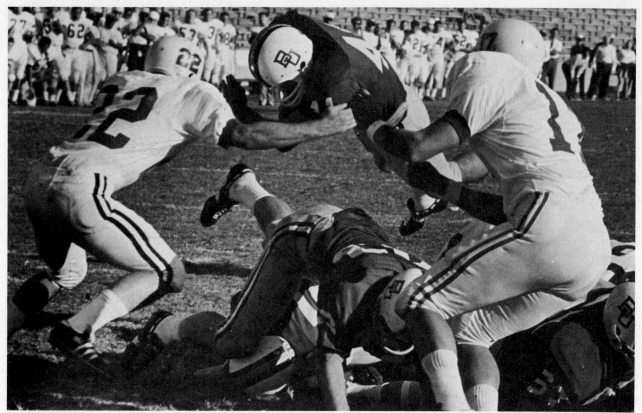

A brief moment of glory for the Bears as Gordon Utgard dives over right guard to score. Defending for TCU are Larry Wright (22) and Ted Fay (17). The scoring play covered one yard.

the Frog lead to 14-0.

The Bears had another opportunity to put their mark on the scoreboard when a TCU punt rolled dead at the 50. This time, they took advantage of the break. It took nine plays to get the score. Tailback Gene Rogers got the biggest bite of that disance with a 34-yard zip up the middle. Ted Fay finally brought Rogers down on the Frog two-yard line. Baylor's first touchdown in seven quarters of play came after Gordon Utgard took all four downs to hammer in, finally, from the one. Terry Cozby finally got a chance at an extra point and made good. The score read 14-7 in favor of the Frogs.

Apparently, all Baylor's score did was to give the Frogs a poke with a sharp stick. In 15 plays, Judy moved his company into the Bruin end zone. It started 70 yards away and a holding penalty on first down moved TCU 85 yards from pay dirt. A pass to Miller brought a first down, then flanker Linzy Cole came up with third-down receptions for 10 and 15 yards. Judy ran for another 16 to the Bear seven. On fourth-and-one, Judy bucked it over for another six points. Merritt's kick was good for a 21-7 lead.

With 10:23 left in the game, Cook took his Bears on an 80-yard trip to pay dirt. It took 15 plays from the Bruin 20 with Cook keeping and throwing op-

tions to Jerry Smith until a Cook keeper covered the last five yards to score. Cozby again kicked true to move the Bears up to a 21-14 gap.

But, it didn't last long. The Bears' sharp stick put the Frogs into high gear again. Passing gear, even. With 9:29 left, Steve Judy stepped on the gas from his own 30 and raced 70 yards to put his Frogs ahead, after Merritt's kick, 28-14. It had happened only three plays after Cook's score. Norman Bulaich cleared the last man away at the Bear 15.

Baylor was allowed possession of the ball for only two plays after the kickoff, then Greg Webb intercepted a Cook pass, returning three yards to the Bear 27. A penalty moved the Frogs back 15, but Judy passed them back to the 24 and Merritt kicked his 41-yard field goal.

	TCU	Baylor
First downs	23	12
Yards rushing	286	192
Yards passing	214	292
Return yardage	7-56	4-19
Passes	19-30-2	6-24-2
Punts	4-39.5	7-41.5
Fumbles lost	1	1
Yards penalized	77	24

TCU	7	0	14	10—31
Baylor	0	0	7	7—14

TCU — Miller 4 pass from Judy (Merritt kick)
TCU — Miller 22 pass from Judy (Merritt kick)
Baylor—Utgard 1 run (Cozby kick)
TCU—Judy 1 run (Merritt kick)
Baylor—Cook 5 run (Cozby kick)
TCU—Judy 70 run (Merritt kick)
TCU—FG Merritt 41
Attendance—25,000

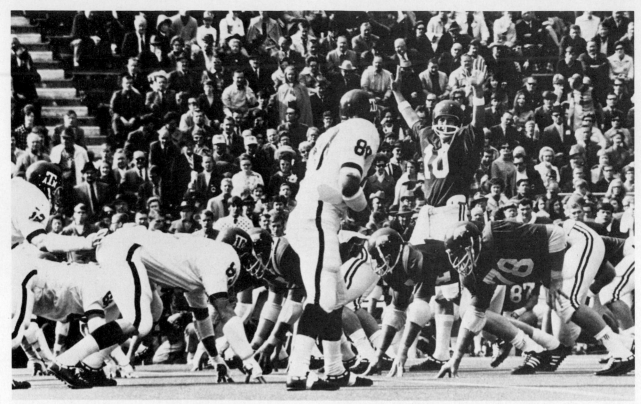

As the Arkansas offense confronts the A & M defense, quarterback Bill Montgomery calls for the Razorback fans to lower the noise level.

ARKANSAS 35-TEXAS A&M 13

The battered Aggie football machine rolled into Razorback Stadium and rolled for a quick score against the mighty Hog defense as though a new day had dawned for A&M. As it turned out, the Cadets had just had their dessert early. Most of the rest of it was medicine. Bad medicine, as far as the Maroons were concerned.

The Hogs kicked off and Dave Elmendorf returned to the Aggie 18. Larry Stegent rammed over guard for 14 yards and Marc Black swept left end for eight. Stegent carried into the line again for seven and again for four. Rocky Self passed to Black to the Hog 40. Stegent continued to pound the Arkansas line for gains of five, three and one yard. Self kept twice for three yards total, then called again for Stegent. Persistence paid off as Stegent bolted over left guard and went all the way. Mike Bellar's kick put the Aggies ahead 7-0.

Arkansas returned the kickoff to their own 27. It was carried by Mike Hendren from the ten. But, a clipping penalty put the Hogs back to their nine. Arkansas picked up two yards on Bruce Maxwell's carry over center, then Bill Burnett banged center again for four. Bill Montgomery passed to Maxwell

at the 26. Burnett's draw play made three and Montgomery skirted end for six. After a run by Burnett for five, Montgomery passed to John Rees at the Aggie 35. Burnett was dumped for a one-yard loss at right end. Maxwell grabbed a pass for seven, then Montgomery was stopped for no gain. With a fourth down at the A&M 25, Bill McClard's field goal try was wide to the left. A personal foul put the Razorbacks back in business at the 12. Burnett carried three times and Montgomery once, the drive ending with Burnett's dive over left tackle for two yards and a TD. McClard's kick tied it up at 7-7.

Starting on their 16, the Aggies moved to the Hog 16 in ten plays, the last two beginning the second quarter. But a pass by Self for the score fell incomplete and the Aggies had to go for a field goal. The 29-yard try by Bellar was wide to the right.

It took an even ten plays for Arkansas to get back on the scoreboard. Montgomery's pass to Pat Morrison picked up 11, Maxwell ran for nine and so did Burnett. Chuck Dicus took Montgomery's pass to the Aggie 26. Russell Cody carried three times for 16 yards and Montgomery passed complete to Dicus for the Hog's second score. McClard kicked the

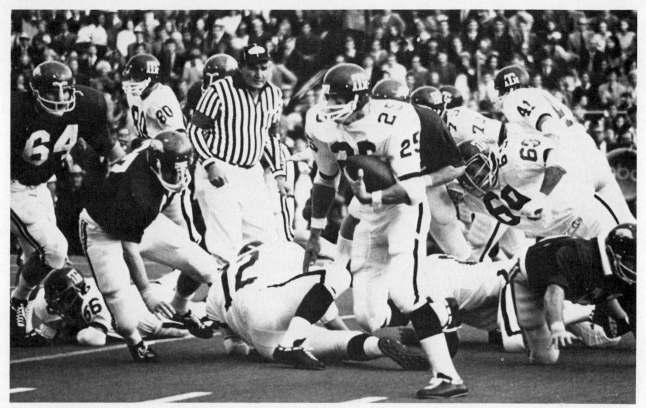

Surrounded, the official freezes, but not Larry Stegent (25) as he goes for two yards. Arkansas players are Cliff Powell (64) and Tommy Dew (87). Aggies, left to right, are Jack Koyar (56), Ross Brupbacher (80), Mike Fields (72), Leonard Forey (69) and Mark Black (41).

Hogs ahead 14-7 with 10:40 left in the half.

Then the Aggies were stung with a second bad break. Self, on his own 41, dropped back to pass and was hit. Controversy raged over whether it was an incomplete pass or a fumble, but the Porkers ended up with the ball on the Aggie 34. The sixth play of the series found Burnett scrambling through right tackle for four yards and another score, putting the Hogs ahead 21-7.

The Aggies failed to move and punted. Rocky Self's 41-yard punt gave Arkansas the ball on their 40. The Aggie defense dug in, forcing Arkansas to punt. Dave Elmendorf made a nine-yard return, but a clipping penalty put the ball on the A&M four. Stegent took a pitchout around left end for two, was hit hard and fumbled. The ball was recovered by Bruce James for Arkansas on the A&M six. Burnett ran for a yard, then Montgomery passed to Pat Morrison to extend Arkansas' lead to 28-7.

The Aggies came howling back. Self passed to Ross Brupbacher for 23 and to Barney Harris for 40 to the Hog six, but the Cadets were stopped at the Arkansas one as the half ended.

The Aggies started the second half by kicking off to Arkansas. Arkansas started the second half by scoring on the Aggies. It took 12 plays to cover the 73 yards. Maxwell figured in seven of them, three

for runs and four passes from Montgomery. His last carry was over right tackle for a yard to score and the Hogs had a lopsided 35-7 lead. There was 10:40 left in the third quarter.

It was late in the fourth quarter before the Aggies were able to battle their way back onto the scoreboard. The Cadets took a Hog punt on their own eight, Elmendorf returning it to the 17. Stegent ran for 12 and five yards. Self passed to Jimmy Adams at the 50 and Stegent ran for nine more. Steve Burks swept left end for 21 yards to the Arkansas 20. Then Self hit Brupbacher in the right flat. He escaped three Hog defenders to score. Self tried for two points, but was thrown for a loss, making the final score 35-13.

	A&M	Ark.
First downs	22	25
Rushing yardage	211	158
Passing yardage	238	207
Return yardage	18	44
Passes	16-30-1	19-29-0
Punts	3-47	5-38
Fumbles lost	2	1
Yards penalized	42	72

Texas A&M	7	0	0	6	13
Arkansas	7	21	7	0	35

A&M — Stegent 28 run (Bellar kick)
Ark — Burnett 2 run (McClard kick)
Ark — Dicus 10 pass from Montgomery (McClard kick)
Ark—Morrison 5 pass from Montgomery (McClard kick)
Ark — Maxwell 1 run (McClard kick)
A&M—Brupbacher 20 pass from Self (pass failed)
Attendance—40,000

SYNOPSIS

7

TOP TEN
1. Ohio State
2. Texas
3. Tennessee
4. Arkansas
5. Penn State
6. Southern Cal
7. UCLA
8. Notre Dame
9. Missouri
10. Purdue

TEAM LEADERS FOR THE SEASON

OFFENSE

Rushing	Texas 2151 yds.
Passing	SMU 1749 yds.
Total	Texas 2706 yds.

DEFENSE

Rushing	Texas 520 yds.
Passing	Texas Tech 830 yds.
Total	Texas 1422 yds.

SWC OFFENSIVE PLAYER OF WEEK
Jim Bertelsen, Halfback, Texas

SWC DEFENSIVE PLAYER OF WEEK
Bruce James, Defensive End, Arkansas

FRESHMAN GAME RESULTS
Oklahoma 50 — Texas Tech 12
Texas A & M 36 — Rice 8
SMU 21 — Texas 14

CONFERENCE	W	L	T
Texas	3	0	0
Arkansas	3	0	0
Texas Tech	3	1	0
SMU	2	2	0
TCU	2	2	0
Texas A & M	1	3	0
Rice	0	3	0
Baylor	0	3	0

SEASON RECORDS	W	L	T
Texas	6	0	0
Arkansas	6	0	0
Texas Tech	4	3	0
SMU	2	5	0
TCU	2	5	0
Texas A & M	2	5	0
Rice	1	5	0
Baylor	0	6	0

Eight Week
November 8

OOOPS! Billy Fondren seems to have lost something and Raider defensive end Richard Campbell isn't about to return it. Campbell had just blocked the kick and recovered it in the end zone for a Tech TD.

TCU 35-TEXAS TECH 26

Texas Tech's hopes of winding up in the Cotton Bowl on New Year's Day were ground up in the jaws of the offense-minded Horned Frogs at Fort Worth. The Frog defense also came in for its share of Raider steak as they held the Tech ground game to a measly 37 yards.

Linzy Cole took the opening kickoff for TCU and roared down the sidelines for 66 yards to the Raider 34. Kevin Ormes was the last Raider to have a shot at Cole and he made it good, knocking Cole out-of-bounds. The Frogs drew a five-yard penalty, but Marty Whelan romped 21 yards to the Tech 18. Quaterback Steve Judy bounced a lateral off the ground and Whelan was there again to recover it. On fourth-and-three from the 11, Judy, with good protection, passed complete to Cole at the back

edge of the end zone. Wayne Merritt kicked the extra point for a 7-0 lead.

Raider defensive end Richard Campbell put together a one-man scoring drive late in the first quarter. Frog punter Billy Fondren was punting from his own five when Campbell tore into the backfield, blocked the punt, followed the bouncing ball into the end zone and recovered it for a Tech score. Jerry Don Sanders kicked for a 7-7 tie.

Early in the second quarter, Tech moved ahead. Ken Perkins returned a Fondren punt 19 yards to the 50. A holding penalty kept the Raider drive going with the first down at the TCU 31. It took nine plays to score. Reagan Young collected from a foot away and Tech led 13-7. Sanders' kick was wide to the left, ending a consecutive PAT record at 64, dat-

took the pigskin for an 81-yard ride to the TD. Merritt's kick put TCU ahead 14-13.

Raider halfback John Kleinert threw a pass to Charles Evans to get the next Tech drive under way. It was complete for 15 yards. Then quarterback Charles Napper tossed a bomb to David May for 47 yards to the Frog 13. The Raiders managed to get as far as the six, but had to settle for a field goal from the 23. Sanders' kick gave Tech a 16-14 half-time lead.

In the third period, Chuck Forney blind-sided Napper, jarring the ball loose and TCU's Clay Mitchell recovered for the Frogs on the Tech 24. Marty Whelan jarred the line for seven, three and two yards. Sammy Rabb ground out ten more before Judy rolled out to his right for the final two yards. Merritt's kick put the Frogs permanently ahead 21-16.

The Frogs drew blood again with three minutes left in the third quarter. Norman Bulaich rumbled over the Raiders for 23 yards on three drives, putting Judy & Co. on the 17 of Tech. From there, Judy rolled right and passed back to his left to hit Jerry Miller for the TD and it was 28-16.

Tech's Ken Perkins returned a 37-yard punt for 41 yards on the first play of the fourth quarter. That put the Raiders in business on the Frog 16. The scoring pass came from Napper to Danny Hardaway for four yards, putting Tech back in the game, trailing 28-23.

The Raiders almost moved back in the lead with a 15-yard pass to Hardaway and a beautiful 39-yarder to Ken Kattner at the Frog 16. But the Frogs jammed Napper for a seven-yard loss and the best the Raiders could do was a field goal from the 31 by Sanders. The game tightened at 28-26.

With fourth down and a foot on their own 44, Judy kept for a first down for the Frogs. TCU almost lost it again when Whelan was hit hard on the Tech 27 and lost the ball. Tech's Bruce Dowdy seemingly recovered, but the referee ruled the ball still belonged to TCU. Six plays later, the Frogs scored their 35-26 win.

TCU quarterback Steve Judy rolls into the end zone on a one-yard keeper in the third quarter. The referee signals the TD despite the efforts of Tech's Larry Molinare (52).

ing back to the second game of the 1966 season.

The Frogs nearly scored again, but Judy's pass to John Hetherly was intercepted in the end zone by Dale Rebold. They didn't let that stop them, though. Linzy Cole was not to be denied his long punt return. This time, he took the ball at his own 19, gathered an impressive array of interference and

	Tech	TCU
First downs	13	20
Yards rushing	37	242
Yards passing	221	140
Return yardage	92	141
Passes	14-28-2	15-28-1
Punts	7-40	8-36
Fumbles lost	2	0
Yards penalized	28	79

Texas Tech	7	9	0	10—	26
TCU	7	7	14	7—	35

TCU—Cole 11 pass from Judy (Merritt kick)
Tech — Campbell 18 covered blocked punt (Sanders kick)
Tech—Young 1 run (kick failed)
TCU—Cole 81 punt return (Merritt kick)
Tech—FG Sanders 23
TCU—Judy 2 run (Merritt kick)
TCU—Miller 17 pass from Judy (Merritt kick)
Tech — Hardaway 4 pass from Napper (Sanders kick)
Tech—FG Sanders 31
TCU—Bulaich 1 run (Merritt kick)
Attendance—25,278.

Aggie end Jimmy Adams (88) takes a pass at the goal line and is immediately dumped by Pony defensive back Larry Tunnell. Mustang defenders are: John Jordan (84), Joe White (58), Bill Wright (69) and Rufus Cormier (56). Ags are: Jim Parker (64), Carl Gough (58) and Leonard Forey (69).

TEXAS A&M 20-SMU 10

There's no place like home. The Aggies are convinced of that, and so, now, are the SMU Mustangs. A&M hosted the Ponies at Kyle Field and preserved their home stand winning streak at two straight. The Mustangs moved well all over the field, but couldn't find the door to the Aggie end zone as they had drives stopped in the second half on the A&M 29, nine, 12 and five with only three points to show for their efforts.

The Aggies took the kickoff on their 22, covering the 78 yards in ten plays to cash in on their first possession. Larry Stegent was responsible for a consistent rush along with fullback Marc Black. Rocky Self called the signals for the drive. With a third-and-five on the Mustang 28, Self dropped back to pass, was rushed hard and had to scramble to his right. Just before being forced out-of-bounds, Self found Ross Brupbacher open at the back edge of the end zone. His leap for the reception nearly carried him out, but he landed safe enough for six points. Mike Bellar kicked and A&M led 7-0.

On the ensuing kickoff, Gary Hammond took Bellar's boot at his own six and wound through the Aggies for 31 yards to the Pony 37. That carry

broke former Texas Tech star Donny Anderson's record for SWC punt returns, bringing Hammond's total return yardage to 550. Anderson's record was 541, set in 1965.

But the Mustangs could only reach the Aggie 31 with a first down. Two more plays were completely smothered by the alert Ag defense, smashing the Ponies back to the 47. Their punt carried to the A&M ten. Now, the SMU defense closed in and the Maroons could not move. Jimmy Sheffield punted short to the Mustang 36.

Between the running of Daryl Doggett and the passing of Chuck Hixson, the Ponies covered the ground to pay dirt in nine plays. SMU halfback Bicky Lesser saved the score for the Ponies. On third-and-one, Gordon Gilder was hit hard at the Maroon one and fumbled into the end zone. But, Lesser was there to recover for the score. Chipper Johnson's kick tied the score at 7-7.

Once again, the Aggies were called to go on a 78-yard march for their reward. And, once again, they did it. Self's passing took the Cadets for 69 of those yards, with Stegent brusing his way into the end zone. It took two smacks from the Pony one to

Rocky Self scrambles into the SMU defense and is hit by Tommy Fraser. Larry Tunnell (41) and Bruce Portillo (38) offer insurance in spite of Ross Brupbacher's (80) block.

do it, but Stegent went in standing up for six points. Bellar's kick put A&M ahead 14-7.

The Mustangs tried to come back for another tie, but a 15-yard penalty for clipping put them out of reach on the A&M 49. Larry Tunnell's punt bounced around on the Maroon one before finally roling into the end zone, putting A&M in business on their 20.

Tailback Steve Burks came in to give Stegent a rest and promptly slipped through right tackle behind Jimmy Adams and Ross Brupbacher for 57 yards. The drive came to an abrupt halt three plays later when Pat Curry intercepted a Self pass on the Pony five.

The Mustangs seemed to put the pieces together in the third quarter . . . except for the piece about scoring. Aggie defense hid that one. SMU took the opening kickoff and marched down to the Aggie 28 before Army stopped Hixson on a fourth down keeper. He needed one inch more. The Methodist defense wrapped up the Aggies, too, though and they punted.

Once again, the Pony offense got in gear and things looked serious for A&M as the Mustangs drove 70 yards to the A&M seven. But Mike DeNiro busted through to drop Hixson for a 14-yard loss and the Pony field goal attempt by Johnson was wide.

At the A&M 49, Self fumbled and Bill Wright recovered for the Mustangs. Three passes by Hixson moved the Ponies to the Maroon 12, but, on fourth-and-four, the best that could be gotten was three points on a field goal by Johnson. The Aggies still led 14-10.

Dave Elmendorf took the kickoff on his own seven and returned it to the A&M 30. Self kept for ten, Burks ran twice for a total of eight, but the Aggies were set back 15 on a holding penalty. With a third-and-17 on their own 33, Self threw to Barney Harris who made a leaping catch for a first down at the Pony 37. It was Steve Burks, again, who carried the mail for all 37 yards as he ripped over right tackle for the score. It gave him 100 yards rushing on just four carries and put the Aggies ahead 20-10 as the kick missed its mark.

	SMU	A&M
First downs	23	14
Yards rushing	131	203
Yards passing	242	145
Return yardage	18	14
Passes	22-33-2	6-16-1
Punts	3-41	5-45
Fumbles lost	1	1
Yards penalized	50	30

SMU	7	0	0	3—10
A&M	7	7	0	6—20

A&M—Brupbacher 28 pass from Self (Bellar kick)
SMU — Lesser fumble recovery (Johnson kick)
A&M—Stegent 1 run (Bellar kick)
SMU—FG Johnson 29
A&M—Burks 37 run (kick failed)
Attendance—33,220.

Stahle Vincent (12) sets up to pass behind Owl protectors Ron Waedemon (75), Paul Strahan (68), Mike Spruill (46) and Larry Caldwell (44).

ARKANSAS 30-RICE 6

On the way to the sixth of December, the Razorbacks made a side trip to Rice Stadium. The side trip almost turned into a side track as the Owls gave Arkansas all it could handle for the first 30 minutes. A crowd of 32,000 sat in on the game in almost 90 degree weather.

Arkansas received the kickoff. Bill Burnett ran for 18 yards which was eliminated by a penalty. Burnett ran for four yards which a penalty wiped out. Bill Montgomery passed to Bruce Maxwell for 23 yards. Burnett made a first down on a run of seven yards. Now at their own 49, Montgomery lost four attempting to pass. After two incompletions, Cary Stockdell punted to the Rice 16.

The Owls picked up a first down then had to punt and Arkansas took up where it left off at its 29. Maxwell ran for nine and Burnett for three, before Maxwell popped through for 19. Maxwell fumbled at the end of the run and Randy Lee recovered in mid air and returned seven yards to the Owl 47.

Rice failed to move and punted into the end zone. Arkansas moved out to their 48 before bogging down and punting to the Owl 13. The Rice offense moved out to the 29 mainly on a 17-yard run by quarterback Stahle Vincent. The 37 was reached

before punt formation came up. The Razorbacks fielded the punt at their 35. Maxwell ran the draw for nine, then Montgomery got loose around right end for 25 yards to the Rice 31. At the 26, Bill McClard was called on and he responded with a 43-yard field goal. Only 23 seconds remained in the first quarter as Arkansas went ahead 3-0. The Hogs had gained a total of 146 yards and had three points to show for it.

After the kickoff and an exchange of punts, Rice owned the ball at their 45. Dale Bernauer reversed for 12 yards and Vincent kept for 20 yards to the Arkansas 23. An incompletion, a completion for five yards, and a seven-yard loss on an attempted halfback pass, brought on Tim Davis. His 41-yard try for a field goal was wide.

The Owls made good the next time they got that close. Davis kicked a 33-yard field goal to tie the game at 3-3. The long gainer was a 34-yard Vincent pass to Mike Spruill.

The Razorbacks decided to put it all together on their next possession. They scored in 10 plays. Burnett and Maxwell handled the ground game as Maxwell had one run of 13 yards and Burnett's longest was a 19-yarder. At the 19, Montgomery passed to

Bill Burnett (33) goes up and over, following blocker Bruce Maxwell (34), to score Arkansas's first touchdown. Rodrigo Barnes (82) goes under Burnett.

Chuck Dicus at the Rice one and Burnett went over on the next play. McClard's conversion was good and with 51 seconds left in the half the Hogs led 10-3.

The Owls came roaring back as Vincent hit Bob Brown for 17 yards, ran for nine yards, then passed to Larry Davis for 17 yards to the Arkansas 20. Tim Davis came in for a field goal but the attempt failed. Arkansas was offsides and Davis made good on his second chance. The half ended with the Razorbacks leading 10-6.

The bubble burst for Rice as Arkansas scored on their first two possessions in the second half. The first score covered 58 yards in 10 plays. The pay-off came on a Montgomery pass to John Rees covering 15 yards. McClard kicked good and Arkansas led 17-6.

The second score came about on a 23-yard bolt over right tackle by Burnett. Preceding this Russ Garber ran the draw for 18 yards for the big gainer. McClard's point try went wide and the Hogs led 23-6.

The third quarter expired and most of the fourth quarter before the Razorbacks pushed across their final touchdown. This score followed a spirited drive by Rice which died a penalty plagued death at the Arkansas 39 after reaching the 19 earlier. A Vincent pass to Joe Henderson picked up 21 yards for the largest gain in the drive.

Arkansas moved from their 39 to score mainly on the passing of Montgomery and John Eichler who replaced him during the drive. Dicus caught passes of 25, eight and 12, although the last was rubbed out by a penalty. Russell Cody gathered in a 21-yarder. Eichler scored from the two and was shaken up on the play. McClard's extra point put Arkansas ahead 30-6. The game ended shortly with no more scoring.

Coach Frank Broyles was not too happy with his Razorbacks play, although winning 30-6. He praised the Owls for coming to play and was concerned that his own troops took the Rice team too lightly. This was Arkansas' 13th straight victory and it didn't come easy. The youthful Owls gave up no points through errors. Every Hog score was earned the hard way on this hot Saturday afternoon.

	Ark	Rice
First downs	21	15
Yards rushing	252	110
Yards passing	149	171
Return yardage	—1	21
Passes	10-24-0	17-35-0
Punts	7-35	8-38
Fumbles lost	1	1
Yards penalized	30	22

Arkansas	3	7	13	7—30
Rice	0	6	0	0— 6

Ark—FG McClard 43
Rice—FG T. Davis 33
Ark—Burnett 1 run (McClard kick)
Rice—FG Davis 24
Ark—Rees 14 pass from Montgomery (McClard kick)
Ark—Burnett 23 run (kick failed)
Ark—Eichler 2 run (McClard kick)
Attendance—32,000

Jim Bertelsen slips the grasp of Bear Dennis Watson (86). Taking up the chase are Gary Sutton (79), Glen Chmelar (80), Brian Blessing (44) and Tom Reaux (77).

TEXAS 56-BAYLOR 14

The 51,000 fans who almost filled Memorial Stadium got a preview of the 1970 Longhorn varsity. The starters only played long enough to get a safe cushion, then the reserves took over. Friday, 30 members of the squad came down with a virus, 14 of these being starters. Unfortunately for the Bears, the starters started.

Texas received the kickoff and Steve Worster reinjured his ankle and left the game. Bobby Callison replaced Worster. Texas couldn't move on their first series and after an exchange of punts started again from their 20. Callison scored the first of his three touchdowns from the one. In the drive Jim Bertelsen had runs of 13 and 53 yards. Happy Feller made it Texas 7 — Baylor 0.

Fred Steinmark intercepted a Laney Cook pass at the Texas 49 to set up the next 'Horn score. Ted Koy ran for 20 years on the first play and James Street ended the lightning thrust with a 20-yard scoring pass to Cotton Speyrer. Feller kicked the extra point putting Texas up 14-0.

A first down fumble by Baylor, following the kickoff, set up the next Texas assault on the Bear end zone. Dave Arledge recovered the fumble at the Baylor 14. Callison, Koy and Street pounded to the two. After two Bruin offsides, Callison tried twice and scored on the second. Feller repeated his efforts and it was Texas 21-0, still in the first quarter.

Early in the second quarter the Longhorns scored again on an 80-yard drive. Street passed to Speyrer for 25 yards. Then alternately Street, Billy Dale and Bertelsen moved the ball to the Baylor 16. Eddie Phillips then took over at quarterback. Koy scored from the six after Baylor was penalized twice and Bruin Glen Chmelar was ejected from the game. Feller kicked good and Texas led 28-0.

Next time Texas had the ball Phillips moved them 65 yards in six plays. The sixth play was a 37-yard scamper by Callison and the adding machine, after Feller's kick, read Texas 35 — Baylor 0.

With most starters sitting on the bench, the Longhorns closed out their first half massacre with the aid

124

Paul Kristynik separates Baylor receiver Derek Davis (83) from the ball to break up the pass attempt. Mack McKinney (42) approaches from the rear.

of an intercepted pass. David Richardson picked off a Steve Stuart pass at the Baylor 27. Phillips hit Randy Peschel with a 13-yard pass on fourth down, which set the ball on the Bear 12. Terry Collins ran for four and Phillips scored from the eight. Rob Layne kicked the conversion and Texas led 42-0.

The Longhorn second team defense took over and Baylor marched 72 yards to score. Stuart used the air as he passed complete to Jerry Smith for seven, 14 and 14. Don Huggins then caught a 30 yarder at the one. Gordon Utgard scored from there and Terry Cozby added the point to make it Texas 42-7, as the first half mercifully ended.

The Longhorns added two more touchdowns in the third quarter to close out the scoring for Texas. The first score was set up by a Jimmy Gunn interception of a Baylor pass at the 50. The 'Horns scored in nine plays. Collins went over from the one and Layne converted to put Texas up 49-7.

The last Texas score came on a six-play drive covering 67 yards. Phillips soloed the last nine yards on a roll out for the score. Layne put the last point on the scoreboard for Texas. As play entered the

fourth quarter, the Longhorns led 56-7.

Baylor, with 2:11 remaining, pushed across another score. Using 14 plays the Bruins marched 64 yards. Utgard did the honors again from one yard out. Cozby kicked Baylor's 14th point. Time ran out shortly and the final read Texas 56 — Baylor 14.

The old saying, "You can't tell the players without a program," was certainly true today as Texas reserves played most of the game. This being the Longhorns' 16th straight victory, a new record was established for Texas. Bear Gordon Utgard broke a SWC record, with nine punt returns. The old record of seven was held by Gordon Wyatt of the 1950 Rice Owls.

	Baylor	Texas
First downs	12	31
Rushing yardage	93	388
Passing yardage	110	167
Return yardage	0	72
Passes	8-27-5	12-23-0
Punts	6-52	4-31.8
Fumbles lost	2	0
Yards penalized	72	40

Baylor	0	7	0	7—14
Texas	21	21	14	0—56

Tex—Callison 1 run (Feller kick)
Tex—Speyrer 20 pass from Street (Feller kick)
Tex—Callison 1 run (Feller kick)
Tex—Koy 6 run (Feller kick)
Tex—Callison 37 run (Feller kick)
Tex—Phillips 8 run (Layne kick)
Bay—Utgard 1 run (Cozby kick)
Tex—Collins 1 run (Layne kick)
Tex—Phillips 9 run (Layne kick)
Bay—Utgard 1 run (Cozby kick)
Attendance—51,000

125

SYNOPSIS

TOP TEN

1. Ohio State
2. Texas
3. Tennessee
4. Arkansas
5. Penn State
6. Southern Cal
7. UCLA
8. Missouri
9. Notre Dame
10. Purdue

TEAM LEADERS FOR THE SEASON

OFFENSE

Rushing	Texas	2539 yds.
Passing	SMU	1991 yds.
Total	Texas	3261 yds.

DEFENSE

Rushing	Texas	604 yds.
Passing	Texas Tech	970 yds.
Total	Texas	1616 yds.

SWC OFFENSIVE PLAYER OF WEEK

Norman Bulaich, Halfback, TCU

SWC DEFENSIVE PLAYER OF WEEK

Mike DeNiro, Defensive End, Texas A & M

FRESHMAN GAME RESULTS

LSU 51 — Rice 40
SMU 30 — Baylor 22
Texas A & M 35 — Texas Tech 0
Arkansas 28 — North Texas State 6

CONFERENCE	W	L	T	SEASON'S RECORDS	W	L	T
Texas	4	0	0	Texas	7	0	0
Arkansas	4	0	0	Arkansas	7	0	0
Texas Tech	3	2	0	Texas Tech	4	4	0
TCU	3	2	0	TCU	3	5	0
SMU	2	3	0	Texas A & M	3	5	0
Texas A & M	2	3	0	SMU	2	6	0
Rice	0	4	0	Rice	1	6	0
Baylor	0	4	0	Baylor	0	7	0

Ninth Week
November 15

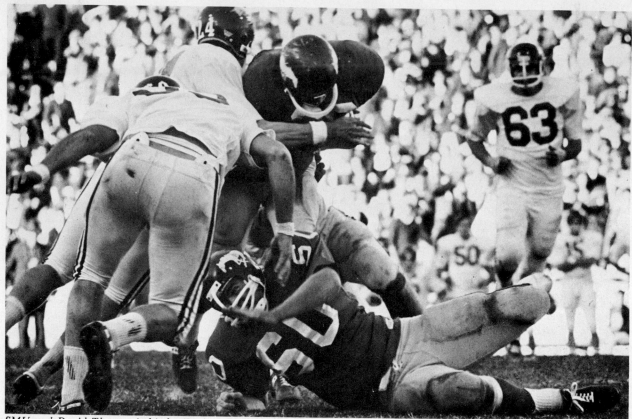

SMU end David Thomas is hit by Terry Stewart (24) and Lynn Garner (53). Roger Harnish (63) sprints in to help as the whole mob is about to fall on Keith Cupples (60).

ARKANSAS 28-SMU 15

Arkansas put their unblemished win string on the line in Dallas and left the Cotton Bowl with a longer unblemished win string. The Mustangs didn't have as much to lose, but they lost it, anyway.

Bicky Lesser kicked off to Arkansas in a strong breeze of 12 mph. The Hogs moved from their 20 in relentless bites to the Pony 20. It took them nine plays, all of them on the ground. But, as quarterback Bill Montgomery made the 20 on a keeper, the Hogs lost 15 on a clipping penalty. Two plays later, Bill McClard's kick for three points was wide to the left.

The Mustangs ran three plays and punted. Terry Stewart took the kick, but fumbled and tackle Bill Jackson recovered for the Mustangs on the Arkansas 33. On the ninth play of the series, Chuck Hixson passed to Walter Haynes in the end zone, but it was called back on an illegal motion penalty. Hixson passed incomplete to Gary Hammond, so Chipper Johnson was called to make good a 27-yard field goal and the Mustangs led 3-0.

The Pony defense held the Hogs in check for the balance of the first quarter. The Mustangs started the second period with two plays and a punt. The Mustangs almost held the Hogs, but, on fourth-and-one, Montgomery kept for a first down at the SMU 47. Chuck Dicus took a pass to the 35 and Bruce Maxwell made the 18 three plays later. A penalty and a strong Pony defense set the Hogs back to the 23. Montgomery passed to Pat Morrison for ten and to John Rees for the score. McClard's kick put the Hogs ahead 7-3.

SMU took the ball on their 20. It took 12 plays to go 80 yards for the go-ahead score. Daryl Doggett carried four times for 24 yards. Hixson kept for five and passed to Ken Fleming for 24, the last 19 was the scoring shot. Gary Hammond took two passes for 13. With 3:11 left in the half, Johnson's kick was wide and the Ponies led 9-7.

On their next possession, Arkansas struck fast. Maxwell swept left end for 14, Montgomery passed to Morrison for five, Maxwell took left end to the SMU 48, Montgomery scrambled for 19 to the Pony 33, then passed to Burnett for the score. McClard's kick made it 14-9.

Hammond took the kickoff to the SMU 30. In

*Arkansas' Bill Burnett plays in heavy traffic pursued by Jim Johnston (62), Joe White (58), Mike Nekuza (45) and Mike Jordan. Hog blockers include **Jerry Dossey (74)**, Bob Stankovich (75), Rodney Brand (57) and John Rees (25).*

nine plays, Hixson passed from the Razorback nine to Hammond in the end zone, but it fell incomplete. With 22 seconds left, Johnson kicked a 27-yard field goal for a 14-12 halftime score.

On their first possession of the second half, the Hogs scored. It took them 12 plays. Only one was a pass; Montgomery to Rees for 17. Russell Cody carried four times for 21 yards. Burnett smacked over the left side for the final four yards and the TD. It was 21-12.

But the Ponies were still very much in the game and they came back looking for pork. SMU took the ball on their 20. The Mustangs made their own 41, punted and got another chance as the Hogs were called for roughing the kicker. With a first down at the Arkansas 40, the Mustangs picked up two on Doggett's run and 14 more to the 24 on a Hixson pass to Hammond. A delay-of-game penalty cost them five, but a pass to Bicky Lesser made ten. Doggett lost two on a pass and Hixson was dropped for a loss of 12. Hixson's pass to Hammond made the Hog 23 and the Mustangs had to settle for a 40-yard field goal by Lesser with 40 seconds left in the third quarter. The Ponies trailed 21-15.

Arkansas failed to make the SMU end zone on their next possession. Twenty yards in penalties had

some effect on their offensive play. So, they kicked to the Ponies.

The Mustangs were forced to punt after the first series of downs. The Hogs got down to the SMU two-yard line, but on fourth-and-goal, Montgomery was stopped at right end for no gain.

The combatants traded punts. Cary Stockdell's punt went out on the Mustang one-yard line and, on second down, Hixson's pass was deflected and intercepted by Bobby Field. It took one play for Burnett to cover the nine yards to pay dirt and Arkansas wrapped it up 28-15.

	Ark.	SMU
First downs	24	17
Yards rushing	284	78
Yards passing	123	196
Return yardage	4	2
Passes	9-10-0	26-39-1
Punts	4-37	6-39
Fumbles lost	1	0
Yards penalized	70	45

Arkansas	0	14	7	7—28
SMU	3	9	3	0—15

SMU—FG Johnson 27
Ark—Rees 13 pass from Montgomery (McClard kick)
SMU—Fleming 19 pass from Hixson (kick failed)
Ark—Burnett 33 pass from Montgomery (McClard kick)
SMU—FG Johnson 27
Ark — Burnett 4 run (McClard kick)
SMU—FG Lesser 40
Ark — Burnett 9 run (McClard kick)
Attendance—35,673.

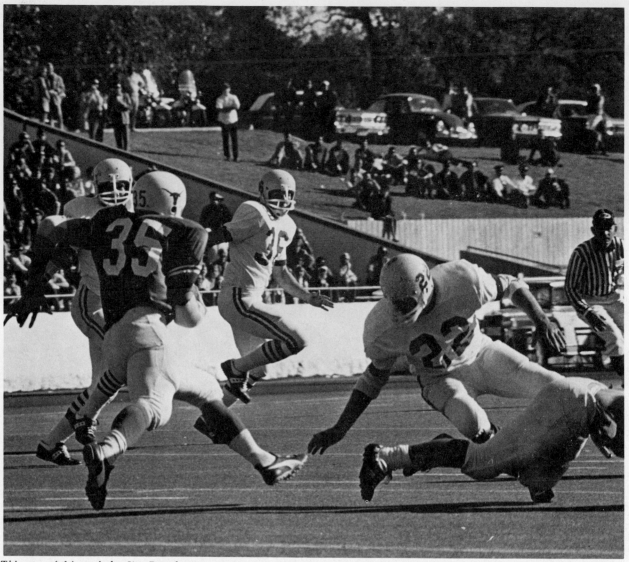

This run of 14 yards by Jim Bertelsen, carried to the TCU one-yard line and set up the fourth Texas touchdown. Horned Frog defenders are James Hodges (36) and Larry Wright (22).

TEXAS 69-TCU 7

A crowd of 51,000 came to the Coliseum (Memorial Staduim) and for the second time this year the Christians were fed to the lions. This time the Texas Longhorns played the part of the lions. The score was the largest Texas has ever mounted against a SWC opponent. Ten touchdowns and nine extra points. Surely some merciful fan somewhere in the stadium must have muttered amid all the cheering, "Someone turn off the Touchdown Machine."

The Touchdown Machine started when, in the first quarter, a fumble by Frog quarterback Steve Judy was recovered by David Arledge at the TCU 26. Five plays later Jim Bertelsen went three yards for the lid opener and with Happy Feller's PAT,

Texas led 7-0.

Following a TCU punt the 'Horns repeated their scoring act. Steve Worster found a hole on the right side and ran 34 yards to paydirt. Add Feller's point and it's 14-0, Texas.

With time running out in the first quarter, Texas beat the clock for another score. Quarterback James Street did the damage this time with a keeper-option run of 10 yards. Feller added one more and as play entered the second quarter, Texas led 21-0.

The only thing TCU had to cheer about during the game came early in the second quarter. Linzy Cole, the Horned Frog speed merchant, gathered in a Scooter Monzingo pass at his 35. He headed for the sidelines, did a 180, then another one before heading up the sideline behind a line of blockers. Steve Worster chased Cole, but to no avail. Sixty-five yards later, as the crow flies, Cole scored. Wayne Merritt kicked the conversion and TCU now trailed 7-21.

The Frogs might have gotten back in the game if a penalty hadn't zapped them. After their kickoff, Greg Webb picked off a Street pass and TCU moved to the Texas 27. Norman Bulaich picked up 16 yards on two carries during the drive. A six-yard run by Sammy Rabb reached the 27. Then a five-yard penalty for delay of game cooled the Frogs. After Steve Judy passed incomplete twice, Busty Underwood tried a field goal from 50 yards. It was wide and Texas took over at their 20.

The Longhorns scored in 12 plays. Billy Dale had a 17-yard run, Bertelsen one for 14 yards, and Worster got the final yard. Feller's kick put Texas up 28-7.

Texas scored once more before the half. Cotton Speyrer returned a punt to the TCU 41. Worster carried twice to put the ball on the 18. Street then dropped back and passed to Speyrer for 18 yards

and a touchdown. Feller missed the extra point to break a string of 38 and Texas led at the half 34-7.

The first time Texas got the ball in the second half they scored again. Dale, on a dive play, exploded for 51 yards to score. Feller returned to form and Texas led 41-7.

The first team retired after that and the Longhorns failed to score again in the third quarter. They made up for it in the final 15 minutes as the subs put 28 points on the board.

Before this took place the Horned Frogs tried one more time. They reached the Texas 20 before losing nine yards. Merritt tried a 45-yard field goal which failed.

Quarterback Eddie Phillips passed to wide open Ken Ehrig for the next Texas TD, the play covering 51 yards. Rob Layne took over the conversion chores and kicked good to put Texas up 48-7.

Donnie Wigginton then took the quarterback position and punched across yet another touchdown for dear old Texas. Before his scoring run of five yards, Bobby Callison carried for 21 yards and Terry Collins for 35. Texas now was ahead 55 to 7, including Layne's extra point.

Jim Williamson recovered a TCU fumble and the "machine" was turned on again. Collins contributed a run of 18 yards and Wigginton scored from the six. Layne kicked good and Texas led 62-7.

Rick Nabors set up the last Texas score with an interception of an Underwood pass and returned it 19 yards to the Frog 26. Tommy Asaff scored from the one following a 16-yard dash by Paul Robichau. Layne added the 69th point.

Paul Kristynik picked off a Frog pass and the Longhorns were approaching the wornout TCU goal line as the game ended. The "Touchdown Machine" had run up against the only thing able to stop it, the final gun.

The win was the 17th in a row for Texas. After all that running they have an open date to rest up before their Turkey Day encounter with the Texas Aggies. TCU, who could be declared a disaster area, will pick up the pieces and host the Rice Owls next Saturday.

Horned Frog quarterback, Steve Judy (18), gets off a pass over the outstretched arms of Bill Atessis (77). Norman Bulaich (23) is on ground behind Judy, after pass protection block.

	TCU	Texas
First downs	12	32
Yards rushing	105	517
Yards passing	76	134
Return yardage	74	96
Passes	8-34-3	8-15-2
Punts	8-40	4-34
Fumbles lost	2	1
Yards penalized	44	24

TCU	0	7	0	0	7
Texas	21	13	7	28	69

Tex—Bertelsen 3 run (Feller kick)
Tex—Worster 34 run (Feller kick)
Tex—Street 10 run (Feller kick)

TCU—Cole 65 punt return (Merritt kick)
Tex—Worster 1 run (Feller kick)
Tex—Speyrer 18 pass from Street (kick failed)
Tex—Dale 51 run (Feller kick)
Tex—Ehrig 51 pass from Phillips (Layne kick)
Tex — Wigginton 5 run (Layne kick)
Tex — Wigginton 6 run (Layne kick)
Tex—Asaff 1 run (Layne kick)
Attendance—51,000

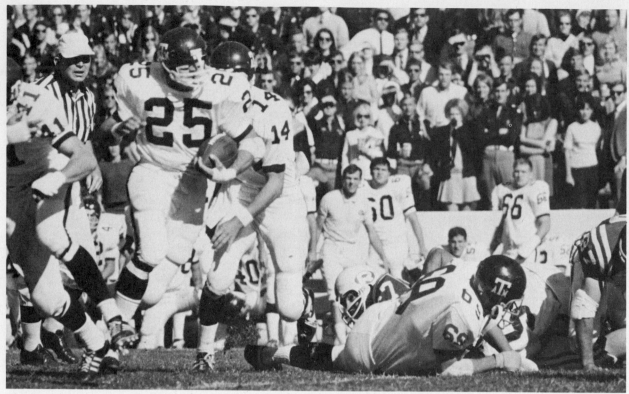

The Aggies' Larry Stegent (25) finds a gaping hole after taking the handoff from Rocky Self (14). Stegent was the Cadets' leading rusher.

RICE 7-TEXAS A&M 6

The Aggies came south to Houston to meet the bedraggled Rice Owls. Rice had not won a Southwest Conference football game since the 1967 finale against Baylor. They had lost six straight games after winning their opener this year. They hadn't been able to put two good halfs together and they hadn't been able to win the close ones. Today they did both and the Owl rooters in the crowd of 41,000 shared this new experience.

The Cadets, with the power running of Larry Stegent, moved goalward on their first possession. The Owls put a stop to this at their 27 and a 44-yard field goal attempt by Mike Bellar was short.

Bucky Allshouse's interception blunted the next Aggie attack. Then early in the second quarter another Owl theft, this one by Jack Faubion, set up Rice in business at their 43. Quarterback Stahle Vincent got the feathered flock moving with a 13-yard pass to Mike Phillips. Facing a third and four at the A & M 36, Mike Spruill bolted the left side for 20 yards to the 16. After two plays netted a loss of two yards the Owls faced another crucial third down. Vincent dropped back to pass, spotted an opening, and ran through the left side for 13 yards and a first down at the Cadet five. From there Spruill scored on

runs of two and three yards. Tim Davis added the extra point, insignificant at the time, to put Rice in the lead, 7-0.

The next time Rice got the ball they moved from their 28 to the A & M 19 before bogging down. Davis missed a field goal attempt from 30 yards. With time running out in the first half Rice got their express in gear once more and zipped to the Aggie nine after Cadet quarterback Rocky Self suffered his third interception of the first half. This one by Monte Hutchinson. From the A & M 34 Spruill ran for 12 yards. Vincent kept for five and then passed to Larry Davis for eight to the nine. A backfield in motion penalty cost five yards. Vincent then passed, intended for Bob Brown, Corky Sheffield blocked the ball and Mike Lord intercepted at the five. With only 38 seconds left, the first half soon ended with Rice clinging to its 7-0 advantage.

Now if the script runs true to form, all sorts of evils swoop down on the Owls in the second half and the opposing team repeatedly laughs all the way to the Rice end zone. On the first Aggie punt, a roughing-the-kicker penalty was called on Rice. From midfield the Owls held and forced a punt. Allshouse, playing with a broken hand, dropped back to punt

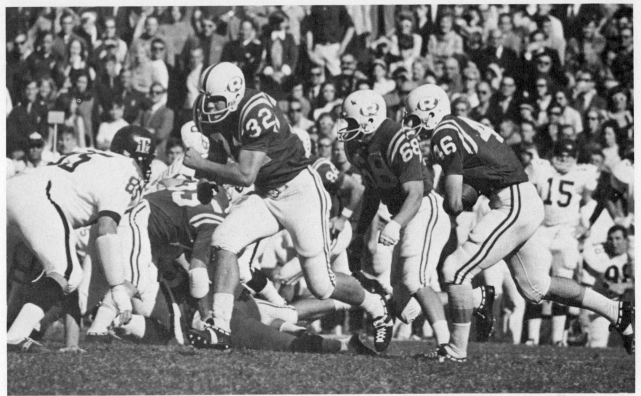

Mike Spruill (46), the game's leading rusher, follows the blocking of Paul Strahan (68) and Kim Malone (32) for one of his 31 carries.

for Rice four plays later and got off a kick of nine yards.

The Cadets had possession on the Owl 33-yard line. Stegent ran for nine yards. Quarterback Jimmy Sheffield passed complete to Bamey Harris for 11 yards and a first down at the Rice five. Rodrigo Barnes stopped Stegent at the line of scrimmage then teamed with Mike Taylor to throw Steve Burks for a four-yard loss. Sheffield hit Stegent with a pass to the three. The Aggies called time, after some head huddling they decided to by-pass the field goal route and go for the TD. Sheffield's pass to Jimmy Adams in the end zone was too high and Rice took possession.

The Aggies got the ball back, after a punt, at the Owl 29. Sheffield passed to Marc Black at the 15. Dale Grounds dropped Stegent for a yard loss. Burks ran for three, stopped by Grounds and Steve Bradshaw, then an incomplete pass brought up fourth down. Bellar missed a field goal from the 29.

On their next possession the Cadets overcame the tenacious Owl defense to put six points on the scoreboard. Starting from their 24, they covered the 76 yards in nine plays. On a Sheffield to Harris pass of 15 yards, Harris set a new A & M pass reception yardage career record. At the Rice 17, quarterback Self kept around the left side and went all the way. With nine minutes left in the game the Aggies went

for two instead of the tie. Barnes put the rush on Self as he dropped back to pass and Mike Taylor deflected the ball away from Harris in the end zone. Rice led by one, 7-6.

The Aggies got the ball again and after reaching their 40 had to punt. With 5:46 to play they never had the ball in their possession again. Starting from their 21, the Owls rolled up four first downs, chiefly on the running of Spruill. At the A & M 35 time ran out and Rice had preserved their one-point margin for a well deserved win.

Today was Homecoming for Rice and the old grads were justly satisfied. The Owls' two victories this year were over Keydets and Cadets. The end result was the same no matter how you spell it. For A & M it was a despairing loss. Favored by 10 points, they would have settled for a one-point win, but in trying for two points they by-passed one. That one point was the difference.

	A&M	Rice
First downs	15	16
Yards rushing	213	185
Yards passing	55	15
Return yardage	8	15
Passes	5-16-3	4-11-1
Punts	4-43	8-32.1
Fumbles lost	0	0
Yards penalized	49	42

A&M	0	0	0	6—	6
Rice	0	7	0	0—	7

Rice — Spruill 3 run (T. Davis kick)

A&M — Self 17 run (pass failed)

Attendance — 41,000

133

Baylor quarterback Laney Cook is stopped just short of the goal in the Bears' lone scoring drive. Adding weight to his lunge are: Terry Jackson (31), Joe Allbright (74) and Ted Gillum (82).

TEXAS TECH 41-BAYLOR 7

The Baylor Bears went to Lubbock in search of a victory, but again played the victim. Baylor ended the half with a tie and an edge over Tech statistically, but the battered Bruins lacked the depth and the roof fell in before the final gun.

Neither team was able to remain on offense for more than five plays during the first four offensive drives. Tech took their third possession on a 44-yard boot by Bear punter Ed Marsh. It went into the end zone for a touchback and the Raiders, directed by quarterback Charles Napper, sent halfback John Kleinert into the Bear left side. He made probes of seven, three, six and three yards. David May caught a toss for ten, then TCU rover Tom Bambrick dumped Kleinert for a four-yard loss at right end. Unshaken, Napper flung a bomb to May past midfield. He raced to the Baylor nine. Kleinert carried to the six. Ed Marsh intercepted a pass, but was out-of-bounds in the end zone. Napper finally hit Charles Evans for the TD. Jerry Don Sanders' kick put Tech ahead 7-0.

The Raiders got a break when a punt by Marsh went only 21 yards to the Baylor 40. Tech's Denton Fox took the kick, but fumbled and the Bear's Ron Evans recovered at the 41. An interference penalty took Baylor to the Tech 19. On fourth-and-two from the 11, Laney Cook passed on target to Jerry Smith in the end zone, but the ball bounced off his shoulder.

The Bears got the ball back on the first Tech play when Miles Langehennig fumbled after a two-yard gain. Tommy Reaux recovered for Baylor at the Tech 13. Derek Davis carried for seven. Gordon Utgard hit the line for no gain. Randy Cooper and Derek Davis escorted Cook around left end for the score. Terry Cozby's kick put the Bears in a tie for the third time this season, 7-7.

The second half opened with Baylor running three plays, then punting. The receiving Raiders had found new life. Steve Perkins took the kick and hauled down the Baylor sidelines for 34 yards to the end zone, but it was ruled that he had stepped out on the Bear 25. Five plays took the Raiders to the Baylor 14. The sixth try was a 33-yard field goal by Sanders, putting the Raiders in the lead, 10-7.

The Bruins were not able to hog the ball and, five

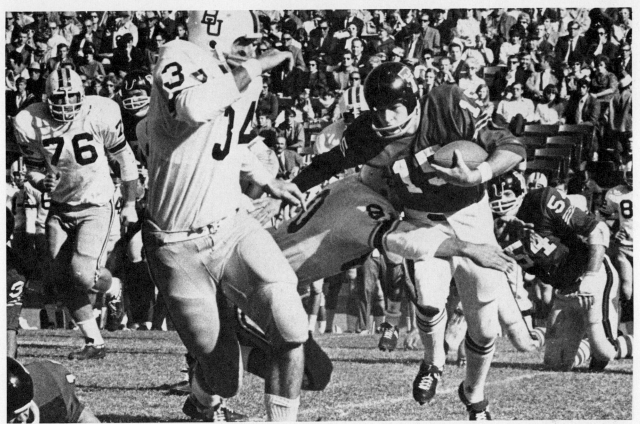

Bears Earl Maxfield (76), Dennis Whitley (34) and Glen Chmelar (80) attempt to corral Raider quarterback Charles Napper. Tech center Mark Hazelwood (54) watches progress of the play.

plays later, politely returned it to the hungry Raiders. It took them eight plays to eat up 67 yards for another score. Big bites came with Napper passing for 11, 13 and 27 yards for the score to Johnny Odom. Danny Hardaway also chewed away with runs of eight and four yards. Odom's TD moved the margin to 17-7.

For the last six minutes of the third quarter, the Bears managed to hang onto the ball. Trying to pass from his own 20, Cook was mobbed for a nine-yard loss. This convinced him to stay on the ground with Davis running wide, Cook carrying keepers and Randy Cooper smacking the middle. Backup quarterback Steve Stuart came in on the first play of the fourth quarter. Attempting to pass from the Tech 43, his pass was batted up by Wayne McDermand and intercepted by Dicky Grigg.

Napper started another march with a 14-yard completion to Evans. Fullback Reagan Young ran for 11 to the Baylor 20. In all, it took nine plays with Hardaway hitting left tackle for the score: 24-7.

The Bears were through. They were worn down and stumbling; their lack of depth had taken its toll. Bruin tailback Terry Jackson fumbled at the Baylor 27 and Dennis Lane recovered for Tech at the 25. The Raiders ran three plays and missed a field goal

attempt. But, it only took four plays for them to get the ball back. Following an offensive pass interference penalty, Marsh's punt carried out to the Bear 37. That's where the next Raider drive started. Larry Hargrave carried for six of the ten plays needed to score. Napper ran for the final two and it was 31-7.

Stuart attempted to pass for the Bears again, but Andy Hoyle intercepted at midfield and returned to the Bear 31. It took seven plays before Sanders' kick made it 34-7. That gave Sanders a SWC record for 11 field goals in a season.

Tom Sawyer came in at quarterback for the Raiders with 2:24 left. He threw a 39-yard scoring shot to Robbie Best for the final 41-7, including Sanders' kick.

	Baylor	Tech
First downs	9	20
Yards rushing	144	172
Yards passing	36	151
Return yardage	11	117
Passes	3-24-2	14-30-1
Punts	11-40	5-49
Fumbles lost	2	3
Yards penalized	84	53

Baylor	0	7	0	0—7
Texas Tech	7	0	10	24—41

Tech—Evans 6 pass from Napper (Sanders kick)
Baylor—Cook 2 run (Cozby kick)
Tech—FG Sanders 33
Tech—Odom 27 pass from Napper (Sanders kick)
Tech—Hardaway 1 run (Sanders kick)
Tech — Napper 2 run (Sanders kick)
Tech—FG Sanders 23
Tech—Best 11 pass from Sawyer (Sanders kick)
Attendance—32,000.

135

SYNOPSIS

TOP TEN

1. Ohio State
2. Texas
3. Arkansas
4. Penn State
5. Southern Cal
6. UCLA
7. Missouri
8. Notre Dame
9. Tennessee
10. LSU

TEAM LEADERS FOR THE SEASON

OFFENSE

Rushing .Texas 3056 yds.
Passing . . . . .SMU 2187 yds.
Total . . . . .Texas 3912 yds.

DEFENSE

Rushing .Texas 709 yds.
Passing . . . . .Texas Tech 1006 yds.
Total . . . . .Texas 1797 yds.

SWC OFFENSIVE PLAYER OF WEEK
Mike Spruill, Tailback, Rice

SWC DEFENSIVE PLAYER OF WEEK
Cliff Powell, Linebacker, Arkansas

FRESHMAN GAME RESULTS
Baylor 2 — Rice 0
Tulsa 22 — Arkansas 15
Texas 37 — TCU 6

CONFERENCE	W	L	T	SEASON'S RECORDS	W	L	T
Texas	5	0	0	Texas	8	0	0
Arkansas	5	0	0	Arkansas	8	0	0
Texas Tech	4	2	0	Texas Tech	5	4	0
TCU	3	3	0	TCU	3	6	0
SMU	2	4	0	Texas A & M	3	6	0
Texas A & M	2	4	0	Rice	2	6	0
Rice	1	4	0	SMU	2	7	0
Baylor	0	5	0	Baylor	0	8	0

Tenth Week
November 22

In this third quarter action, Norman Bulaich (23), almost loses ball upon being tackled, but retained possession for a 13-yard gain. Jerry Cooper (69) throws a helping block.

TCU 21-RICE 17

The Horned Frogs, before 19,786 fans in Amon Carter Stadium, closed out their 1969 season with a victory over the Rice Owls. Behind 10 points going into the fourth quarter, TCU pulled it out on the clutch running of seniors Marty Whelan and Norman Bulaich. The Frogs 549 yards on total offense broke the TCU single game record which Rice backfield coach Gil Bartosh helped set in 1950. Jerry Miller broke the TCU record for pass receptions and quarterback Steve Judy broke the legendary Dave O'Brien's season passing yardage record. After last weeks disaster, the season ended on a good note for the Frogs.

TCU scored on their first possession as Judy moved them 62 yards in six plays. The big plays in the drive came on two Judy pass completions. Linzy Cole caught one in the right flat and made 29 yards on the pass-run. Miller grabbed one for 20 yards. From the nine Bulaich pounded up the middle, found

no opening, then cut to his left and scored standing up. Wayne Merritt kicked the extra point and TCU led 7-0.

The Owls came back like gangbusters to tie up the game. In only three plays they moved 72 yards. The third play covered 64 yards of the 72. Mike Spruill, behind great blocks by David Stockwell and Brownie Wheless, broke clear and went all the way for the score. Tim Davis kicked the conversion and the game was deadlocked 7-7.

The Frogs, with Judy passes, came pounding goalward. Only a great defensive effort saved Rice from another TCU touchdown. Cole, after grabbing a Judy pass, was hit hard by David Keys. Cole and the ball parted company and Jack Faubion recovered for Rice at the Owl 11-yard line.

Rice kept the pressure valve open on this series as quarterback Stahle Vincent darted 34 yards on a keeper, then on a fourth down play passed complete

After a successful run of 26 yards, Marty Whelan (40) has the ball stolen by David Keys (43), who retained possession for Rice. Dale Grounds (34) is Rice defender on right.

The Owls spent most of the scoreless third quarter deep in their own end of the field. The one time they did get out of their territory, having a first down at the Frog 47, went for naught as TCU held Vincent to three yards on three carries. Allhouse punted to the TCU 10-yard line.

The Horned Frogs moved 86 yards to the Rice four with Whelan's 29-yard run up the middle being the big gainer. With one yard needed for a first down at the four, Randy Lee stopped Bulaich for no gain and the Owls took over. With Rice unable to move, Allhouse punted from the end zone out to the Owl 37.

The fourth quarter began as TCU turned the ball over to Whelan. Six straight times Whelan carried up the middle, for two, five, 16, six, five and three yards. The last carry terminated in the Owl end zone. Merritt added the PAT and TCU trailed 14-17.

Following the kickoff, Rice started from their 22. Phillip Wood had replaced Vincent at quarterback and Wood stuck to the ground. Using up the clock the Owls ran thirteen running plays. With Wood, Larry Caldwell and Kim Malone taking turns the ball was moved to the TCU five. Spruill made the first down on fourth and one, but the football popped loose and Jimmy Tidwell grabbed the pigskin for TCU at the four.

This time Bulaich got the calls as he carried for five, six, two, 15, five and 11 yards. The Frogs reached the Rice 34 and Judy dropped back to pass. Cole caught the pass at the 20, shook loose Faubion and fled down the sidelines for the winning touchdown. Merritt closed out the scoring with his point after.

Rice, with 2:30 remaining, owned a first and 10 at the 50. But a victory for Rice was not to be as Wood threw three incompletions and fumbled the snap on fourth down. The clock on the scoreboard reached zero and TCU owned a 21-17 win.

The Owls trouble most of the year cropped up again. They played a great first half, but after intermission nothing seemed to work. They never quit trying, the pieces just wouldn't get together. The win clinched fourth in the conference for the Frogs and they could end up tied for third, depending on the outcome of the Arkansas-Texas Tech game.

to Larry Davis for 17 yards. This placed the ball on the Horned Frog eight with a first and goal. Spruill made the two on two carries, but Vincent was thrown for a seven yard loss on third down. Tim Davis entered the game at this time and booted a 26-yard field goal. The Owls now led 10-7.

There was no more scoring until midway through the second quarter. Bucky Allshouse punted 44 yards to the TCU three. Rice held and Billy Fondren punted for the Frogs. Phillip Wood received the ball and ran to the right, cut back to the left and shook loose from clutching hands to return 43 yards to the TCU six. On second down, Spruill bombed over right tackle from the four for the towndown. Tim Davis added one more with his successful kick and Rice led 17-7.

Penalties thwarted scoring drives for both teams as the first half ended with no more points being scored.

	Rice	TCU
First downs	15	20
Yards rushing	292	323
Yards passing	36	226
Return yardage	43	33
Passes	4-12-0	16-22-0
Punts	7-41	4-32
Fumbles lost	2	4
Yards penalized	69	32

Rice	10	7	0	0—17
TCU	7	0	0	14—21

TCU—Bulaich 9 run (Merritt kick)
Rice—Spruill 64 run (T. Davis kick)
Rice—FG T. Davis 26
Rice—Spruill 4 run (T. Davis kick)
TCU—Whelan 3 run (Merritt kick)
TCU—Cole 34 pass from Judy (Merritt kick)

SMU's Daryl Doggett dives to the Pony 20 behind blocking of Kemp McMillan (68) and Stan Poulos (57). Earl Mayfield (76), Tom Reaux (77) and David Jones (89) defend for Baylor.

SMU 12-BAYLOR 6

The Mustangs' record of last year was 7-3 for the season. They closed out this season with the same numbers, but the order is 3-7. There's no Bluebonnet Bowl to look forward to, just a better season next year. The Bears have one last hope. They will travel to Houston to play Rice next week; a team that had a winless season last year, but did manage a tie. If the Bears lose that one, they'll be sole owner of the dubious distinction of being the first SWC team to go 0-10 for the season.

The Bears, still waiting for Lady Luck to turn The Big Play, found her suited up in red and blue. The Bruins were given a boost by the wind with 5:32 left in the first quarter. Baylor took possession on their own 49 and used eight plays to move within kicking range. Bear fullback Randy Cooper had a lot to do with moving the ball deep into Mustang territory. He rushed for gains of 17, 15, seven, two and three yards. But the drive stalled on the Pony 34 and Terry Cozby came in to try a placement. With the wind at his back and blowing a brisk 23

miles-per-hour, Cozby put the ball through the uprights. His kick broke the old Baylor record set by Jack Jones, a drop-kicker, set in 1925. Jones' record was 48 yards. Lo and behold! The Bears had scored in the first quarter and moved ahead of the Methodists 3-0.

So much for the wind. The Bruins had reaped all the riches good fortune would allow and the Mustangs were on the way. SMU took the ball on their own ten and drove 90 yards in nine plays. The Ponies acquired possession when an interception by right cornerback Pat Curry killed a Bear attack. Daryl Doggett carried three times for a total of 39 yards and Gordon Gilder tacked on another 13 with two runs. Then, it was sophomore Gary Hammond, playing with a rib separation, sprinted through an end-around play, taking the ball from quarterback Chuck Hixson and threw 40 yards to flanker Sam Holden. He was brought down on the Baylor five. Hixson faked a pass and skirted end to run in the six points. Chipper Johnston added the extra point

Baylor fullback Randy Cooper is finally dragged down after a 15-yard gain by Mike Nekuza (45), Jim Johnston (62) and Mike Jordan (46). Action took place in the first quarter.

and the Mustangs led 7-3.

With 3:05 left in the half, the Mustangs had stalled on the Baylor 45. The wind was now at their backs and Johnson came in to kick a field goal from the 42. His 52-yard boot was the second longest in the SMU record book. Bicky Lesser's record of last year with a pair of 53-yarders against Texas Tech still stands. The Mustangs led 10-3.

As the half came to a close, the Bears fought back deep in Mustang territory. Bear quarterback Steve Stuart filled the air with passes. Mike Nekuza and John Jordan each knocked passes out of the air to force the Bears to go for a field goal with three seconds left in the half. The line of scrimmage was on the Mustang four-yard line. Cozby stepped in for the necessary 21-yard boot and the half closed with the Bears trailing 10-6. It was the climax of a 12-play series for 75 yards. Don Huggins had run for eight and nine yards and caught two passes for 21 yards. Rollin Hunter made a fine leaping catch for 11 and Randy Cooper ran for nine.

The combatants wrestled neck-and-neck through the third quarter, but no one got loose to put any points on the board. In fact, almost two-thirds of the

fourth quarter had passed before the final two points were added to the Mustang tally.

It happened like this: The Mustangs had driven to the Baylor six, where they had a fourth-and-one. Daryl Doggett slammed right tackle, was stopped and tried to bounce to the outside. John Miller, Ed Marsh and Russell Serafin stopped him for no gain and the Bears took over on downs. Cooper rammed the line for no gain. Derek Davis had to scramble after a wild pitchout, recovering it on the one-yard line. Davis skirted left end for seven, bringing up fourth-and-nine. Laney Cook faded into the end zone for a last pass. He found his receivers covered and knelt for a safety. That ended the scoring with SMU ahead 12-6.

	SMU	Baylor
First downs	20	16
Yards rushing	208	188
Yards passing	193	101
Return yardage	40	60
Passes	19-37-2	9-22-3
Punts	6-36	4-45
Fumbles lost	0	2
Yards penalized	50	42

SMU	0	10	0	2—12
Baylor	3	3	0	0— 6

Bay—FG Cozby 52
SMU — Hixson 5 run (Johnson kick)
SMU—FG Lesser 52
Bay—FG Cozby 21
SMU — Safety (Cook tackled in end zone)
Attendance—20,000.

SYNOPSIS

10

TOP TEN

1. Texas
2. Arkansas
3. Penn State
4. Ohio State
5. Southern Cal
6. Missouri
7. Michigan
8. Notre Dame
9. LSU
10. Tennessee

FRESHMAN GAME RESULTS

Texas 21 — Texas A&M 6
TCU 22 — SMU 21

OPEN DATE: Texas, Texas A&M, Arkansas, Texas Tech

TEAM LEADERS FOR THE SEASON

OFFENSE

Rushing .... Texas 3056 yds.
Passing .... SMU 2380 yds.
Total .... Texas 3912 yds.

DEFENSE

Rushing .... Texas 709 yds.
Passing .... Texas Tech 1006 yds.
Total .... Texas 1797 yds.

FINAL FRESHMAN

	W	L	T
Texas	4	1	0
Arkansas	4	1	0
Texas A&M	4	1	0
TCU	3	2	0
SMU	3	2	0
Texas Tech	1	3	0
Rice	1	4	0
Baylor	1	4	0

CONFERENCE	W	L	T	SEASONS RECORDS	W	L	T
Texas	5	0	0	Texas	8	0	0
Arkansas	5	0	0	Arkansas	8	0	0
Texas Tech	4	2	0	Texas Tech	5	4	0
TCU	4	3	0	TCU	4	6	0
SMU	3	4	0	Texas A&M	3	6	0
Texas A&M	2	4	0	SMU	3	7	0
Rice	1	5	0	Rice	2	7	0
Baylor	0	6	0	Baylor	0	9	0

Eleventh Week
November 27, 29
December 6

NOTE: The Texas vs. Arkansas game was moved from October 18 to December 6 to accommodate TV coverage. This game is included in the Eleventh Week.

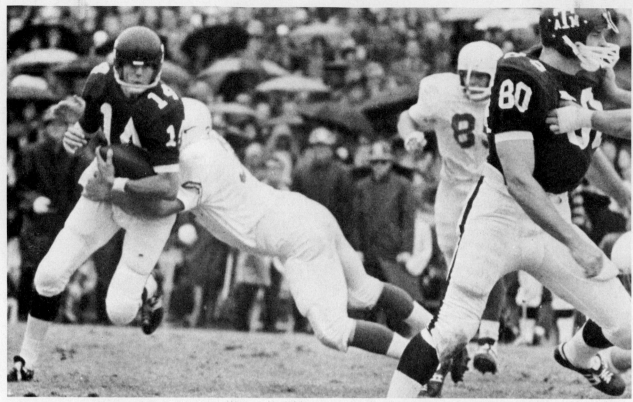

Aggie quarterback Rocky Self is thrown for five-yard loss by Greg Ploetz as he is forced to run from the pass pocket.

TEXAS 49-TEXAS A&M 12

It was raining a little in College Station as the Aggies welcomed the Longhorns for their traditional Thanksgiving Day battle. Most of the black clouds gathered in the Aggie dressing room after the game, however. In the 76 years of the series, Texas never scored as many points before and the 37-point spread was third highest. The crowd of 51,160 was the largest in the history of Kyle Field.

Texas scored the first time it had the ball. The Aggie kickoff was downed in the end zone and the Horns took possession on their 20. On their first three offensive plays, Texas gained 17 yards. Then, they broke it loose when James Street faked to Steve Worster and handed off to Jim Bertelsen over right tackle. Bertelsen cut up the middle and went 63 yards to score. Happy Feller added the seventh point.

On their next turn at bat, the Longhorns bashed the Aggies for another score. It was an 81-yard march on the ground. The best chunk was clipped off by Worster over right guard for 21 yards. The 13th play saw Worster rip left guard for two yards and the score. Feller missed for the second time in 41 conversions this year and the Steers led 13-0

with 7:05 left in the first quarter.

The Aggies, kicking with the wind, got off a 35-yard punt to set Texas in action on the A&M 46. Seven plays did it. It was early in the second period by the time Worster smashed off left tackle and fell backward into another six points. Feller kicked true for a 20-0 lead.

Aggie quarterback Rocky Self was dumped for a 10-yard loss by Bill Atessis and David Arledge. Jimmy Sheffield's punt went only 22 yards and the Horns were back in business on the A&M 37. A holding penalty against Texas put them back to their own 48, but it took only three plays to romp for another six. Cotton Speyrer took Street's pass for 28 yards after one incompletion and Worster ripped off 16 more. Street carried around right end for eight yards to score. With 10:58 remaining in the half, Feller's kick made it 27-0.

Tom Campbell stung the Maroons with an interception of a Self pass, returning it 30 yards to the A&M four before Self forced him out-of-bounds. Street fumbled and barely recovered. Now running from the seven, he pitched back to Bertelsen who followed Ted Koy's block for the TD. Rob Layne

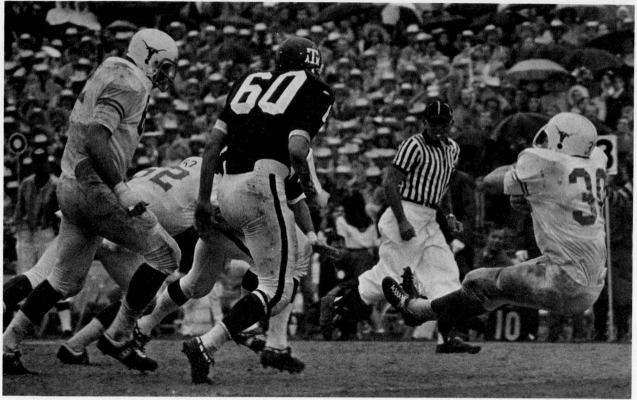

Longhorn fullback Steve Worster scores sitting down. Aggie linebacker Buster Adami (60) arrives too late.

stepped in to kick and bounced the ball off the up-right, so it remained 33-0.

The Big Orange picked up another quick score when linebacker David Richardson busted Larry Stegent, causing a fumble. Arledge recovered for Texas. Speyrer threw a 37-yard pass to Randy Peschel for another addition to Texas' riches. Layne bounced his second PAT attempt off the goal post. Texas' lead stretched to 39-0.

That was the end of the game for the TU first string offense. With 4:50 left in the half, the Aggies were able to make it past their own 40 for the first time. They managed the Texas 36 before Atessis killed it by dropping Self for a nine-yard loss.

Texas lost the ball on a fumble deep in their own territory at the 16, but a broken play scrambled the Aggies offense at a crucial moment and the Steers took over on downs at their own 13.

With 4:42 left in the third quarter, Texas' second team drew some more Aggie blood. Their drive had bogged down on the A&M 26. Happy Feller came in to kick a 43-yard field goal and Texas led 42-0. That's when the first defensive unit retired for the day.

Scooter Monzingo got off a short, 12-yard punt, giving A&M the ball on the Texas 27. Then, Texas was slapped with pass interference and holding pen-alties, moving the Aggies to the three. From there, Rocky Self passed complete to Ross Brupbacher deep in the end zone to break the drouth and put A&M on the board. A pass for two failed and the score was 42-6.

A minute later, the Aggies scored their final tally when Jim Piper blocked a Steer punt at the four and carried it in to give A&M another six. Again, the try for two failed.

Texas' last score came when safety Rick Nabors intercepted a Self pass at the Maroon 45. Quarter-back Eddie Phillips guided the drive and carried a bootleg for the four-yard scoring run. Feller's kick was good for a final 49-12 lead.

	Texas	A&M
First downs	22	12
Yards rushing	330	88
Yards passing	111	67
Return yardage	103	9
Passes	6-14-1	6-18-4
Punts	5-17	6-32
Fumbles lost	1	2
Yards penalized	80	25

Texas	13	26	3	7—49
Texas A&M	0	0	0	12—12

Tex — Bertelsen 63 run (Feller kick)
Tex—Worster 2 run (kick failed)
Tex—Worster 3 run (Feller kick)
Tex—Street 8 run (Feller kick)
Tex—Koy 7 run (kick failed)
Tex—Peschel 37 pass from Speyrer (kick failed)
Tex—FG Feller 43
A&M — Brupbacher 3 pass from Self (pass failed)
A&M—Piper 4 ret. blocked punt (pass failed)
Tex—Phillips 4 run (Feller kick)
Attendance—51,160.

Bill Montgomery, who has quarterbacked the Razorbacks to 15 straight victories, drops back to pass on a rainy Thanksgiving Day.

ARKANSAS 33-TEXAS TECH 0

Thanksgiving Day in Little Rock, and what could be more appropriate than an afternoon of football. Texas Tech and Arkansas provided the teams as 38,000 turkey-filled fans settled down for the greatest show on earth — college football.

With the Razorbacks facing an earth-shaking collision with Texas on December 6th, it would have been easy for them to look past the Red Raiders. The only looking past Tech was down-field to the enemy endzone, which after sighting they visited often.

Arkansas scored their first touchdown just 12 seconds before the first quarter ended. Quarterback Bill Montgomery took them 59 yards mainly on his passing. A pass to John Rees covered 16 yards and ended up inches away from the Tech goal. Bill Burnett went across on fourth down and with Bill McClard's kick, the Razobacks led 7-0.

A 28-yard screen pass to fullback Russ Garber and a 14-yard pass to Rees put the Hogs in position

for McClard to kick a field goal from the 19. Garber was subbing for the injured Bruce Maxwell. With the field goal the Razorbacks upped their lead to 10 points.

Before the half Montgomery flipped another screen pass to Garber. After a run of 43 yards, Garber was downed on the Red Raider five. Burnett carried twice and scored Arkansas' second touchdown. McClard kicked the conversion and Arkansas led 17-0.

The Hog's defense, burning on all 11 cylinders, blunted any and all Tech threats at the Arkansas goal line. Early in the game Eddie Windom blocked a Razorback punt and Tech had possession on the Arkansas 48-yard line. Four yards was picked up by Larry Hargrave, but then quarterback Charles Napper was dumped for a five-yard loss. On third down Napper was again downed five yards behind the line of scrimmage. End of possession, end of threat.

Dick Bumpas grabs Larry Hargrave's leg as he goes by and Razorback Lynn Garner jumps in to make tackle secure.

On their first six possessions, the Red Raiders were still looking for a first down.

Late in the first half Napper passed complete to David May for 22 yards. Next Danny Hardaway caught a pass for 11 yards and a first down at the Razorback 19. The Hog defense, who leads the nation against scoring, stone-walled Tech and the half ended with Arkansas leading 17-0.

McClard started the second half scoring by kicking a field goal from 33 yards out. This successful boot put the Razorbacks out front 20-0.

Burnett, who leads the SWC in scoring, took over the conference rushing leadership as he gained 100 yards on 20 carries. He scored his third touchdown of the day in the third quarter. Chuck Dicus caught a 12-yard pass to put the ball on the Red Raider eight-yard line. Burnett grabbed the handoff from Montgomery and started over left tackle. The hole closed and he reversed himself to the right and went across standing up. McClard kicked good and Arkansas increase their lead to 27-0.

Late in the third quarter the Red Raiders got their

hopes up again. Mainly on the running of Hardaway they reached the Hog seven-yard line. The stone wall formed again and Dick Bumpas dropped Napper for a 20-yard loss to end any Tech scoring threat.

The Razorbacks put one more drive together. Russell Cody ran over from the nine to close out the scoring as McClard missed the extra point. The game ended with Arkansas on the long end of a 33-0 score.

With their goal line uncrossed, the stone wall defense retired to the dressing room to contemplate what happens when an irresistible force meets an immovable object. On the sixth of December we'll all know the answer to that.

	Texas Tech	Ark
First downs	17	21
Rushing yardage	34	150
Passing yardage	216	315
Return yardage	12	74
Passes	17-43-5	19-33-0
Punts	9-37	7-28
Fumbles lost	1	0
Yards penalized	30	37

Texas Tech	0	0	0	0— 0
Arkansas	7	10	10	6—33

Ark—Burnett 1 run (McClard kick)
Ark—FG McClard 29
Ark—Burnett 1 run (McClard kick)
Ark—FG McClard 33
Ark—Burnett 8 run (McClard kick)
Ark—Cody 9 run (kick failed)
A—38,000.

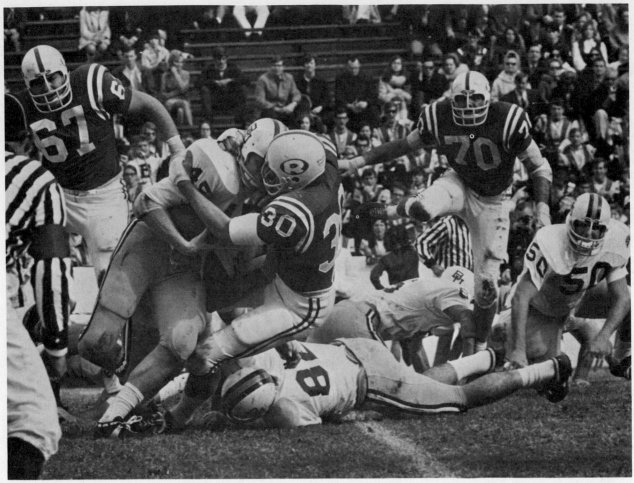

A Bear gets hugged by Owl Ron Marsh (30). Randy Cooper (45) carries, followed by Owls Roger Roitsch (67) and Steve Bradshaw (70). Bear blockers are: Ted Gillum (82), Jim Sartain (65) and Calvin Hunt (50).

RICE 34-BAYLOR 6

Rice set a SWC record last year with their 0-9-1 season. But, as long as there is some room at the top, or the bottom, someone will eventually be there to find it. The depths were plumbed this year in Rice Stadium by the Baylor Bears. They have removed the Owls, mercifully, from their perch at the bottom of the record book by plunging a half game deeper. No one will ever do more, or less, than a 0-10. Unless the season goes to 11 games.

Rice took the opening kickoff on their own 25. Quarterback Philip Wood ran for 14 yards and passed for 60 on three tosses. Baylor defense rose to the occasion as Earl Maxfield and Tommy Reaux dropped Wood for a four-yard loss to the Bear 25. Tim Davis' field goal attempt failed.

The Bruin offense was mauled for a minus-one in three plays and Ed Marsh punted out-of-bounds on the Rice 43. It took three plays for the Owls to score. Wood passed to Larry Davis for seven, then

ran a keeper around left end for 48 to the Bear two. John Miller finally bumped him out. Larry Caldwell rammed left tackle for the score. Tim Davis' kick put the Owls ahead 7-0.

Baylor missed a field goal attempt of 54 yards after quarterback Steve Stuart made a good 16-yard run behind the effective blocking of Randy Cooper.

Early in the second quarter, the Owls put another mark on the board. Their attack was almost smothered when Baylor safety John Miller intercepted, then fumbled. Rice's David Stockwell recovered on the Baylor 29 for a first down. Wood lost a yard, but Mike Spruill roared off-tackle for the 30-yard scoring romp. With 10:54 left in the half, Davis' kick put the Owls 14 points ahead.

Rice came back for more points less than four minutes later. After taking possession on the Bear 45, the Owls' Bob Brown made a good gainer in the series with a 24-yard reception on the Baylor eight.

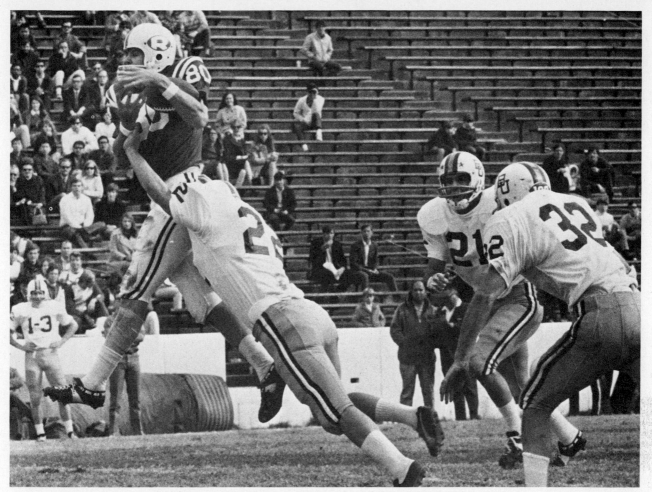

Split end Larry Davis is hit by Ed Marsh as Baylor teammates John Miller (21) and Tom Bambrick (32) follow up. Yes, Virginia, there really is a no. 1-3, like it says in the program. He's kicker Terry Cozby (far left).

A holding penalty set the Owls back to the 22. It was Brown again with an athletic snag at the nine. A face-mask penalty put the Owls on the four. Spruill made it all the way through the Bruin line. A missed conversion left the Owls ahead 20-0.

The Bears got warm again just before the end of the half. They moved from their own 21 to the Rice 14. A penalty put them back on the 29, but another face-mask call put the ball back on the Owl 16. Laney Cook's pass intended for Rollin Hunter was broken up by Bucky Allshouse. That ended the threat and the half.

The Bears' only touchdown came late in the third quarter. Taking possession on their own 20, Baylor rose up on its hind legs and marched the full distance in 12 plays. The scoring jab was a 12-yard pass from Stuart to Rollin Hunter. It was Hunter's first college TD. Terry Cozby's extra point try failed. The Bears trailed 20-6 with 3:34 left in the third quarter.

Baylor momentarily caught fire when they recovered their onside kick, but they were unable to make a first down.

Two-thirds of the way through the fourth quarter, Jack Faubion intercepted a Stuart pass on the Owl 48. Dale Bernauer ran for five to add six to Rice's score. Davis' kick was again good for a 27-6 margin.

The Bears had the ball on their own 40 when the Owls stung them again. Laney Cook dropped back to pass, was dropped for a 12-yard loss and fumbled. Mike Kramer recovered for Rice. They had only 28 yards to go. And, they went. Owl quarterback Mike Kramer threw to Bob Brown to the Bear 11. Mike Spruill carried to the two. The Bear defense got tough and it took three plays before Spruill went for the last yard. Davis' kick ended the scoring at 34-6.

	Baylor	Rice
First downs	16	14
Rushing yardage	151	207
Passing yardage	112	191
Return yardage	15	58
Passes	12-29-6	16-27-2
Punts	5-34	7-43
Fumbles lost	2	1
Yards penalized	79	157

Baylor	0	0	0	6— 6
Rice	7	13	0	14—34

Rice—Caldwell 2 run (T. Davis kick)

Rice — Spruill 30 run (T. Davis kick)

Rice—Spruill 4 run (kick failed)

Bay—Hunter 12 pass from Stuart (kick failed)

Rice—Bernauer 5 run (T. Davis kick)

Rice — Spruill 1 run (T. Davis kick)

Attendance—17,000.

Bill Burnett dives over for Arkansas's first touchdown. In the crowd are Scott Henderson (61), Rodney Brand (57), Glen Halsell (67), Jerry Dossey (74) and Mike Campbell (86).

TEXAS 15-ARKANSAS 14

The eyes of Texas and the nation were on Fayetteville, Arkansas as the number one team in the country, Texas, met the number two team, Arkansas. With "Sooey, Pig" and "Hook 'em Horns" the battle cries of the day, the Razorbacks and Longhorns played one of the greatest football games of all time.

Arkansas won the coin toss and elected to take the wind and kicked off to Texas. McClard kicked over the end zone and the Longhorns put the ball in play at their 20. On their second play, Ted Koy fumbled at the Texas 22 and Bobby Field recovered for Arkansas. After two incomplete passes, quarterback Bill Montgomery passed complete to John Rees at the Texas two-yard line. Bill Burnett picked up a yard and then scored on his second carry. McClard kicked the extra point and Arkansas led 7-0.

Texas started from their 20 again as McClard kicked off into the end zone. With Steve Worster and Koy running the ball the Longhorns picked up three first downs and reached the Arkansas 46. On second down quarterback James Street passed deep for Cotton Speyrer. Terry Stewart stepped in front of Speyrer and intercepted at the Arkansas eight.

Burnett carried twice for six yards. Montgomery then kept for eight and a first down. Montgomery kept again and ran for 14 yards. Following a five yard illegal-shift penalty the Razorbacks faced a third and thirteen when Montgomery passed complete to Chuck Dicus for a first down at the Texas 45. On third and seven Montgomery hit Dicus again at the Texas 26. On the next play Dicus made a great fingertip catch as he crossed the goal line, but the touchdown was nullified by an offensive interference penalty against Arkansas. Montgomery was thrown for a 23-yard loss back to the Hog 36. Bruce Maxwell ran for six. Cary Stockdell punted to Speyrer who returned to the Texas 30.

The first quarter ended shortly and on the second play of the second quarter, Scooter Monzingo punted to the Hog 18. Unable to move, Arkansas punted to the Texas 37. After an exchange of punts, Texas moved from their 18 to the Arkansas 31, unleashing their bruising ground game, but there the Razorbacks stiffened and took over the ball.

Arkansas missed a first down by six inches and Stockdell's punt was blocked by Scott Henderson. Bill Zapalac recovered for Texas, but the gun went off ending the first half with Arkansas leading 7-0.

McClard, after two out-of-bounds kickoffs, finally got one down the middle to Speyrer at the Texas nine. Speyrer returned to the 37, but fumbled and Ronnie Price recovered for Arkansas. Texas held and Stockdell punted into the end zone. After reaching their 35, Street passed complete to Speyrer on

150

James Street escapes the grasp of Dick Bumpas and the onrushing Rick Kersey (72) as he scrambles for 42 yards and a Texas touchdown.

third down. Speyrer reached the Hog 47, but fumbled when hit. Stewart recovered for Arkansas.

Burnett ran for seven yards. Montgomery lost four yards, but on the next play ran for 19 yards and a first down at the Texas 31. Maxwell carried for two yards. Montgomery then passed complete to Dicus for 29 yards and a touchdown. Pat Morrison threw a great block to take out the last Longhorn defender. McClard added the point and Arkansas led 14-0.

Texas took the kickoff and moved from their 29 to the Arkansas 49. The big play was a Street to Speyrer pass good for 19 yards. Street was then intercepted by Dennis Berner at the Hog 24. Arkansas moved to the Texas 37, but Montgomery was then thrown for a five-yard loss and Stockdell punted.

The Longhorns had moved from their 20 to the Arkansas 42 as the third quarter ended. On the first play of the fourth quarter, Street, unable to find a receiver, scrambled out of the pocket and broke two or three tackles as he ran 42 yards for a Texas touchdown. The 'Horns went for two. Street kept and went over to make the score 14-8, Arkansas.

The Razorbacks came back on Montgomery's passing as he hit Dicus for 20 yards and Rees for 14. At the Texas 24, the Longhorns were penalized to their nine for holding. On third down at the seven, Montgomery's pass was intercepted in the end zone by Danny Lester and run back to the Texas 20.

Street guided the Longhorns to the Arkansas 38-

yard line as he hit Randy Peschel on a 15-yard pass and handed off to Speyrer on the end-around for 14 yards. On third and three at the 38, Koy fumbled a bad lateral and Gordon McNulty recovered for Arkansas at the Hog 42. The Texas defense forced a punt and Texas had the ball again at their 36.

The Longhorns moved to their 43 where they faced a fourth and three. The 'Horns were going for it and surprise, Street drops back to pass. Peschel, fleeing down the left sideline, made a spectacular catch at the Hog 13. He caught the ball over his head with two Razorbacks hot on his heels. Koy barreled his way to the two. Jim Bertelsen scored on the next play and Happy Feller's point after put Texas ahead 15-14.

Arkansas took the kickoff and with Montgomery's pin-point passing moved to the Texas 39. Getting near field goal range, a Montgomery pass to Dicus floated too long and Tom Campbell intercepted for Texas at their 21. Two running plays and the curtain fell on 1969 football. Next stop, Notre Dame for Texas, Mississippi for Arkansas. It could've just as easily been the other way.

	Texas	Ark.
First downs	19	18
Rushing yardage	244	103
Passing yardage	124	204
Return yardage	47	—2
Passes	6-10-2	14-22-2
Punts	2-36	7-31
Fumbles lost	4	0
Yards penalized	30	40

Texas   0 0 0 15—15
Arkansas 7 0 7 0—14
Ark—Burnett 1 run (McClard kick)
Ark—Dicus 29 pass from Montgomery (McClard kick)
Texas—Street 42 run (Street run)
Texas — Bertelsen 2 run (Feller kick)
Attendance—44,000

151

11

FINAL PRE-BOWL TOP TEN

1. **TEXAS**
2. Penn State
3. **ARKANSAS**
4. Ohio State
5. Southern Cal
6. Missouri
7. Michigan
8. LSU
9. Notre Dame
10. UCLA

TEAM LEADERS FOR THE SEASON

OFFENSE

Rushing	Texas 3630 yds.
Passing	SMU 2380 yds.
Total	Texas 4713 yds.

DEFENSE

Rushing	Texas 900 yds.
Passing	SMU 1277 yds.
Total	Texas 2259 yds.

CONFERENCE	W	L	T	SEASONS RECORDS	W	L	T
Texas	7	0	0	Texas	10	0	0
Arkansas	6	1	0	Arkansas	9	1	0
Texas Tech	4	3	0	Texas Tech	5	5	0
TCU	4	3	0	TCU	4	6	0
SMU	3	4	0	SMU	3	7	0
Rice	2	5	0	Rice	3	7	0
Texas A&M	2	5	0	Texas A&M	3	7	0
Baylor	0	7	0	Baylor	0	10	0

Wrap-Up

By Dave Campbell,
President, Football Writers Association of America
Editor-Publisher, Texas Football Magazine

SEASON REVIEW

Arkansas quarterback Bill Montgomery faded and threw and as the ball spiraled through the air 40,000 hearts stood still, and then Texas defensive halfback Tom Campbell reached in front of the receiver and took the ball away and the Texas bench went wild, and that was the way the season ended, both with a bang and a heartbreak.

Two passes that went awry and one that didn't, plus two gutty, scrambling payoff runs—those were the decisive plays in the tell-tale moments of the tell-tale game of the 1969 Southwest Conference football season, and they all belonged to Texas. The heartbreak belonged to Arkansas.

Amazingly and yet fittingly, what began in mid-September all came down to the fourth quarter of the season's final game. Then came those five plays. They enabled Texas to overtake and nose past Arkansas, 15-14, in the game that had everything and settled everything: the conference champion, the national champion, the winner of the special Presidential Plaque that was presented personally by Richard Nixon, the berth in the Cotton Bowl opposite the Fighting Irish of old Notre Dame.

The key figure in that fourth quarter was James Street.

By dawn's early life, dressed in ordinary campus attire, on his way to the athletic dining hall, Street is just another bright-eyed young University of Texas student currently in pursuit of a higher education. He stands only 5-10, weighs a mere 175. It is only on Saturday, when he dons cleats, pads and that orange jersey, that Street becomes 10 feet tall.

It was Street who ran 42 yards on the first play of the fourth quarter for Texas' first touchdown, at a moment when the rampaging Razorbacks were leading by 14 points. Then it was Street who ran for the two-point conversion that opened up a whole new world for the Longhorns.

Those were the two big runs. There were two crucial interceptions that also turned the game around. Tom Campbell's theft, at the Texas 21, was the final one; it wrapped up what Danny Lester's steal a few moments earlier in the Texas end zone had opened up. And then there was the pass that did fly true, the biggest pass of the 1969 season. Street threw it.

Months earlier, a journalist one day had asked Darrell Royal if he thought Street might be underrated as a passer. "I don't know how others rate him," Royal replied. "He pleases us." In the fourth quarter, when it was fourth-and-three at the Texas 43 with 4:47 left to play and Arkansas leading, 14-8, Street did more than please his coach; he delighted and rescued him. As Royal, supposedly the arch conservative, gambled in an incredible way, Street threw a perfect 44-yard pass that Randy Peschel caught at the Arkansas 13, setting up the winning points that Jim Bertelsen and Happy Feller provided a moment later.

It was, said President Nixon, "one of the greatest games of all time," and it climaxed an unusual season for the Southwest Conference. It was a season that began with Arkansas and Texas on an obvious collision course at the summit, but they followed different paths in getting there.

Texas' route was all stampede. No team in conference annals ever scored like the Longhorns did (414 points) or attacked with such a devastating infantry featuring the thundering runs of Bertelsen, Street, Steve Worster and Ted Koy. The Longhorns' 49-point spree against Texas Tech in their conference opener was merely a hint of things to come. When those things did come, the Longhorn regulars, even such defenders as Bill Atessis and Glen Halsell, seldom were around to enjoy them for any length of time. They usually spent the second half of the game on the bench, the verdict already wrapped in orange.

In their headlong rush to their fateful meeting with Arkansas, the Longhorns never scored less than 31 points against a conference opponent. All through November, as they blistered SMU and Baylor and TCU and A&M, they heard themselves praised in a monotonous refrain: "Greatest team I ever saw or played against."

Arkansas never did have Texas' raw power or physical strength. The Razorbacks had to depend on pin-point execution, and when the development of that execution was delayed by a series of injuries, first to Montgomery and then to Chuck Dicus and Bruce Maxwell, the Hogs had to get there first with defense. That they did, as linebacker Cliff Powell set a dazzling pace for the best defense against scoring in all college football. Although the Razorbacks kept winning, they hardly won by Texas-style scores, and it wasn't until the day of The Big Shootout in Fayetteville that they finally managed to convince the skeptics even as they lost the game.

So it all came down to Texas and Arkansas, just as the form chart had said it would. Where the form chart missed badly, along with the coaches themselves, was in appraising what lay beneath the summit. What lay beneath was weak and mushy.

This was the season the conference was to have been at peak strength. In one manner of speaking, it was. Texas emerged as the nation's No. 1 team and once-beaten Arkansas as the No. 3 team. The conference has had No. 1 teams before but never has it had two teams that ranked in the top three nationally at the end of the regular season.

None of the other six teams, however, won more games than it lost; none scored more points than it surrendered. For the first time in conference history, one team, Baylor, played a full 10-game schedule and lost every game. Another team, TCU, twice saw an opponent put more than 60 points on the scoreboard. A&M gave up the most points it has ever surrendered to a Longhorn team. Rice again failed to win a game on the road. After just two weeks, every conference team had lost a game except Texas and Arkansas. And so it went.

"The conference proved to be much weaker than any of us had anticipated," said Arkansas coach Frank Broyles at the finish. "For one thing, a number of teams were having to go with new, inexperienced quarterbacks. That can always mean trouble. At one point, five teams—Tech with Charles Napper, A&M with Rocky Self, Baylor with Si Southall, TCU with Steve Judy, Rice with either Stahle Vincent or Phillip Wood—were starting sophomores at quarterback.

Logically then, the other three — Texas with Street, Arkansas with Montgomery and SMU with Chuck Hixson — should have been the Big Three. Logic was only two-thirds correct.

While Hixson was having another outstanding year statistically, finishing second nationally in pass completions, the Mustangs sought in vain for big playmakers of the Jerry Levias-Mike Richardson type. They began by losing three squeakers in a row, and although they rallied at one point — beating TCU and Rice as prize soph receiver Gary Hammond and mini-tailback Daryl Doggett teamed well with Hixson—their defense seldom measured up to their 1968 norm. Their final 3-7 figure left them out of first division.

Of the teams with sophomore quarterbacks, Tech and TCU fared best, sharing third place with 4-3 conference slates. Tech had a rather uneven season while going 5-5 overall. The Raiders, who had put their trust in a defense led by Denton Fox and Richard Campbell, saw that defense often wobble in key situations. When two November opponents, TCU and Arkansas, put the Raiders down, the Texas Tech board of directors voted to make a coaching change. J. T. King, promoted to full-time athletic director, was asked to select his own successor.

Although TCU suffered humiliations against both Ohio State and Texas, the Frogs finally found what they had been seeking for years—an accomplished quarterback. His name is Judy and it is worth marking down; Judy is sure to be a strong factor in conference play for the next two years. Judy, with excellent help from Linzy Cole, Jerry Miller, Marty Whelan and (late in the season) Norman Bulaich, made big plays almost every Saturday. Sometimes that was enough, as against Baylor, A&M, TCU and Tech, and sometimes it wasn't. Although Judy broke Davey O'Brien's school total offense record, the Frogs finished at 4-6 as their defense broke down.

Baylor, riddled by injuries, was never a factor. The Bears did construct a fright for Arkansas, forging a 7-7 tie for three quarters, but they eventually lost that game and all the rest. Their lone bright spot was provided by punter Ed Marsh, who led the nation with a 43.6-yard average.

Although sophomore-burdened Texas A&M got all-conference seasons from ends Mike DeNiro and Ross Brupbacher, tailback Larry Stegent and defensive lineman Lynn Odom, they generally found themselves armed with only a low-grade offense in a high-octane year. Like Rice and SMU, they finished 3-7 for the season; like Rice, they finished 2-5 in conference play and tied for sixth.

For the Owls, that represented improvement. They had failed to win a game in 1968. In the second half of the 1969 campaign, they began to make a few impressive tracks as some of their good sophomores—Vincent, Wood, tailback Mike Spruill on offense; end Rodrigo Barnes (the league's top soph defensively), linebackers Dale Grounds and Randy Lee and halfback Mike Tyler on defense — began to mature.

The long-range outlook for 1970 would have to consider the Owls, along with the Frogs, the Aggies (who had 1969's best freshmen) and the Mustangs. But the 1970 form chart doubtless would start where the 1969 chart had started: with Texas and Arkansas.

1969
SOUTHWEST CONFERENCE
CHAMPIONS

TEXAS LONGHORNS

Head Football Coach: Darrell Royal
Team Captains: James Street, Ted Koy,
Glen Halsell

17	California	0
49	Texas Tech	7
56	Navy	17
27	Oklahoma	17
31	Rice	0
45	SMU	14
56	Baylor	14
69	TCU	7
49	Texas A&M	12
15	Arkansas	14
414		**102**

1969 SEASON RECORDS

ARKANSAS

39	Oklahoma State	0
55	Tulsa	0
24	TCU	6
21	Baylor	7
52	Wichita State	14
35	Texas A & M	13
30	Rice	6
28	SMU	15
33	Texas Tech	0
14	Texas	15
331		76

BAYLOR

15	Kansas State	48
10	Georgia Tech	17
8	LSU	63
7	Arkansas	21
0	Texas A & M	24
14	TCU	31
14	Texas	56
7	Texas Tech	41
6	SMU	12
6	Rice	34
87		347

RICE

55	VMI	0
0	LSU	42
21	California	31
14	SMU	34
0	Texas	31
14	Texas Tech	24
6	Arkansas	30
7	Texas A & M	6
17	TCU	21
34	Baylor	6
168		225

SMU

22	Air Force	26
21	Georgia Tech	24
15	Michigan State	23
19	TCU	17
34	Rice	14
24	Texas Tech	27
14	Texas	45
10	Texas A & M	20
15	Arkansas	28
12	Baylor	6
186		230

TEXAS

17	California	0
49	Texas Tech	7
56	Navy	17
27	Oklahoma	17
31	Rice	0
45	SMU	14
56	Baylor	14
69	TCU	7
49	Texas A & M	12
15	Arkansas	14
414		102

TEXAS A & M

6	LSU	35
0	Nebraska	14
20	Army	13
9	Texas Tech	13
6	TCU	16
24	Baylor	0
13	Arkansas	25
20	SMU	10
6	Rice	7
12	Texas	49
116		192

TCU

35	Purdue	42
0	Ohio State	62
6	Arkansas	24
17	SMU	19
16	Texas A & M	6
9	Miami	14
31	Baylor	14
35	Texas Tech	26
7	Texas	69
21	Rice	17
177		293

TEXAS TECH

38	Kansas	22
7	Texas	49
10	Oklahoma State	17
13	Texas A & M	9
26	Mississippi State	30
27	SMU	24
24	Rice	14
26	TCU	35
41	Baylor	7
0	Arkansas	33
212		240

1969 ALL-AMERICAN TEAMS

AP

OFFENSE
E Jim Mandich, Michigan
E Walker Gillette, Richmond
T **BOB McKAY, TEXAS**
T John Ward, Oklahoma State
G Bill Bridges, Houston
G Chip Kell, Tennessee
C **RODNEY BRAND, ARKANSAS**
Q Mike Phipps, Purdue
B Steve Owens, Oklahoma
B Bob Anderson, Colorado
B Jim Otis, Ohio State

DEFENSE
E Jimmy Gunn, Southern Cal
E Phil Olsen, Utah State
T Mike Reid, Penn State
T Mike McCoy, Notre Dame
G Jim Stillwagon, Ohio State
L Steve Kiner, Tennessee
L Dennis Onkontz, Penn State
L Don Parish, Stanford
B Jack Tatum, Ohio State
B Tom Curtis, Michigan
B Buddy McClinton, Auburn

SECOND TEAM
G Jerry Dossey, Arkansas
B Steve Worster, Texas
L Cliff Powell, Arkansas

FOOTBALL COACHES (KODAK)
OFFENSE
E Jim Mandich, Michigan
E **CHUCK DICUS, ARKANSAS**
T Jim Reilly, Notre Dame
T **BOBBY WUENSCH, TEXAS**
G Bill Bridges, Houston
G John Ward, Oklahoma State
C Chip Kell, Tennessee
Q Mike Phipps, Purdue
B Steve Owens, Oklahoma
B Charlie Pittman, Penn State
B Warren Muir, South Carolina
F Carlos Alvarez, Florida

DEFENSE
E Jim Gunn, Southern Cal
E Floyd Reese, UCLA
T Mike Reid, Penn State
T Mike McCoy, Notre Dame
G Jim Stillwagon, Ohio State
L Steve Kiner, Tennessee
L **CLIFF POWELL, ARKANSAS**
L George Bevan, LSU
L Mike Ballou, UCLA
B Jack Tatum, Ohio State
B Buddy McClinton, Auburn
B Glenn Cannon, Mississippi

FOOTBALL NEWS
E Carlos Alvarez, Florida
E Jim Mandich, Michigan
E Elmo Wright, Houston
E Jim Gunn, Southern Cal
T Mike McCoy, Notre Dame
T Mike Reid, Penn State
T Al Cowling, Southern Cal
T **BOB McKAY, TEXAS**
T Sid Smith, Southern Cal
G Chip Kell, Tennessee
G Al Samples, Alabama
G Steve Greer, Georgia
G Jim Stillwagon, Ohio State
C **ROD BRAND, ARKANSAS**
C Ken Mendenhall, Oklahoma
HB Steve Owens, Oklahoma
HB Mack Herron, Kansas State
HB John Isenbarger, Indiana
HB Mickey Cureton, UCLA
LB Steve Kiner, Tennessee
LB Jack Reynolds, Tennessee
LB Dennis Onkontz, Penn State
LB **GLEN HALSELL, TEXAS**
LB Mike Ballou, UCLA
DB John Tatum, Ohio State
DB Tom Curtis, Michigan
DB Buddy McClinton, Auburn
DB Tommy Casanova, LSU
QB Rex Kern, Ohtio State
QB Mike Phipps, Purdue
QB Archie Manning, Mississippi

FOOTBALL WRITERS (LOOK)
OFFENSE
E Walker Gillette, Richmond
E Jim Mandich, Purdue
T **BOB McKAY, TEXAS**
T John Ward, Oklahoma State
G Bill Bridges, Houston
G Chip Kell, Tennessee
C **RODNEY BRAND, ARKANSAS**
Q Mike Phipps, Purdue
B Steve Owens, Oklahoma
B Jim Otis, Ohio State
B **STEVE WORSTER, TEXAS**

DEFENSE
E Jim Gunn, Southern Cal
E Bill Brundige, Colorado
T Mike Reid, Penn State
T Mike McCoy, Notre Dame
L Mike Ballou, UCLA
L George Bevan, LSU
L Steve Kiner, Tennessee
L Dennis Onkontz, Penn State
B **DENTON FOX, TEXAS TECH**
B John Tatum, Ohio State
B Buddy McClinton, Auburn

UPI
OFFENSE
E Carlos Alvarez, Florida
E Jim Mandich, Michigan
T Sid Smith, Southern Cal
T **BOB McKAY, TEXAS**
G Chip Kell, Tennessee
G Larry Dinaro, Notre Dame
C **RODNEY BRAND, ARKANSAS**
Q Mike Phipps, Purdue
B Steve Owens, Oklahoma
B Jim Otis, Ohio State
B Bob Anderson, Colorado

DEFENSE
E Jim Gunn, Southern Cal
E Phil Olsen, Utah State
T Mike McCoy, Notre Dame
T Mike Reid, Penn State
G Jim Stillwagon, Ohio State
L Steve Kiner, Tennessee
L Dennis Onkontz, Penn State
B Jack Tatum, Ohio State
B Tom Curtis, Michigan
B Neal Smith, Penn State
B Buddy McClinton, Auburn

SECOND TEAM
E Charles Speyrer, Texas
B Steve Worster, Texas
T Leo Brooks, Texas

NFL-AFL DIRECTORS OF PLAYER PERSONNEL (SPORTING NEWS)
OFFENSE
SE Ken Burroughs, Texas Southern
TE Steve Zabel, Oklahoma
T Sid Smith, Southern Cal
T **BOB McKAY, TEXAS**
G Ron Saul, Michigan State
G Mike Carroll, Missouri
C Ken Mendenhall, Oklahoma
Q Mike Phipps, Purdue
B Steve Owens, Oklahoma
B Bob Anderson, Colorado
FL Walker Gillette, Richmond

DEFENSE
E Al Cowlings, Southern Cal
E Phil Olsen, Utah State
T Mike McCoy, Notre Dame
T Mike Reid, Penn State
L John Small, The Citadel
L Steve Kiner, Tennessee
L Don Parish, Stanford
CB Steve Tannen, Florida
CB Tim Foley, Purdue
CB Jack Tatum, Ohio State
S Glenn Cannon, Mississippi
S Ted Provost, Ohio State

1969 ALL-SOUTHWEST CONFERENCE TEAM

Player of Year: James Street, Texas
Offensive Sophomore of Year: Garry Hammond, SMU
Defensive Sophomore of Year: Rodrigo Barnes, Rice

CONSENSUS

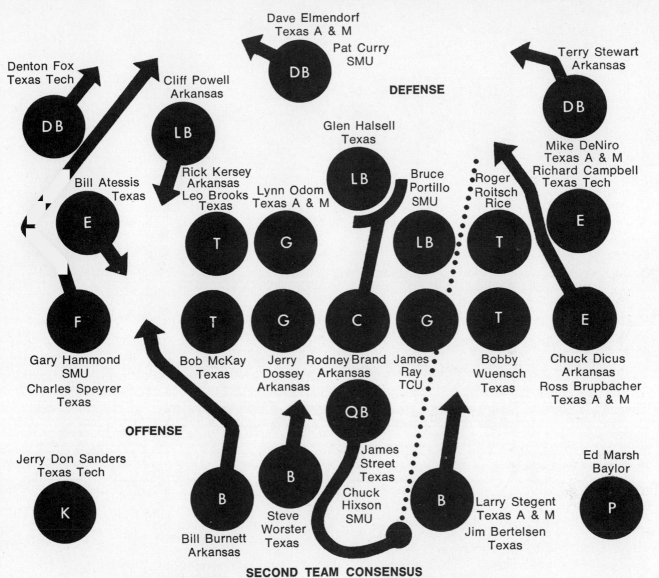

Dave Elmendorf
Texas A & M

Pat Curry
SMU

DB

DEFENSE

Terry Stewart
Arkansas

DB

Denton Fox
Texas Tech

DB

Cliff Powell
Arkansas

LB

Glen Halsell
Texas

LB

Mike DeNiro
Texas A & M
Richard Campbell
Texas Tech

E

Bill Atessis
Texas

E

Rick Kersey
Arkansas
Leo Brooks
Texas

T

Lynn Odom
Texas A & M

G

Bruce
Portillo
SMU

LB

Roger
Roitsch
Rice

T

Gary Hammond
SMU
Charles Speyrer
Texas

F

Bob McKay
Texas

T

Jerry
Dossey
Arkansas

G

Rodney
Arkansas

C

Brand
James
Ray
TCU

G

Bobby
Wuensch
Texas

T

Chuck Dicus
Arkansas
Ross Brupbacher
Texas A & M

E

OFFENSE

QB

James
Street
Texas
Chuck
Hixson
SMU

Ed Marsh
Baylor

P

Jerry Don Sanders
Texas Tech

K

Bill Burnett
Arkansas

B

Steve
Worster
Texas

B

Larry Stegent
Texas A & M
Jim Bertelsen
Texas

B

SECOND TEAM CONSENSUS

OFFENSE		DEFENSE	
E	Jerry Miller, TCU	E	Rodrigo Barnes, Rice
E	Ken Fleming, SMU	E	Bruce James, Arkansas
T	Bill Jackson, SMU	T	Tom Reaux, Baylor
T	Bill James, SMU	T	Rufus Cormier, SMU
T	Richard Stevens, Baylor	T	Dick Bumpas, Arkansas
T	Mike Kelson, Arkansas	G	Steve Bradshaw, Rice
G	Ronnie Hammers, Arkansas	L	Andy Durrett, TCU
G	Bobby Mitchell, Texas	L	Scott Henderson, Texas
G	Leonard Forey, Texas A & M	L	Joe Stutts, SMU
C	Forrest Wiegand, Texas	L	Larry Molinare, Texas Tech
Q	Bill Montgomery, Arkansas	L	Buster Adami, Texas A & M
B	Ted Koy, Texas	B	Jack Faubion, Rice
B	Norman Bulaich, TCU	B	Fred Steinmark, Texas
B	Bruce Maxwell, Arkansas	B	Jerry Moore, Arkansas
F	Linzy Cole, TCU		

1970 COTTON BOWL

January 1, 1970

TEXAS 10-0-0 vs NOTRE DAME 8-1-1

Previous Games
1913—Notre Dame 30—Texas 7
1915—Notre Dame 36—Texas 7
1934—Texas 7—Notre Dame 6
1954—Notre Dame 21—Texas 0

School Nicknames and Colors:
Notre Dame—Fighting Irish
Blue and Gold
Texas—Longhorns
Orange and White

Texas				Notre Dame	
Head Coach: Darrell Royal				Head Coach: Ara Parseghian	
17	California	0		35	Northwestern	10
49	Texas Tech	7		14	Purdue	28
56	Navy	17		42	Michigan State	28
27	Oklahoma	17		45	Army	0
31	Rice	0		14	Southern Cal	14
45	SMU	14		37	Tulane	0
56	Baylor	14		47	Navy	0
69	TCU	7		49	Pittsburgh	7
49	Texas A & M	12		38	Georgia Tech	20
15	Arkansas	14		13	Air Force	6
414		102		334		113

1970 SUGAR BOWL

January 1, 1970

ARKANSAS 9-1-0 vs MISSISSIPPI 7-3-0

Previous Games
Mississippi has won 13
Arkansas has won 12
No Ties

School Nicknames and Colors:
Mississippi—Rebels
Red and Blue
Arkansas—Razorbacks
Red and White

Arkansas		Mississsippi	
Head Coach: Frank Broyles		Head Coach: John Vaught	
39	Oklahoma State	0	28	Memphis State	3
55	Tulsa	0	9	Kentucky	10
24	TCU	6	32	Alabama	33
21	Baylor	7	25	Georgia	17
52	Wichita State	14	69	Southern Miss.	7
35	Texas A & M	13	11	Houston	25
30	Rice	6	26	LSU	23
28	SMU	15	21	Chattanooga	0
33	Texas Tech	0	38	Tennessee	0
14	Texas	15	48	Mississippi State	22
331		76	307		140

FINAL SWC STATISTICAL LEADERS

*Total Offense .... Texas 4713 yds.
Total Defense .... Texas 2259 yds.
*Rushing Offense .... Texas 3630 yds.
Rushing Defense .... Texas 900 yds.
Passing Offense .... SMU 2380 yds.
Passing Defense .... SMU 1277 yds.
Rushing .... Bill Burnett, Arkansas, 900 yds.
Passing .... Chuck Hixson, SMU 2313 yds.
Receiving .... Gary Hammond, SMU, 722 yds.
Scoring .... Bill Burnett, Arkansas, 120 pts.
Punting .... Ed Marsh, Baylor, 43.6 avg.
Punt Returns .... Linzy Cole, TCU, 306 yds.
Total Offense .... Chuck Hixson, SMU, 2202 yds.
†Touchdowns .... Bill Burnett, Arkansas, 20
*Field Goals .... Jerry Don Sanders, Texas Tech, 11
*Extra Points .... Happy Feller, Texas, 43
*New SWC Records
†Ties SWC Record

1970 SCHEDULES

	BAYLOR	RICE	SMU	TEXAS A&M	TCU	TEXAS TECH	TEXAS	ARKANSAS
Sept. 19	@ Army	VMI	@ Tennessee	@ LSU	@ Purdue	@ Kansas	California	Okla. State
Sept. 26	Pittsburg	@ LSU	New Mexico State	@ Ohio State	@ Wisconsin	Texas	@ Texas Tech	Tulsa
Oct. 3	@ LSU	California	@ Northwestern	@ Michigan	Arkansas	Calif. of Santa Barbara	UCLA	@ TCU
Oct. 10	@ Arkansas			Texas Tech	@ Okla. State	@ TexasA&M	Okla. (Dallas)	Baylor
Oct. 17		@ SMU	Rice	TCU	@ Texas A&M	@ Miss. State	Arkansas	@ Texas
Oct. 24	Texas A&M	Texas	@ Texas Tech	@ Baylor		SMU	@ Rice	Wichita State
Oct. 31	@ TCU	Texas Tech	@ Texas	Arkansas	Baylor	@ Rice	SMU	@ Texas A&M
Nov. 7	Texas	@ Arkansas	Texas A&M	@ SMU	@ Texas Tech	TCU	@ Baylor	Rice
Nov. 14	Texas Tech	@ Texas A&M	@ Arkansas	Rice	Texas	@ Baylor	@ TCU	SMU
Nov. 21	@ SMU	TCU	Baylor		@ Rice	Arkansas		@ Texas Tech
Nov. 26				@ Texas			Texas A&M	
Nov. 28	Rice	@ Baylor	@ TCU		SMU			

These schedules are subject to change for TV purposes.

Past Records

FIFTY-YEAR ALL-SOUTHWEST FOOTBALL TEAM

Selected by Southwest members of the Football Writers' Association of America
in connection with the centennial year celebration of college football

ENDS: Raymond Matthews, TCU 1927
Wear Schoonover, Arkansas 1929
James Williams, Rice 1949

TACKLES: Robert Lilly, TCU 1960
Truman Spain, SMU 1935
Charley Krueger, Texas A & M 1957

GUARDS: Tommy Nobis, Texas 1965
Barton Koch, Baylor 1930
Weldon Humble, Rice 1946

CENTERS: Charles Aldrich, TCU 1938
Clyde Turner, Hardin-Simmons 1939

BACKS: Doak Walker, SMU 1949
*Sammy Baugh, TCU 1936
John Kimbrough, Texas A & M 1940
Joel Hunt, Texas A & M 1927
Bobby Layne, Texas 1947
Chris Gilbert, Texas 1968
Harrison Stafford, Texas 1932
Kyle Rote, SMU 1950

SECOND TEAM — ENDS: Lawrence Elkins, Baylor 1964; Lawrence McCullough, Texas 1922. **TACKLES:** I. B. Hale, TCU 1938; Loyd Phillips, Arkansas 1966. **GUARDS:** Joe Routt, Texas A & M 1937; Bud McFadin, Texas 1950. **CENTER:** E. J. Holub, Texas Tech 1960. **BACKS:** Davey O'Brien, TCU 1938; Jim Swink, TCU 1956; John David Crow, Texas A & M 1957; Donny Anderson, Texas Tech 1965; Bobby Wilson, SMU 1935. **BACK-END SPECIALIST:** Jerry Levias, SMU 1968.

*Made 50 Year All-American Team

SOUTHWEST CONFERENCE CHAMPIONS

1915 BAYLOR, OKLAHOMA	**1934** RICE	**1953** RICE, TEXAS
1916 TEXAS	**1935** SMU	**1954** ARKANSAS
1917 TEXAS A & M	**1936** ARKANSAS	**1955** TCU
1918 TEXAS	**1937** RICE	**1956** TEXAS A & M
1919 TEXAS A & M	**1938** TCU	**1957** RICE
1920 TEXAS	**1939** TEXAS A & M, SMU	**1958** TCU
1921 TEXAS A & M	**1940** TEXAS A & M	**1959** TEXAS, TCU, ARKANSAS
1922 BAYLOR	**1941** TEXAS A & M	**1960** ARKANSAS
1923 SMU	**1942** TEXAS	**1961** ARKANSAS, TEXAS
1924 BAYLOR	**1943** TEXAS	**1962** TEXAS
1925 TEXAS A & M	**1944** TCU	**1963** TEXAS
1926 SMU	**1945** TEXAS	**1964** ARKANSAS
1927 TEXAS A & M	**1946** RICE, ARKANSAS	**1965** ARKANSAS
1928 TEXAS	**1947** SMU	**1966** SMU
1929 TCU	**1948** SMU	**1967** TEXAS A & M
1930 TEXAS	**1949** RICE	**1968** TEXAS, ARKANSAS
1931 SMU	**1950** TEXAS	**1969** TEXAS
1932 TCU	**1951** TCU	
1933 ARKANSAS	**1952** TEXAS	

SWC NATIONAL CHAMPIONS

1938 TCU (L. R. MEYER)   **1963** TEXAS (DARRELL ROYAL)
1939 TEXAS A & M (HOMER NORTON) **1964** ARKANSAS (FRANK BROYLES)

COTTON BOWL RECORD

The Cotton Bowl Game was first played in 1937 and an agreement to have the Southwest Conference Champion be the host team began with the 1941 game. The 1939 and 1940 games were the only ones in Cotton Bowl history that did not have a Southwest Conference team involved. Texas Tech played in the 1939 game but was not a conference member at that time.

1937—TCU 16, Marquette 6	**1954**—Rice 20, Alabama 6
1938—Rice 28, Colorado 14	**1955**—Georgia Tech 14, Arkansas 6
1939—St. Mary's 21, Texas Tech 13	**1956**—Mississippi 14, TCU 13
1940—Clemson 6, Boston College 3	**1957**—TCU 28, Syracuse 27
1941—Texas A&M 13, Fordham 12	**1958**—Navy 20, Rice 7
1942—Alabama 29, Texas A&M 21	**1959**—TCU 0, Air Force 0
1943—Texas 14, Georgia Tech 7	**1960**—Syracuse 23, Texas 14
1944—Texas 7, Randolph Field 7	**1961**—Duke 7, Arkansas 6
1945—Oklahoma A&M 34, TCU 0	**1962**—Texas 12, Mississippi 7
1946—Texas 40, Missouri 27	**1963**—LSU 13, Texas 0
1947—Arkansas 0, LSU 0	**1964**—Texas 28, Navy 6
1948—SMU 13, Penn State 13	**1965**—Arkansas 10, Nebraska 7
1949—SMU 21, Oregon 13	**1966**—LSU 14, Arkansas 7
1950—Rice 27, North Carolina 13	**1967**—Georgia 24, SMU 9
1951—Tennessee 20, Texas 14	**1968**—Texas A&M 20, Alabama 16
1952—Kentucky 20, TCU 7	**1969**—Texas 36, Tennessee 13
1953—Texas 16, Tennessee 0	

Since 1941: SWC 13 wins, 12 losses, 4 ties

Records of SWC teams in other Bowl games:

1921 DIXIE CLASSIC (DALLAS): Texas A&M 21, Centre 14

1934 DIXIE CLASSIC (DALLAS): Arkansas 7, Centenary 7

1936 ROSE BOWL: Stanford 7, SMU 0
SUGAR BOWL: TCU 3, LSU 2

1938 SUN BOWL: West Virginia 7, Texas Tech 6

1939 SUGAR BOWL: TCU 15, Carnegie Tech 7

1940 SUGAR BOWL: Texas A&M 14, Tulane 13

1942 ORANGE BOWL: Georgia 40, TCU 26
SUN BOWL: Tulsa 6, Texas Tech 0

1944 ORANGE BOWL: LSU 19, Texas A&M 14

1947 ORANGE BOWL: Rice 8, Tennessee 0

1948 SUGAR BOWL: Texas 27, Alabama 7
SUN BOWL: Miami (Ohio) 13, Texas Tech 12
DIXIE BOWL: Arkansas 21, William & Mary 19

1949 DELTA BOWL: Mississippi 13, TCU 9
DIXIE BOWL: Baylor 20, Wake Forest 7
RAISIN BOWL: San Jose State 20, Texas Tech 13
ORANGE BOWL: Texas 41, Georgia 28

1950 PRESIDENTIAL CUP: Texas A&M 40, Georgia 20

1952 ORANGE BOWL: Georgia Tech 17, Baylor 14
SUN BOWL: Texas Tech 25, College of the Pacific 14

1954 GATOR BOWL: Texas Tech 35, Auburn 13

1955 GATOR BOWL: Auburn 33, Baylor 13

1956 SUN BOWL: Wyoming 21, Texas Tech 14

1957 SUGAR BOWL: Baylor 13, Tennessee 7
GATOR BOWL: Tennessee 3, Texas A&M 0

1958 SUGAR BOWL: Mississippi 39, Texas 7

1960 BLUEBONNET BOWL: Texas 3, Alabama 3
GATOR BOWL: Arkansas 14, Georgia Tech 7
BLUEBONNET BOWL: Clemson 23, TCU 7
GATOR BOWL: Florida 13, Baylor 12

1961 GOTHAM BOWL: Baylor 24, Utah State 9
SUGAR BOWL: Mississippi 14, Rice 6
BLUEBONNET BOWL: Kansas 33, Rice 7

1962 SUGAR BOWL: Alabama 10, Arkansas 3

1963 BLUEBONNET BOWL: Baylor 14, LSU 7
SUN BOWL: Oregon 20, SMU 14
SUGAR BOWL: Mississippi 17, Arkansas 13

1965 SUN BOWL: Texas Western 13, TCU 12
GATOR BOWL: Georgia Tech 31, Texas Tech 21
SUN BOWL: Georgia 7, Texas Tech 0
ORANGE BOWL: Texas 21, Alabama 17

1966 BLUEBONNET BOWL: Texas 19, Mississippi 0

1969 SUGAR BOWL: Arkansas 16, Georgia 2
BLUEBONNET BOWL: SMU 28, Oklahoma 27

SWC: 20W, 23L, 2T

Home
Sweet
Home

RICE STADIUM

The Rice Owls play their home games in Rice Stadium, which is located on campus in Houston.

Construction on the stadium was started in January 1950 and was completed nine months later in September. The first game played in the new stadium was between Rice and Santa Clara. Before 68,000 the Owls won the game 27-7.

Rice Stadium is a complete bowl of 40,000 seats, with two upper decks on the east and west sides holding 15,000 each, for a total capacity of 70,000. With a student body of just over 2,000 Rice Stadium can seat more "general public" than any other university stadium in the United States.

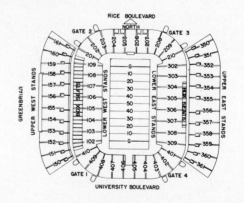

KYLE FIELD

The Texas A & M Aggies play their home games in Kyle Field, which is located on campus in College Station.

Kyle Field is named for the late Edwin Jackson Kyle who was Dean of the School of Agriculture and Chairman of the Faculty Committee on Athletics. He graduated from Texas A & M in the class of 1899.

The concrete U-shaped stadium was built in 1929 with original seating capacity of 34,000. South end zone stands were erected in 1947, upping the capacity to 40,000. In 1967 the stadium was double-decked on both the east and west sides. The south bleachers were removed and replaced by a landscaped flower garden. This brought the seating to its present capacity of 48,000. Every other year 6,000 chair seats are added for the Texas game.

The first game played in Kyle Field was on Thanksgiving Day, November 28, 1929. The Aggies defeated Texas 13-0.

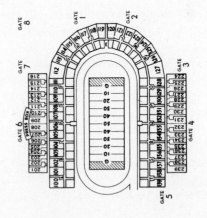

BAYLOR STADIUM

The Baylor Bears play their home games in Baylor Stadium, which is located two miles from the campus in Waco.

The stadium is a concrete bowl with the playing field 26 feet below the surrounding ground level. It was built in 1950. The inaugural game was played on September 30, 1950 between Baylor and the University of Houston. The Bears won the game from the Cougars, 34-7.

Seating capacity in 1950 was 48,000 and remains so today. Lights, yielding 384,000 watts on the playing surface, were added in 1954.

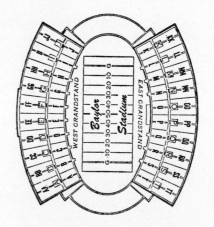

COTTON BOWL STADIUM

The Southern Methodist Mustangs play their home games in the Cotton Bowl The stadium is located on the State Fair grounds in Dallas and is owned and operated by the State Fair of Texas.

Construction on the bowl was begun in 1930. The new stadium was dedicated on October 25, 1930. The Mustangs met the Indiana Westerners and although Indiana was favored, the Mustangs won handily by the score of 27-0.

Original seating capacity was 45,507. In 1948 it was raised to 67,431 and one year later increased to 75,504. During remodeling in 1968, the seating was reduced to 72,032. At this time the wooden benches were replaced by individual aluminum seats. These seats can be raised to allow easier passage.

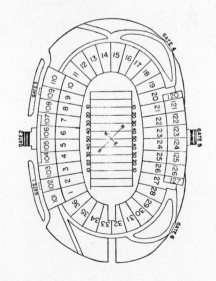

TCU-AMON CARTER STADIUM

The Texas Christian Horned Frogs play their home games in TCU-Amon Carter Stadium, which is located on campus in Fort Worth.

The stadium is named for the late Amon Carter, noted Fort Worth philanthropist, who was president of the original stadium committee.

Construction began in 1929 and the stadium was dedicated on October 11, 1930. Texas Christian met the Razorbacks of Arkansas on that day and the Horned Frogs made the dedication a happy one by defeating Arkansas 40-0.

Original seating capacity was 22,000. Through additions, made in 1948, 1951, 1953 and 1956, the capacity was raised to its present level of 46,000.

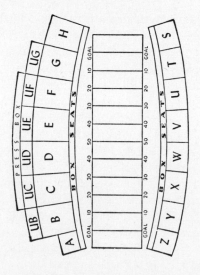

RAZORBACK STADIUM

The Arkansas Razorbacks play their home games in Razorback Stadium, which is located on campus in Fayetteville.

The stadium was built in 1938. It was first named Bailey Stadium, after then Governor Carl E. Bailey. In the 1938 dedication game, Baylor defeated the Hogs by the score of nine to six. Original capacity was 13,200. It has been boosted periodically since, to its present capacity of 43,000. This year the playing surface will be all-weather AstroTurf.

L. L. Brown, who was director of building and grounds for the university when he designed the original concrete structure, recalls that Arkansas was the first Southwest Conference school to use steel pipes for goal posts. A campus plumber came up with the idea to replace the wooden uprights.

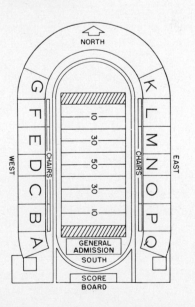

MEMORIAL STADIUM

The Texas Longhorns play their home games in Memorial Stadium, which is located on campus in Austin.

The stadium was constructed in 1924. The first game in the new stadium was played on November 8, 1924 between Texas and Baylor. The Bears, who were on their way to the conference championship, defeated the Longhorns 28-10. At the dedication game, played on November 27, the Longhorns defeated Texas A & M 7-0.

Original capacity was 40,000. In 1948 it was increased to 66,397. Extensive remodeling is under way and in 1970 the capacity will reach 81,197. Included in these plans is an AstroTurf playing surface which will be ready for the 1969 season.

The stadium was named to honor those of the university who died in World War I.

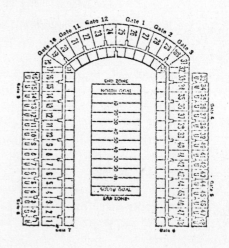